HOW TO BUILD A *GODDAMN* EMPIRE

ABRAMS IMAGE, NEW YORK

HOW TO BUILD A GODDAMN EMPIRE

BY ALI KRIEGSMAN

ADVICE ON CREATING YOUR BRAND WITH HIGH-TECH SMARTS, ELBOW GREASE, INFINITE HUSTLE & A WHOLE LOTTA HEART

For Mom, Ben, and Alana

In memory of David Getman, who never doubted me when I doubted myself. I miss you every day.

Editor: Samantha Weiner
Designer: Jess McGowan
Production Manager: Rachael Marks

Library of Congress Control Number: 2020931089

ISBN: 978-1-4197-4290-3
eISBN: 978-1-68335-809-1

The interviews in this text have been lightly edited and condensed for clarity.

Printed and bound in the United States
10 9 8 7 6 5 4 3 2 1

Abrams Image books are available at special discounts when purchased in quantity for premiums and promotions as well as fundraising or educational use. Special editions can also be created to specification.
For details, contact specialsales@abramsbooks.com or the address below.

Abrams Image® is a registered trademark of Harry N. Abrams, Inc.

ABRAMS The Art of Books
195 Broadway, New York, NY 10007
abramsbooks.com

CONTENTS

A NOTE TO YOU . . .

If you are reading this book, you may have decided to start your own business, build your own brand, make a radical career shift, or pursue a once-distant dream. Whoever you are, you've likely decided to make some sort of big life change. Or maybe you haven't *quite* decided yet, but you're plagued by "what ifs" and a short list of roads not taken; you've spent hours, months, or years pining for a more fulfilling work experience but have put those aspirations in a nice little pile and told yourself to look away "for now." Maybe you have a passion you wish to turn into a career. Maybe you feel trapped in some drab-ass 9-to-5 and wonder, "Is this *really* it? But like . . . *really* though?" Maybe you're currently unemployed and looking to break into a brand-new industry, or you're cobbling together a handful of part-time gigs and looking to pick—or create—a profession where you can grow and establish yourself. Well—whoever you are, and whatever brought you here, I want you to know where I stand. I want you to know how I feel. Because I was once a nine-to-fiver who felt unfulfilled and wanting, staring down the scary prospect, and implications, of a big life change, too. But I am not a self-empowerment guru who wants you to find your inner "girlboss." I don't think I've found her. I don't try to "manifest" or actively practice any sort of positive thinking. In fact, I can't stop myself from the practice of *negative* thinking. I don't believe that hard work and resilience equals a foolproof recipe for success. I've seen hardworking people fail. I've worked my ass off and failed *big-time*. And I don't think running your own shit will suddenly bring you unadulterated, toxin-free happiness. I don't have it. That's not what you should expect, despite what influencers, inspirational Instagram accounts, and even other entrepreneurs might be peddling. I want you to know that doing something new is *hard*. Building your life around any entrepreneurial effort, if you're doing it seriously, will feel like an emotional and intellectual Cyclone drop. Because building an empire doesn't happen overnight. And you may get few or no early signals that it will even happen at all. That shit sucks. No number of motivational sticky notes plastered on your mirror or afternoon affirmations will change the fact that sometimes, being your own boss and paving your own way feels like a total. fucking. hellscape.

I can't give you a three-step manual for how to deal with your hellscape moments, because there isn't one. And I can't share any cutesy, pithy mantras to make you feel like a #badass in your times of self-doubt or hardship, because in my experience, they don't really work. But what I can do is tell you what's coming, as candidly and as openly as possible. I can share my moments of weakness, of desperation, and of total and utter fear. I can tell you what I think I did right and what I definitely did wrong. I can introduce you to dozens of other entrepreneurs who turned hellscape moments into learning opportunities. And I can show you that no matter how big a business gets, how many fans it has, how much money it makes, how much funding it takes—no one is spared the rollercoaster ride of uncertainty and defeat, of mastery and euphoria.

NO ONE IS SPARED THE ROLLERCOASTER RIDE OF UNCERTAINTY AND DEFEAT, OF MASTERY AND EUPHORIA.

Almost every founder I've interviewed, with some prodding, spoke openly about what I call their "I'm-gunna-fucking-quit" moment. Actually, make that moments, plural. There's a real bleak side to entrepreneurship, and I think all of us (but women especially) have been trained to suffer these depressive episodes alone. We are ashamed of them, because it isn't cool or sexy or inspiring or "boss-like" to address these hurting times head-on. Social media has only exacerbated the problem: every day, you open your Instagram feed to household-name founders decked out in designer getups, you're fed power mantras from uplifting, candy-colored grid posts, you see other entrepreneurs all-smiles on their stories as they rush from meeting to meeting. Female founders, in particular, are quietly expected to both govern and influence, run their companies *and* build a personal brand. Often, these personal brands—mine included—exude empowerment, an effortless sense of perfection, and an unyielding stylishness. There is minimal mess—and when there is, it can feel calculated, an *Us Weekly*–style reminder that "successful founders—they're just like us!" All the while, you may feel a deep, unshakeable sense of inadequacy. You may be home, stuck on the couch, overcome by so much darkness that even the *thought* of power-strutting into a meeting feels overwhelming. Or maybe you're genuinely broke, running out of cash in both your personal and professional bank accounts. It's really hard to feel like you're on the right track when you measure your own financial reality against immaculately styled IG outfits and "get that bread" money memes. My company, Bulletin, can reluctantly count itself as part of the problem. We have both promoted and shaped the "girlboss" ethos so many of us have come to loathe. We posted those money memes. I still wear the fanciest shit I own to panels and public events. And because all of us are flexing in our own ways, in different doses, it's become too easy and automatic to compare yourself to other people. Founders rarely cry, scream, sulk, or stream their distress "on the air," so to speak, so when you're at your worst, you feel like a total loser. A weak-willed failure. Impostor syndrome takes hold and convinces you of the sinister lie you've been telling yourself from day one: I don't know what the hell I'm doing, and I'm not equipped to do this. It crawls its way up through the muddy bowels of your self-doubt, looks you straight in the eye, and asks, Who do you think you are?

Whatever change you're about to embark on: a new venture, a side hustle, a brand—you name it—you are signing up for struggle. You are signing up for days riddled with anxiety and uncertainty. You are signing up for problems you don't know how to solve, and for mistakes that might make you feel incompetent and foolish. You will feel pain when something goes wrong and you let your team or your customers down. You will feel pain when you run out of money and you're not sure the business can survive. You will feel pain when you turn down birthday dinners or happy hours and disappoint your friends because you have orders to fulfill or a crowdfunding campaign video to finish. When you are working on something you love, something that's yours, your highs become higher and your lows become lower. The pain feels like an 18/10. Being an entrepreneur means you have an unpredictable and endless stream of these 18/10 moments, really. Often, they're prompted by triggering events or experiences: you lose an important client, screw up a pitch, or can't make payroll. But there's also a more insidious, lingering pain that's always there, humming below the surface. This pain has a voice, and it talks to you: it worries about failure, and what happens if your dream simply . . . doesn't work out. Wrestling with that voice is the hardest struggle of all.

WHEN YOU ARE WORKING ON SOMETHING YOU LOVE, SOMETHING THAT'S YOURS, YOUR HIGHS BECOME HIGHER AND YOUR LOWS BECOME LOWER.

I'm not trying to scare you away from doing something bold, risky, and meaningful with your life. In fact, I'm trying to do the exact opposite. I want you to turn the dial up on your side hustle, pursue a passion, make that career change, take the risk, build that empire—however big or small. But in order to (1) simply get started and (2) continue to do it with any sanity, you need to try to quiet the nagging voice that worries about failure. And to do that, it may be worth rethinking what "success" really means to you. After years of catastrophizing and anxiously asking, What if we don't make it? I had to do this exercise myself.

Success is not *just* your company going viral, your brand becoming famous, your sales quadrupling, a glowing piece of press, an acquisition, an IPO, winning a huge account, getting X number of followers, raising Y amount of funding. There's that cheesy line (creative liberties here): it's not about the destination, it's all about the journey. And yeah, I might be batshit, but I think that cheesy line speaks the absolute truth. In fact, I think you've found some degree of success if you're taking the journey at all. So many people are content to stay stuck. Most would pick stability, silence a passion, forget a dream. So, if you've unglued your feet from the floor, begun to build something from nothing, and are trying to do work you care about—to me, that makes you successful. You don't need a multimillion-dollar enterprise or a "verified" badge on Instagram to prove it.

What I've learned over the past few years is that success means waking up every day and deciding to keep going, making the best decisions you can with the information you have, and always trying to improve your business and bring value to your team, if you have one. You have to think about how many fires you've put out, how many important decisions you've made, how many compromises you've had to make, how many small, proud moments you've had, how many new skills and lessons you've learned, how much brainstorming you've done, how much time you've put in, how many complex emotions you've felt. You will find and feel success along your jagged journey if you learn from those moments. That learning needs to feel like a reward in and of itself or you're going to drive yourself mad.

There will always be entrepreneurs and businesses who have more money, more clout, more funding, more fame, more followers, more traction. But this is your life. This is your journey. We're all gunna die anyway (hehe!)— but seriously, it's really not about them. Don't let it be about them. Let it be about your big wins and your small ones, all the mundane and crazy shit you've had to figure out so far. Because the more you focus on them (what other people think, how you stack up, what your competitor's got cookin') the less successful you will feel. It's a simple equation. I'm not a statistician, but you can trust me. I've spent full-on spirals stalking our competitors and I never emerge feeling anything but winded and overwhelmed.

Know the truth. If you build your empire, you will feel like absolute shit. You will have dense Chipotle burrito nights and cry in the shower. You will feel a special kind of pain when things go wrong. You will compare yourself to others, even if briefly and silently, and you may find success in all the wrong things. But you will also feel deeply proud of yourself and find moments of strength you did not know existed. You will develop skills that make you valuable now, and wherever you end up next. You will create something from nothing and experience moments filled with utter magic both alone and with those who build alongside you. So, as you keep charging forward, I hope that your mistakes make you feel frustrated and foolish. Let your hard lessons feel hard. But give yourself license to let those shitty feelings die a quick and painless death so you can learn and move on.

WHATEVER YOU'RE BUILDING, REMEMBER TO DO IT FOR YOU.

I hope you realize it is cool, sexy, and inspiring to be open and vocal about your hurting times with both friends and fellow entreprenuers. Those moments are more relatable than the ones where you win and shine, and being vulnerable will help you find encouraging, supportive allies when your "I'm-gunna-fucking-quit" moments take the stage. Whatever you're building, remember to do it for you. Remember to pat yourself on the back. Remember to find success in your work every day.

And remember, you could be plagued by "what ifs" and a short list of roads not taken. But instead, you're here.

A BIT ABOUT BULLETIN

I t's funny to peek back at Bulletin's early days. Throughout 2015, I chipped away at Bulletin a mere few hours a week alongside our CEO and my co-founder, Alana Branston. We did it to escape the banal, repetitive nature of our day jobs and treat ourselves to some creativity. There was no family money lying around. Zero Silicon Valley connections. No real-life experience modeling a business plan, optimizing a website, or building a brand. We felt idle and unfulfilled—and then, we had a small idea. We stole away to Alana's apartment after work, ordered Joe's pizza too many times, and worked on our little website. It was low pressure. It was fun. It was for us.

Now, $9 million in funding, a full team, and a software business later, I sometimes find myself yearning for a simpler time. A time when my day ended at 6 P.M. and I could do whatever I wanted. A time when a steady paycheck, livable salary, and free weekends were my only goal. A time when someone else would tell me what to do at work and I didn't have to figure out so much shit on the fly. But that time is over. And as an unexpected, non-traditional "founder," I've learned a ton since then. I've learned how to deal with no paycheck. I've learned how to deal with no weekends. I've learned how to manage people. I've learned how to lay them off. I've learned how to be a good partner and how to be a shitty one. I've learned how to have difficult, intimate conversations with our team about our company culture, or why we have to shrink to survive. I've learned how to put out fires. Big ones, like buoying the business through a global pandemic. Small ones, like our platform breaking after a massive launch. I've learned how to do PR and promote my own business. I've learned how to pitch and sell an idea. I've learned how to identify bad business ideas. I've learned how to position a business in the market. I've learned how to raise money from investors. I've learned how to create a brand voice. I've learned how to pivot. I've learned how to fail.

But I've also learned how to believe in myself and my potential. I've learned how to quiet doubts and manage impostor syndrome (most of the time). I've learned how to prove myself wrong. And I've learned how to mess up without hating myself for it. I started Bulletin when I was twenty-four. I was a naive, inexperienced version of myself. A first-time entrepreneur with no business background—and no clue. Alana was just twenty-eight. We were babies. Sometimes, I think back and truly don't know how we survived.

IF WE COULD DO IT, SO CAN YOU. AS LONG AS YOU'RE WILLING TO TAKE SOME CHANCES, KEEP YOUR HEAD UP, AND MAKE A LOT OF MISTAKES.

This is the story of Bulletin, but it's also the story of Alex, who crowdsourced millions of dollars to launch a sexual wellness and vibrator company. It's the story of Jasmine, who turned a poetry career into a bona fide brand and product line. It's the story of Michelle, who turned a love for illustration and graphic design into a beloved greeting card company. I've spent two years interviewing entrepreneurs from different backgrounds, means, and walks of life, all building brands and selling products. Their stories are different, but in hearing them recount their ups, downs and in-betweens, one thing is clear: if we could do it, so can you. As long as you're willing to take some chances, keep your head up, and make a lot of mistakes.

Bulletin is a platform that helps independent brands grow and scale, and it has taken many faces and forms over the past few years. We began as an e-commerce site featuring products and stories from cool indie brands. Then we decided to think big and began (trying) to build a scalable business. We learned that these digital brands wanted to sell their products in more stores. That led us to pop-up markets. We built and ran our own markets every weekend for ten consecutive months—and we made bank! But then we burnt out. So, we opened a permanent store other people could run. We opened another, and another. And then we built some software. Bulletin 3.0, as I call it, is a platform that makes it easy for modern, e-commerce brands to expand into brick-and-mortar retail. We are a two-sided marketplace. On the one side, we have our brands. This is our network of Shopify and Squarespace and Etsy sellers that are looking to get their products into retailers around the country. On the other, we have our retailers. This is our paying customer. They come to our site to discover our brands and shop inventory for their stores. To flex a bit: we've graduated from a well-known accelerator program in Silicon Valley, raised more than $9 million in venture funding, and scaled our team from two to ten to twenty. That's the high-level, sixty-second overview of Bulletin—who we are, where we've been, and what we've seen—but there's obviously plenty more to share.

But, please, keep in mind: having funding and a team and a multiyear business doesn't mean I know what I'm doing all the time. I am writing this in real-time, from the trenches of ignorance, panic, and constant self-doubt. I take every day as it comes and, given Bulletin's jagged history of shifts and pivots, I know full well the future is a black box—or at least a dark gray box. Sometimes I wonder if tomorrow's the day I'll feel wise and all-knowing, like I can see exactly how this is all going to play out. That day never comes, and it never will, and I feel just as uncertain as I did the day before. My hope is that writing from that place will make your climb a little less scary. And that the candor will help you find humor—not failure—as you hobble your way to the top.

A big point of this book (spoiler alert!): you can only get to the top if you aim for it. At one very distinct point in time, Alana and I decided to at least try to build a massive company. Then even if we failed, at least we would know we tried to go big. Women often suffer from being taught to think small. They worry they don't have the traits, resources, or vision necessary to bring an industry-disrupting idea or pipe dream business to life. It's partially a representation issue: there are far fewer women CEOs running the companies or brands we interact with every day. And the media—Netflix, news, Twitter, reality TV—plays a huge role in shaping and defining our sense of who gets to innovate and lead. While that has been slowly improving, in most of the TV shows and movies that exist, a white man plays the president. Or the top exec. Or the leader of the pack. News coverage, reflecting our actual political reality, is flush with headlines about old dudes changing and shaping the world, for better or for worse.

When a founder does see her company through an IPO, gets a coveted political seat, or becomes CEO at a Fortune 500 company, it's treated as some sort of exception or miracle, like a three-legged horse on Xanax just won the Kentucky Derby ("We never saw it coming! What a day, folks!"). Even within our own community, across social media, panels, and networking groups, we use words like "she-e-o" and "female founder," which makes normal identifiers like the plain old "CEO" or "founder" feel wrong or reserved for men. We deserve those identifiers, those titles, those positions. We need to start using language that normalizes women taking positions of power. Because you deserve to be hyperambitious and take your hustle, project, or business as far as you want it to go. Some people believe in themselves and others don't. Try to be the version of you who genuinely thinks, Hey, wait. Maybe I *can* do this. Why the hell not? Kill your potential-dysmorphia and stretch your interpretation of how far you can take your career. You'll be surprised at how many opportunities open up if you let yourself stretch, even a little.

While Bulletin is a retail start-up, I didn't come from retail, and Alana didn't really either. It's okay to have zero experience in your new career or venture. Don't think less of yourself for being ignorant about certain concepts or terms off the bat. But be ready to learn—and you'd better ask for help. First-time founder? *Everyone was a first-timer once.* Zero clue how to code? Sign your ass up for a General Assembly class. Know nothing about makeup but want a coveted job at a rising skincare brand? Start reading. Interview a dermatologist. Chat up everyone on the floor at Sephora. Join free Slack communities or networking groups for founders in your industry. I don't necessarily know the path for every career out there or every role on the planet. No one ever could. But I do know that asking industry people lots of questions is key, and that requires both pausing your pride and silencing insecurity. This is hard to do when certain industries or careers feel like a total boys' club. I remember having no clue what a start-up valuation was in a room full of Silicon Valley dudes who seemed to live and breathe tech terminology. Alana and I literally forced a founder acquaintance to write us a script for our first investor conversation. This book is going to try to demystify that culture and some business terminology, the way I wish someone had explained it to me.

ALANA AND I LITERALLY FORCED A FOUNDER ACQUAINTANCE TO WRITE US A SCRIPT FOR OUR FIRST INVESTOR CONVERSATION.

I've talked to dozens upon dozens of female entrepreneurs who have built viable brands and businesses, and I'm honored to share their insights with you. These brands are all at completely different growth stages, sought varying means of capital, and represent a funky blend of part-time and full-time entrepreneurs. As I mentioned earlier, this isn't just my story. That would be kinda conceited (wouldn't put it past me, though!) and, ultimately, not that helpful. My hope is that even if you don't relate to me, or my path, you'll feel inspired by and connected to these other brands and businesses—to *their* empires.

So, to all of you: The ones who worry they aren't ready to break off and start a business. The ones who worry they don't have the proper network in place, or the tools or resources to start something from scratch. The ones who worry they aren't cool enough to launch a consumer brand or don't have enough "influence" to inspire sales. The ones intimidated by the logistics and financial aspects of becoming a freelancer, launching an LLC, or hustling paycheck to paycheck. The ones who have big, murky, terrifying decisions ahead of them: raising capital, finding a business partner, pivoting, doing their own PR, managing a team . . .

I'm about to demystify the journey from the inside. This isn't intended to be some glossy, editorialized look at two female founders, bopping around in crisp, stylish outfits and "crushing it." This is a look at two real women who evolved into entrepreneurs from the dilapidated couch of a stuffy, lightless apartment, where dreams would be made, risks would be taken, and businesses would be born.

TAKEAWAYS!

KILL YOUR POTENTIAL-DYSMORPHIA.

DELUSION IS REQUIRED.

IT'S OKAY TO BE GREEN.

CHAPTER ONE

YOU GOTTA START SOMEWHERE

Let's get down to brass tacks here.

Who am I?

And how did I get here?

I am not a household name, and you may want some background info on me because, well, I'm giving you advice.

That's fair.

I lived twenty-four eventful years prior to launching Bulletin with Alana, and while my ten-year battle with chronic acne or brief stint as a horse lover may serve up some juicy entertainment, there is very little to learn from some drawn-out autobiography about my early life. And that's kind of the point, here. I didn't have parents plugged into the tech community, a well-connected group of founder friends, or financial resources at my fingertips. I never thought about entrepreneurship, launching a brand, or weaseling my way into Silicon Valley. I never joined a business club or got an MBA or even followed founders on social media. But business nestled its way into my lap, and into my life.

I had frantic entrepreneur parents that fled New York right after I was born because raising a baby in the city seemed literally impossible. They'd just started a small production company and, after nine months of carrying my stroller up a six-floor walkup, moved to LA, where they could, presumably, have a more steady, predictable life in the media and entertainment industry.

My family is (not super, but very) Jewish, and so they sent me to a religious day school through age eighteen. I knew the same one-hundred-or-so classmates until college. As I got older, if I wanted something, I had to buy it myself. I started working at the age of fifteen as a barista at a local bakery and did a whole camp counselor-tutor-babysitter shuffle. My life in LA was very non-LA, or at least, not the LA reflected in *Beverly Hills, 90210* or *The Hills*. When I tell people I'm from the sunny West Coast, I always have to add that no, I didn't see celebs on the daily. And no, I didn't go to any of the LA clubs or hot spots they've seen on

Keeping Up with the Kardashians. I spent most of my Friday nights at Shabbat dinner or flopping around the house with my closest friends.

My parents were entrepreneurs, hustlers, hunter-gatherers. Some years were fruitful, and others weren't so much. For the most part, though, my early years were very privileged and very steady. I always had a beautiful roof over my head, food on the table, clothes on my back, a great education, and woke up knowing how each day was going to go. My parents gave me the world and worked their asses off to build a business that supported our entire family.

We spent my later high school years struggling with my dad's medical issues, our financial woes, and their marital tension. All three things converged into a giant, unruly tornado that threw our lifelong stability out of whack and turned every day into a suspenseful fourteen-hour slog for me and my younger brother. My parents struggled to make consistent money, we were drowning in hospital bills, and my brother and I were acutely aware that shit was hitting the fan. (Hi, Ben! I love you. We made it!) To make things significantly worse, because of our tight-knit community, our fall from grace was quite public. A lot of *other* people knew shit was hitting the fan, too. It was one of the most challenging, upsetting periods in my life. When it was time to go to college, I was eager to move very, very far away. I wanted to expand my worldview, meet new people, break out of my narrow day school bubble, and start living a life I could fully control. I got into the University of Pennsylvania off the waitlist, and I'm pretty sure I peed, cried, and booked my ticket to orientation that same day.

Outside of classes, I gorged on extracurriculars—a cappella, theater, sorority stuff—and was a work-study employee at a literary nonprofit on campus called the Kelly Writers House. The Writers House was a magical place. They had famous authors, journalists, and playwrights visit almost every day, and I helped run the readings and Q+As, which really meant I cut up baguettes and cheese and spent most of the night talking books with my brilliant co-workers and trying to steal sips of wine during the receptions.

Then, right before my sophomore year, my parents decided to divorce, their shared business finally fell apart, and it was up to me and my mom to cover tuition. To make sure I could graduate, I spent my summers working at restaurants, tutoring, teaching kids to sing, staffing a boutique—literally anything to make some money. I eventually took on another part-time job during the school year writing copy at a local ad agency, where I got to dress up in my Urban Outfitters blazer and feel professional.

When graduation reared its head, I did what every type-A freakazoid overachiever kid does: OCR, which stands for "on campus recruiting." Despite my math and Excel anxiety, I applied to endless consulting, banking, and finance jobs. I just wanted money. A stable income. Financial security for the first time in a long time. I thought zero about my own strengths, skills, and pleasures, but I studied really hard and begged my Wharton friends to train me (insert a *Rocky*-style montage here). By the end of the first semester, I landed a job, which I would start after graduating. It was in asset management, which meant a $60K salary, benefits, and the envy of my employment-thirsty peers. At the time, I was making an average of $10 an hour and saving like a maniac. $60K a year would dramatically change my life.

Then, I quit. I quit before I even started. As May loomed, I started to think of my actual day-to-day in said asset-management role, and I kind of wanted to jump out a window. It just didn't feel quite right, like being in an unhealthy relationship you know is doomed to end. I didn't want to spend my days deep in Excel, dealing with numbers, building a career in financial services. I'm not knocking anyone who does this—it just didn't seem fulfilling to me personally. It didn't play to my strengths. I didn't have a backup job, but I knew I'd be comfortable in a ton of other roles, whether working at a store again, finding another barista gig, bartending, or becoming a hostess—

all jobs I'd happily done before. I was set on moving to New York and making it work no matter what. I called up the HR department and asked them to void my contract.

I met my first boss, Alison, at an a cappella reunion at University of Pennsylvania. She was forty, in the midst of a divorce, and needed an assistant. She worked in the marketing department at Condé Nast and without a job description, salary, or really even knowing her for more than five minutes, I said yes. I loved magazines. I grew up reading *Vogue* and *Allure* (and *OK!* magazine and *Us Weekly* and *Life & Style*, of course). When I was young, I used to cut up my mom's old magazines and make new, original magazines with Elmer's glue. I knew I'd be doing bitch work, but I figured I'd be doing it at the most prestigious magazine publisher in the world while working for a woman I admired. That, to me, was light-years better than faking my way through managing some rich guy's money.

I worked at Condé for about a year, and yeah, I was totally right—I did a ton of bitch work. I had to supplement my abysmally low salary with babysitting on weeknights and weekends, so I was working seven days a week that whole year. I was a Hamptons au pair throughout my first summer, so I was there Friday nights through Sunday nights. And in the fall, I trekked from Astor Place to the Upper West Side, my Saturdays and Sundays lived on and off the 6 train. And because I was broke, I shared a bedroom with my boss's seven-year-old daughter for six months. In exchange for free housing, I was an on-call babysitter and would help out around the house. I slept on a twin trundle bed beside Eden, her youngest, and commuted with Alison to work every morning. I know the privilege of going to a prestigious school with a strong alumni network afforded me this opportunity and others, but not every alum gives a fresh New Yorker a place to live and food to eat. I am forever indebted to Alison for making my New York life possible. Without her, I would not have been able to move to the city after graduating. My trajectory, and my entire professional life, would have looked very different had Alison not opened her home to me.

Thanks to Alison—for both the job and the free rent—my first year in New York was pretty magical. Sure, I was mostly making copies, getting coffee, and booking conference rooms, but I also sat in on every meeting I could. I shadowed older employees who I thought did interesting things, and I asked my bosses to give me mini research projects. Alison always obliged and gave me every feasible opportunity. I was exhausted, but I was home.

After a year, I hit a ceiling. Alison had left. I wanted to do more than my limited role required. It was clear that proactive projects weren't necessarily welcome or expected, especially from an entry-level employee. No one in my department, aside from Alison, was going to give me interesting work. I was a department coordinator. That's all they needed and wanted from me.

I like to say I was poached by a company called Contently because it just sounds so *divine* to be poached. But really, I did some very aggressive stalking and the LinkedIn equivalent of sliding into my soon-to-be new boss's DMs. Elisa had come to the office to pitch Contently, and, from my desk, I heard the entire meeting go down. I knew instantly that I had to get in touch with her. Contently provided an editorial team on-demand. Meaning, if brands needed content—video, articles, infographics—Contently would vet and recruit the perfect freelancers to make it happen.

I hit up Elisa via a thoughtful LinkedIn message, and she responded that same day. By the end of the week, I had interviewed with the Contently founders, got poached, and had a new employment contract in hand. It was enough of a salary bump that I could finally stop working weekends. That's all I needed to know.

My title was sales strategist, which sounded mega-fancy. But really, I was just helping my sales executive close deals with brands that needed quality content. My exec got let go within the year, and I was haphazardly tasked with filling the gap. As it turned out, I was damn good at sales. I was a smooth talker, sharp, and a little cheeky. But most important, I knew content better than most others on my team because of my time doing all that bitch work and squatting in meetings at Condé. I got promoted twice in a year's time, was pulling in a six-figure salary, and making bank on my commission. I was able to help my mom pay for my brother's college tuition and get her thoughtful gifts for her birthday. At twenty-four, I was proud of myself.

But the repetitive nature of my sales role eventually started to wear on me. I was having the same quasi-scripted pitch conversations every day, even telling the same stale joke at the start of every call. I loved that I was able to fuse together my content expertise and sales skills to make a ton of money, but when I got frank with myself, I didn't want to sell writers to big brands. I wanted to be a writer.

And this is the part of the story where Alana changes my life.

Around the time of this realization, I became friends with my very cool, very chic co-worker Alana. She was four years older than me, a bleached blonde beauty, and always perfectly styled. And she laughed at my jokes. Alana was (and still is) a force to be reckoned with. She's a strategic, bold bitch from Long Island who, I think in hindsight, knew she was meant for something big. She graduated from Wake Forest with an economics degree and meandered through bizarre finance-adjacent jobs for a few years after college. She eventually landed a gig at 3x1, a luxury denim start-up in SoHo, managing their concept store and overseeing business development, which really meant placing thousand-dollar jean orders for Jack Dorsey and other high-powered dudes with too much money. We started at Contently on the same day, and we were desk-mates.

One day, while we were sitting in our open-concept office space, she mentioned she was thinking of launching a side project: her own digital magazine that would showcase and celebrate the coolest internet brands nobody had heard of yet—the little guys on Etsy, Shopify, and Instagram that were hard to find. Alana had read some of the stuff I'd written over the past few years, so she asked me to join her as editor in chief. This cool girl? Wanted *me*? To write for her? I was working a cushy 10-to-6 gig and had tons of free time after work and on the weekends. It seemed like the perfect way to add writing samples to my portfolio without totally abandoning my lucrative career.

Because I had never envisioned working on something entrepreneurial alone *or* with a partner, I never thought through who that partner might be or what their skills or temperament might look like. But I didn't flinch when Alana asked me to come on board. I didn't sit and weigh her strengths against my weaknesses, assess her priorities against mine, or think through her ability to be a leader and CEO. I didn't do an ounce of probing, critical thinking, or questioning. I *knew* this person. I admired her as a colleague, I saw her work ethic firsthand, and, even without trying, she inspired me. It didn't feel like this heavy, big, will-dramatically-change-the-course-of-your-life decision. It was a friend I looked up to asking me to do something fun.

From the start, where I saw obstacles, Alana saw opportunities. When an artist could only meet at 4 P.M. on a Thursday, I'd flip. Meanwhile, Alana would fake a meeting on our work calendars so we could sneak out to Brooklyn and do the interview. In the early days, we were like two giddy tweens keeping a juicy secret. A handful of brand interviews and after-work brainstorm sessions later, I had caught her bug and began to see my future as a blank canvas rather than a linear story.

We'd scour websites and retail stores for brands with cool products we wanted to feature. We picked brands that made stuff we loved. We picked brands that made stuff we thought other people might love. Using our sales skills from Contently, Alana and I would find these brands' e-mail addresses, explain our business, and ask if they'd like to be featured. I pitched them on a long-form, in-depth editorial piece about their aspirations and aesthetic. We would take 40 percent of every online sale and the brand would keep 60 percent. Alana had run a small e-commerce side hustle before called Barb and Bear, so she took a lot of what she'd learned and applied it to our business model. She advised that we do drop-ship, meaning we didn't own any of the featured product, we'd just notify brands once we generated an order and they would fulfill it themselves and send the item to the customer. That way, we could reduce our overhead and keep things lean. We didn't have a grand plan, and just tried to improve bit by bit. We were exploring and executing at the same time. Which, in retrospect, is a great definition for entrepreneurship.

Bulletin took us to the edge of Red Hook, where we interviewed a guy named Reed Hansuld, who made stunning furniture, like the walnut-framed rocking chair we put on our first business cards. It took us to Chinatown, where George Venson was hand-painting wilted penises, colorful koi, and rouged lips on delicate wallpaper under the brand Voutsa. And it took us to Greenpoint, where the late Laura Busony designed stunning, otherworldly jewelry that made you feel like a rich intergalactic princess. We bopped around the city interviewing designers who caught our eye, immersing ourselves in their world for just an hour or two. We'd throw my editorial features up with high-res pictures of their products and send off little "news bulletins" via e-mail when we had new brands to share. Hence, the company name.

WE HELD EACH OTHER ACCOUNTABLE AND RESPECTED EACH OTHER ENOUGH TO COME THROUGH.

We would work over Gchat and e-mail. We'd do our respective tasks at our leisure. I'd write the featured editorial over a week or two. Alana would tinker with Squarespace to make things look clean and build brands' products onto the site when she had time. There was no ticking clock or any crazy external pressure. But we held each other accountable and respected each other enough to come through.

We felt so committed to our brands. We cared a lot about each and every designer we interviewed, and the nature of our project meant we knew them pretty intimately, even if from afar. Because their lives inspired products, their experiences could dictate an entire collection, and, as small businesses, they were very vocal about "making it" as struggling creatives in New York. We wanted Bulletin to work—we wanted to make them money—because after meeting these creatives, we genuinely hoped they would succeed. And, even if irrational, we felt somewhat responsible to help make that happen. That accountability kept us moving forward.

Starting Bulletin 1.0 wasn't scary. It wasn't stressful, and it wasn't all-consuming. I still grabbed happy hour wine with friends, milked my weekend downtime, traveled, and fell asleep at 11 P.M. Often, inspirational Instagram accounts or #bossbabe influencers will frame entrepreneurship as this all-consuming, all-or-nothing choice. And trust me, if you reach a certain scale, or if you're trying to, running a business will Pac-Man the fuck out of your life and eat up any leisure time you've got. But often, "starting a business" can just mean "monetizing a hobby," and that's something you can do on your own terms and in your own time.

Whatever you start, and whoever you start with, just be sure you care a lot. Pick something you want to keep coming back to, so when it's 10 P.M. on a Sunday and your activity choices are an hour of bingeing Netflix vs. an hour of biz-time, you feel an urgency and excitement around your project and are 23 percent juiced up to work on it. That 77 percent is always gunna yearn for a lazy nightcap with *The Great British Bake Off*—trust me, this will never change. But your project should matter enough to prevent you from abandoning it slowly as time goes on or when shit hits the fan.

"STARTING
A BUSINESS"
CAN JUST MEAN
"MONETIZING
A HOBBY,"
AND THAT'S
SOMETHING
YOU CAN
DO ON YOUR
OWN TERMS
AND IN YOUR
OWN TIME.

PICKING A CO-FOUNDER!

I copped to this earlier—but yes, I did minimal-to-zero vetting when deciding to work alongside Alana. But the *last* thing I want to do is evangelize the idea that you can blindly enter a business partnership. So, to cover my ass and (hopefully) help you out a smidge, here's a checklist I made with the help and guidance of various Bulletin brands and their founders. Some unlocked lifelong friendship and prosperity, while others were met by lawsuits and loss. My Spidey senses tell me we're going for the former, so listen up!

☐ **Look for someone who shares your values.** You know how sometimes you and a college friend outgrow each other because you're just kind of—I dunno—living on two different planets? Yeah—don't start a company with someone like that, aka someone you just flat out can't relate to or fundamentally don't understand. You and your co-founder kind of need a hive mind, so you should baseline "get" each other.

YOU AND YOUR CO-FOUNDER KIND OF NEED A HIVE MIND, SO YOU SHOULD BASELINE "GET" EACH OTHER.

☐ **Don't just pick someone out of circumstance or convenience.** You're stuck with them for years and years to come, so don't just bet on what feels easy or simple right now. I had a close friend move in with her boyfriend straight out of college because she didn't know anyone else looking for a roommate in NYC. They broke up within four months. That's the type of convenience-driven decision-making I'm talking about. You don't want to end up dissolving your company because you shacked up with your partner too quickly because it was easy.

☐ **If you plan to go full-time with your business, find someone you can talk to candidly about money.** Sometimes, it's easier to partner with someone who has similar financial means or a similar risk profile. What are each of you really putting on the line? What's going to keep you both up at night? You should both have serious skin in the game to feel the weight of your undertaking and work as hard as humanly possible, and it can be kind of awkward when one founder has to seriously worry about money and the other is livin' cushy clean. It might breed resentment or generate tension that could be tough to navigate. At the very least, find someone who makes you feel like money-talk is okay. Maybe you come from wildly different means—and that's fine. They could easily be the perfect match for you. But put that financial shit out in the open and be candid about your risk profile so one person isn't being sucked dry while the other has no idea.

☐ **Find a complement.** The yin to your yang. So much of entrepreneurship is learning to divide and conquer. Pick someone who fills gaps in your skillset and can own an entire piece of the biz early on. You can't do everything, but everything needs to be done well. It's nice to rest easy at night knowing your partner has a handle on things that are out of your wheelhouse.

HOW FAR WILL SOMEONE GO, HOW HARD WILL THEY WORK, AND HOW MUCH CAN THEY ACCOMPLISH—EVEN WHEN NO ONE IS LOOKING?

☐ **Try to find a builder.** Someone you've seen actually start something and see it through to completion. Before Alana brought me on to do editorial work for Bulletin, she watched me conceptualize, film, edit, and market a documentary I had made after graduating...just because. It wasn't for work or money or any sort of prize. It was a creative project I was excited to sink my teeth into. And I was able to peruse Alana's previous e-commerce site, Barb and Bear, the brand she built years before meeting me. A lot of this is about accountability: how far will someone go, how hard will they work, and how much can they accomplish—even when no one is looking?

■ **Someone you'd consider a friend, even if you didn't have to work with them.** Not necessarily a best friend or a close friend, but someone you genuinely like. This person will be by your side, either physically or digitally, for most of your waking hours for the foreseeable future. Like them. It makes it easier. And obviously way more fun.

■ **Ego is a no-go.** Growing a business requires vulnerability. The entire premise of "starting a business" requires you to try to keep tabs of what is and isn't working. And ideally, you're comfortable admitting when something's off or not contributing to your company's growth. People with crazy ego are never truly vulnerable—their self-perception serves as a weapon against critical feedback or failure. Here, ego gets in the way of making smart decisions. You need a partner who can admit when they're wrong, pivot in the face of failure, and ask for help. Ego makes this way less likely, and you don't want that shit stinking up your company. It makes for bad leadership and toxic energy.

YOU NEED A PARTNER WHO CAN ADMIT WHEN THEY'RE WRONG, PIVOT IN THE FACE OF FAILURE, AND ASK FOR HELP.

I am extremely fortunate that Alana checks all of these boxes; but she is much more than a technically compatible partner. She is an ego-free, proactive person that I can laugh with and trust in and count on. Yes, we can talk about money and other "taboo" topics openly and without judgment. We bring different strengths and skills to the table, and we share the same values and expectations. But most important, she believed in me despite knowing I wasn't perfect; despite coming to learn my flaws. She is judicious, strategic, and careful when I get rash, distracted, and careless. She helps anchor my lofty creative ideas to actual tasks and next steps. She is optimistic, clear-eyed, and encouraging when I get nihilistic, irrational, or discouraged. She saw potential in me and helped me expand my sense of self. She accepts me, even when I'm messy; even when I'm down. The boxes are important, but finding someone who believes in you supersede every empty check box.

EIGHT WAYS TO BUILD CONTACTS IN YOUR INDUSTRY

Maybe you're scouting for a co-founder, seeking a mentor, or simply looking for a door into your industry. Often, you don't have these contacts at your fingertips. You'll need to hunt for the right people who can help refine or launch your idea.

1. (Thoughtfully) Attend Networking Events

I've met and interviewed *so* many founders who credit an in-person networking event for finding their long-term business partner, or someone more one-and-done, like a short-term advisor who can make helpful intros or increase your industry knowledge. You can find free industry networking events on sites like Eventbrite or Meetup, or google larger conferences or industry events in your city if you're able to pay a ticket price.

If there are certain players in your industry that you admire—a blogger, CTO, founder, or creator—follow them on all their social channels and keep tabs on any panels they're joining or conferences they'll be attending. Don't be afraid to gun for a front-row seat and linger by the stage after they present or speak. It might be worth asking what *they* did to break into their industry and build the right network—and always politely ask if you can send them a few questions over e-mail. They might say no—we're all busy creatures with our own boundaries and commitments; but some—in fact many—might say yes.

Set intentions and goals before any in-person event: What outcome will mean this event was worth your time, or your ticket? Do you want to meet six new people in your industry? Are they folks you can brainstorm with, or learn from? See, those are two different things. Do you want to get the e-mail address of at least one featured panelist? Or do you simply want to go and absorb more industry know-how? Understand why you're going, and then map out how you'll reach that outcome. But most important, don't be shy. You really do have to put yourself and your idea out there to get value from any in-person programming or networking opportunity.

2. Attend Digital Workshops and Events

The pandemic fundamentally changed the way we do business. Online conferences, panels, meetups, and mentorship sessions are all the rage. It's a blessing for entrepreneurs and side hustlers everywhere: You now have free or affordable access to people, conversations, and networking opportunities that would normally be more expensive or exclusive. Heavy hitters in your industry—whether it's tech, wellness, beauty, logistics, fashion, health care; you name it—are posting on Twitch, IGTV, YouTube, and more to share their insights. In many cases, you can actually see the other people attending these webinars and chat with them in real time. I've seen countless entrepreneurs use this chat real estate to quickly share both what they're building and their e-mail addresses. It's great for those who are a bit uncomfortable with the forced introductions and pressure of an in-person event.

3. Do Some Cold Outreach

I get cold DMs and e-mails from aspiring retail entrepreneurs all the time. Even if I can't answer them immediately, I do my best to respond and provide guidance when and where I can. Obviously, I err on the side of wanting to help and support other founders and aspiring entrepreneurs—I'm writing this book after all! Many founders won't have the bandwidth to respond. But there are those who, remembering their own desperate days trying to milk insights or words of wisdom from entrepreneurs *they* admired, will, in due time, throw you a bone. With this in mind, make a long list (long, like . . . fifty to seventy-five people) of founders and senior executives in your industry that you want to reach out to. You can find those senior execs by using LinkedIn. Remember, though: when you build your list, don't aim *too* high. I mean it. You'll decrease the likelihood of anyone getting back to you. If you're looking to start a speed-dating business, the CEO of Bumble is probably out of pocket—indefinitely. But an events or partnerships manager at Bumble probably would be flattered to hear from you and is more likely to read your note and reply.

After finding these contacts on LinkedIn, search for their Instagram handles or Twitter profiles and craft a short but effective message that puts *them* in the driver's seat. Ask if they'd be available for a fifteen-minute call whenever is most convenient, or if they'd prefer that you send a list of three questions via e-mail. Be sure to double and triple check their information before you hit send: Did they leave that role recently? Does their profile explicitly say "no outreach please?" Much like IRL networking, cold outreach requires that you be bold. It also requires that you be gracious, thoughtful, patient, and attentive. Don't send a barrage of questions up front or make your message too long and unwieldy. Know what you want to learn from this person, keep your communication tight, and respect both their time and their boundaries.

4. **Stalk and Scrape the Comments Section of Instagram**

   Okay, this one is a bit . . . unconventional. If you're not a fan of digital or IRL programming as a form of networking, or you don't feel comfortable cold e-mailing already established founders or senior execs, you can find other entrepreneurs at your level all over IG. If you currently follow those already established founders on social media or keep tabs on other industry players on Instagram, you can find and network with other aspiring or early founders by stalking the ever-entertaining comments on their posts. In many cases, followers will comment in droves and post about their own companies, or even start full-blown conversations in IG comments. This is a great way to meet and connect with other business owners or aspiring founders who are just starting out, whether you're looking to build a small community of peers so you can help each other stay accountable, or want advice from folks who appear a few paces ahead of you.

5. **Join Industry Slack Groups**

   Many know Slack as an internal communications tool for companies far and wide, but it has also become a community hub and discussion platform for founders, creatives, and entrepreneurs everywhere. You need not be working for a company using Slack to use Slack yourself. Many microcommunities—likeminded marketers, developers, designers— have launched and joined Slack "channels" to network, problem-solve, and share resources with one another. Most are free, and some have an application process or a membership fee. Google around for Slack groups by industry, region, city, profession, and more.

6. **Tap Your Alumni Network**

   If you went to high school, college, junior college, or community college, you can find alumni in your industry and ask them for mentorship or guidance, whether by thoughtfully e-mailing them (if your school gives you that info) or by sending them a quick note on LinkedIn. It's super-easy to find alumni on Facebook, and in some cases, schools even have their own digital databases you can access and sift through. Also, attend all the reunions. Do it. Even if a small part of you worries it'll be lame. I met my first boss at my dream company while singing a cappella at a college reunion. I didn't go to my ten-year high school reunion, and I truly regret it. Your community is your best resource.

7. Download the Apps

There are a ton of apps, groups, and platforms out there that literally LIVE to help people network: Mogul, Ladies Get Paid, Freelancing Females, Dreamers & Doers, Bumble Bizz. They are, in most cases, free to join and use. Some have built their own apps; others leverage platforms like Slack and Facebook to do their community-building. But all the aforementioned apps serve the same purpose of connecting and supporting female entrepreneurs.

8. Creep Crowdfunding Campaigns

Entrepreneurs are launching crowdfunding campaigns on Kickstarter, IFundWomen, Indiegogo, and Patreon every day. Of course, those folks are in the thick of a major campaign—if they're in the throes of crowd-funding, they may not be inclined to drop everything and get on a call or get back to your e-mail right then and there. But you can surf these sites to find entrepreneurs in your space and stash their company info and e-mails and try to hit them up post-campaign. It's definitely worth chipping in to a few of these campaigns, if you can, as I bet those entrepreneurs will be even more likely to respond to your cold e-mail or DM if you supported them when they needed it most.

HOW DID YOU GET STARTED?

ASHLEY MOLESSO
ASH + CHESS

I met my boyfriend and business partner, Chessie, online, and we fell pretty hard pretty fast. At the time, I was working at a wallpaper company and went to tons of exhibitions like the National Stationery Show and International Contemporary Furniture Fair. These fairs let vendors showcase their products in the hopes of getting a wholesale deal with a retailer. I was a full-time graphic designer but always envisioned building a brand or running my own business. As a middle-schooler, I handmade these little wallets and flip-flops out of duct tape and chokers from rubber bands and sold them to all my friends. My goal was to buy a pink yacht someday. That was like, my North Star. My priorities have changed, but I always wanted to play by my own rules, I guess.

So, I started going to those exhibitions and collected catalogs and lookbooks from brands that I thought were cool, just in case they'd come in handy down the line. After getting together, I asked Chessie to walk the National Stationery Show with me. We were so inspired. We were walking around, so happy and so in love, and we realized we could do this. We could do this together. It was this feeling of, well, why not? The following year, we launched our brand, Ash + Chess, and bought a booth at the show. It cost us $3,000, which felt really scary and kind of risky, but I was confident. I knew what I was doing. I had seen other vendors do it for years, so knew how to showcase the brand.

We started producing stuff for the show but had somewhat of a rocky start. We were initially doing letterpress pieces that were really time consuming and costly. And then we moved into digital printing, but our first production place was insanely expensive and killed our margins. We eventually found the right production partner and got to work producing an initial line of cards and prints. The show was a major turning point for us. We booked a handful of stockists and everyone was just really surprised it was our first year in business because we made sure to present everything perfectly.

Cut to now, and we've evolved from a small card company to a multi-category brand that's worked with Forever21, Belletrist, and Urban Outfitters. We sell all around the country—and even in Japan. That makes us, like, a global brand! Which is nuts. But it started out with us falling in love and a few baby steps. It's still this fun, stress-free activity we share. I get to design stuff I like and put it out into the world—something I wanted to do since seventh grade. And Chessie has a passion project outside of his full-time teaching job. We decided to do what makes us happy and take a few risks. It's all about focusing on what you want and making small changes to get there.

TRINITY MOUZON WOFFORD

GOLDE

I've always been a wellness-y person. I grew up in Upstate New York in the '90s—also known as Birkenstock land at the time. I was raised by a single parent with a debilitating auto-immune disease. When my mom started seeing more holistic MDs and then rapid improvement of her symptoms, it was a really pivotal moment for me. After a while, she had to stop seeing those doctors because it was so expensive. That really angered and upset me, and I became hyperaware of how disgusting and unfair the health care system is in this country.

After graduating from NYU premed with a psych degree, I wasn't really sure what I wanted to do. I fell into a career in marketing at a start-up, and I absolutely loved it. I totally became "that" co-worker who was constantly recommending herbal remedies and telling people to eat garlic cloves. (They really work, by the way!) I knew I had to get back into wellness somehow and focus on accessibility.

My business partner and high school sweetheart, now fiancé, Issey, was really the missing piece. His family has run their own small business for more than twenty years, and learning about them growing profitably and sustainably helped us realize we could do this. We could consider launching a company. We were both still at our full-time jobs but slowly decided we wanted to launch a product-based company in the wellness space, so we just kind of started playing around. We formulated the first series of products ourselves, spending months finding the best possible raw materials, trying infinite combinations of the ingredients to make sure it tasted really good but had strong wellness benefits, too.

From a packaging perspective, we were very bootstrap-y. A friend through Issey's job, who was a professional graphic designer, helped us out. The first product we launched was the turmeric latte blend. We were, what, twenty-three? We didn't have funding or experience, but I think not having that background is okay. We could do this.

LAURA SCHUBERT
FUR

I've known Lillian since our seventh-grade orientation. We did high school gymnastics together, we went to college together, and we even ended up getting our MBAs together. I became really interested in entrepreneurship while getting my MBA and knew that someday I was going to start my own business. In 2014 I was talking about body hair with my sister and realized there were no specific products for body hair. I left my consulting job and started working on the idea. Of course, I'm working on this beauty brand, so I have to call up my old girlfriend, Lillian, who works at L'Oréal doing beauty marketing. I learned that she was in the same place in her career where she was in midlevel management, wondering, Is this my calling? Is this what I want to be doing?

We were at the same holiday party in late 2014 and I had an early version of Fur oil in my purse. I approached her and said, I want you to try this. And I think you should do this with me. All I had was a formula. I didn't have a name. But she left L'Oréal in early 2015 to become my co-founder and our CMO. You have to worry if starting a business with your best friend makes things too personal. But actually, it feels like we were destined to be business partners. It's a very interesting relationship, and one you can't have with everybody.

LILLIAN TUNG

FUR

I hated the idea when she first pitched it to me. I thought it was a terrible idea. I know that shelf space is so crowded, and with pubic hair oil, you have to convince a consumer to spend money on something they've never had or tried before, and convince retailers to free up shelf space. It was a huge, but totally unproven category. I'm a pretty risk-averse person. I was coming from Corporate America Beauty. Laura had taken entrepreneurship-specific classes in business school, but I had never thought of becoming an entrepreneur. I'm a beauty person, a packaging person, and one night in 2014 Laura slips me a sample directly from the lab. It was completely unmarked . . . I just didn't get it at first. But then I tried the product—and the product was good. I slowly realized that if the product is good, which it was, and if I can market it, which I could, the whole thing will make sense. Because I knew I would work well with Laura. Talking about hiring issues, monetary issues, and legal issues can really test a friendship. We've known each other since we were twelve, and I knew who I was signing up for. Whatever your dynamic is from the start, it isn't going to change, it's just going to deepen.

POLLY RODRIGUEZ

UNBOUND

I grew up in the Midwest, where marriage, children, and buying a house were major bucket list items within my community. That's just, like, what you did. I was diagnosed with colorectal cancer at age twenty—literally, cancer of the butt. My chemo and radiation caused early onset menopause. I was infertile, and really confused about the state of my body and the future of my sex drive. A nurse recommended I buy a vibrator, but the entire shopping experience made me distressed and grossed out. I'd end up on trashy, vulgar websites hawking cheaply made sex toys or in the deep clinical K-hole of WebMD.

I ended up working in politics, consulting, and start-ups, but that shopping experience never left me. I simply couldn't find a brand that made me feel good and confident about investing in my own pleasure. While I was working at a start-up, Grouper, a former employee started a networking group on Facebook called Dreamers & Doers. I joined, and that's where I met my co-founder, Sarah Jayne. We launched this skeleton of a subscription box company where customers would get sexual wellness and pleasure products sent to them every month. Neither of us was working on it full-time, I didn't come from money, and I had no idea how to raise venture capital or take this small thing and make it bigger.

All I really knew for sure was to learn as much as possible, so I read a ton, held a lot of focus groups, and learned where the opportunity was. I always felt like I had no idea what I was doing, but I kept showing up and struggling and trying to make it work. I couldn't have kids, and I just kind of decided that this company was what I would raise and build and put out into the world. I was superstubborn and foolishly kept going, even when it meant insane credit card debt and lying to my parents. I made the leap into doing it full-time and kind of lied to myself about how it would all work out. I didn't ask myself, What if it doesn't work out? What happens when your money runs out? My parents couldn't financially support me, and, early on, the company definitely wasn't doing well. I had to get a handful of part-time jobs.

I remember one time my boyfriend showed up at the gala I was working at part-time and here I was, in some dumb T-shirt wearing a headset and a messy bun selling raffle tickets. I ran to the bathroom and started crying in embarrassment, only to realize, like, Why am I embarrassed? I am killing myself to put something out into the world and create something that's mine. I am building my dream. Not giving up in the early years is the same thing as success. Effort plus time is the magic equation.

VICTORIA ASHLEY
LAUNDRY DAY

I was looking for something to do in my spare time, so I started leatherworking. I put a few pieces up on Facebook and a local coffee shop owner responded and wanted to order them. When I got that response, it sparked something in me. I began working at a retail store and started putting my leatherworking stuff in there. I could see that people wanted what I was making, and soon the leathermaking went from this thing I was just doing to pass time in my apartment to something that was generating orders and bringing in some money. I had been doing it for a couple of months, and then my friend invited me to share a studio space.

The only place we could find in our budget was this weird little old house in an alley that used to be a retail location. I signed that lease when I was nineteen, and I was so scared. I was shaking and my friend had to convince me to see it through and sign the lease. The store is called Merge and we ran it together for three years. I tapered off from my leatherworking eventually—I didn't enjoy making products with my bare hands anymore and started to get way more interested in merchandising and packaging from working in the store.

Around then, I started having serious health issues. I was going back and forth to the doctor for three years for IUD problems that were being mis-diagnosed. I turned to cannabis for pain relief. My cannabis usage became something I wanted to take ownership of. I decided to make my own piece. I wanted a pipe that I wouldn't be ashamed of. I was using, like, my high school boyfriend's ugly pipe that he hid in a sock drawer. Merge was my platform to test out the prototypes and see if there was any customer interest. Seeing girls get excited about weed and hearing them ask, Why doesn't this already exist? was really validating.

I had planned a trip to New York and spoke with Polly, the co-founder of Unbound, a sexual wellness company. She changed my life. She kind of challenged me to shift my mind-set from this is a crafty little thing I am doing in my small town to maybe I've found a product and a story that speaks to people, and I can give women something they are looking for within this very male-dominated industry. She made me bring a piece to New York and present it to her team. I was so nervous I thought I was going to pass out. But in that encounter, I realized the brand and this more decor-oriented approach might appeal to masses of women. That opened up my eyes and encouraged me to pursue this new, bigger direction, which no one else had encouraged me to do.

CHAPTER TWO

THAT MAGICAL AND MISERABLE BEGINNING

Once you start something, you're committing to working on some-thing. And yes, a healthy cocktail of excitement, ambition, patience, and resilience can help you make that something great. But let's not get too delusional too quickly and act like we burp up viable, lucrative business ideas after lunch every day. It's obviously important to address the reali-ties of your pursuit, whether you're looking to launch a company or take any major career risk. Nailing down a meaty idea you can fund, execute, grow, and monetize is hard. It requires a ton of research, conversation, and education. And to do it well, you have to relinquish some ego and learn to hear and digest a lot of critical feedback.

I'm not some know-it-all business guru and I'm still in the trenches, just like you, but I am comfortable insisting that the magic behind any good idea is product-market fit (PMF). If you have product-market fit, then people want—and are using—your service or product. Alana and I learned the concept back in 2016, and since then, it has been the framework through which we adjust and grow our business. The first thing to really consider when launching something from scratch, then, is, Do people want this? And if so, how do I know that? I added that little follow-up question because it forces you to confront your own bias and ego. You may think people want something—a brand, a product, a service—because family and friends have said it was a good idea. But are they in your target market? Are they potential power users? How many people did you interview? Are they incentivized to give you their most informed, educated, and honest answer? I'm not sitting here assuming your parents said, "Go get 'em tiger!" so you abruptly quit your job to launch a brand or become an actor, throwing caution to the wind! I think most of us are prudent and risk-averse enough to gut-check an idea a bunch before chasing it. But uncovering the most accurate answer to "do people want this" requires a lot of legwork: interviewing hundreds of poten-tial users, reading about existing or potential competitors, and meeting relevant players already in your space.

The annoying part: this type of fact-finding can feel superrepetitive, unproductive, and tedious. "Talking" can feel like a waste of time because it isn't concrete or because you're getting similar feedback over and over again. You'll want to jump the gun and start building as soon as Person Three says they "love" the idea. But don't listen to that antsy-ass gremlin! Because here's what you'd be missing: the rewarding part. The rewarding thing about hunting down product-market fit in earnest is this: the more validation you get for the idea, the more excited you are to build it, and the more resilient you are when you fail. It's easier to give up on your idea if you secretly know that you didn't do the legwork to validate it. But when shit gets messy and you have a survey with all responses pointing to "I want this," you're more likely to retool the idea's execution, not abandon it.

When Alana and I launched Bulletin, we did not have product-market fit. Not even close. We were building something no one wanted. Bulletin began as an Etsy 2.0 that was highly editorial and way more curated. It would read like a digital magazine or publication—a Refinery29 or the Cut—that only featured thoughtful pieces about cool emerging brands and the designers who launched them. We'd sprinkle products throughout the stories so readers could shop the brand. This idea was far from revolutionary, and, in many ways, it already existed: Of a Kind, Tictail, and Bezar, all now resting in peace, were all doing the exact same thing. In our minds, the mere existence of competition spoke to the viability of the product and format. Bezar had raised more than $2 million in venture funding and tons of friends subscribed to the Of a Kind newsletter. We were just going to do it better, faster, cooler. And then brands and customers would pour into the site and make us millions!

WE PACED AROUND THE KITCHEN EATING ONE OF TWO MEALS—AN EGG AND BEAN BURRITO OR A PIECE OF AVOCADO TOAST—STRESSING OVER OUR SLOW SALES, NONEXISTENT CUSTOMERS, AND LACK OF TRACTION.

That's not what happened. From January 2016 to April 2016, we burrowed deep in Alana's apartment and tried to grow Bulletin, the shoppable magazine, to no success. We paced around the kitchen eating one of two meals—an egg and bean burrito or a piece of avocado toast—stressing over our slow sales, nonexistent customers, and lack of traction. We FaceTimed various advisors and mentors and tried to hash out our roadblocks and problems. But ultimately, we had to admit what we kind of knew all along: this digital magazine thing was a flop, and we had no viable business model.

As much as Alana and I wanted to own a booming digital magazine, it was becoming increasingly obvious that no one actually wanted one. We were in the middle of Y Combinator Fellowship at the time, and as the program neared its end, we met up with our YC advisor, Kevin, at a hotel lobby near Union Square in NYC. After two and a half months of hardcore slogging to get this digital magazine thing to take off, we sat with Kevin as he looked at our revenue numbers and told us what we already knew—but weirdly had to confirm—which was that this wasn't going to work. But right before the thirty-minute meeting ended, he pointed out one noticeable spike in our revenue buried deep in December 2015. "What's that?" he asked. Well, it was this event we did called Winter Break, a small preholiday weekend pop-up, to promote the site as a gifting destination. About thirty brands each paid $150 for a booth in this cozy Canal Street showroom and we had boozy hot chocolate and a stunning deejay. We had sworn to never do a pop-up again: it was exhausting, it was very poorly attended, and we *hated* the pressure of getting shoppers in the door. "But that's more revenue in one day than you made in two months of online sales. So, do that. Do it again." We were like *what?* Do another pop-up market? We left feeling totally dizzy and dazed and disheveled. It was a jarring thought: the notion we should ditch our digital platform, this passion project, in favor of some gimmicky weekend market concept we already knew we hated. Was Kevin crazy?

With Kevin's feedback in mind, we looked our stagnant business in the eye and thought, Hmm, what can we do with you? Then we realized, why ask ourselves when we can ask the brands directly? We needed to talk to our users. We decided to call the brands on our site to understand what solution we could build or help we could offer to increase their sales or improve their businesses. We didn't sit around reading thought leadership articles about e-commerce or look at recently funded retail companies on Crunchbase or call up more advisor-types for a second opinion on our tragic diagnosis. In isolation, that's wrong. Yes, you should get a second and third opinion from thoughtful, successful elders you trust. Yes, it is obviously wise to stay up-to-date on competitors or challengers or other industry disruptors via Crunchbase and TechCrunch and bunch-a-crunch. And of course, read about your industry and know it inside out. Use all of these strategies to gut-check your assumptions and educate yourself. But nothing should or can replace having an open line of communication with your customer. The answer is not in a Medium piece, and it isn't in some brilliant mentor's feedback, either. It's in your user. They should be your primary source of education and pave the path toward building something people want.

After chatting up dozens upon dozens of brands who sold with us on the site, we grew more and more convinced that Kevin was right. We learned that for many brands on Shopify, Squarespace, and Etsy, online channels weren't their true moneymakers. Often, they earned more in a weekend doing a good pop-up market than selling product through their website or any online marketplace in the same two-day span. We asked why they didn't join more pop-ups around New York, and they explained that while they were game to pay for pop-ups, many were simply too expensive or too exclusive, and that some even required you to commit to eight weekends up front. We saw a very clean, straight calculation of $1 + 1 = 2$. Brands want to do more pop-ups + brands would pay to do pop-ups = hello, new business model! Pop-ups here we *come*.

NOTHING SHOULD OR CAN REPLACE HAVING AN OPEN LINE OF COMMUNICATION WITH YOUR CUSTOMER. THE ANSWER IS NOT IN A MEDIUM PIECE, AND IT ISN'T IN SOME BRILLIANT MENTOR'S FEEDBACK, EITHER. IT'S IN YOUR USER.

We weren't approaching this idea with no inkling it would work: in fact, we were form-fitting our business to what brands were asking for. If we were able to successfully host a series of fun, well-attended markets that brands could afford to join, we'd make money, the brands would make money, and we'd be useful to our customer. So, we decided to help brands "go offline" by launching Bulletin Market, a series of weekend pop-ups all around Brooklyn that featured dozens of independent brands selling their wares directly to customers. We charged brands a couple hundred bucks a weekend to join, and we set up tables and tents for them to use and sell in. Our first Bulletin Market series was at Lot 45 in Brooklyn in April 2016, and we eventually started leasing our own 18,000-square-foot outdoor parking lot in Williamsburg by June. We booked all types of vendors: jewelry designers and falafel food trucks and soap makers galore. We partnered with a local group of guys to install and run a bar with beer and wine, and, over time, they added games and Slip 'N Slides to the mix. We hosted local deejays and gave out free rosé popsicles. We did anything and everything in our power to drive foot traffic to that market and make it work. The brands wanted offline sales? A chance to sell their wares in person? We'd do it, and we'd do it big. We pushed for major press coverage, did local wheat-paste campaigns, and commissioned Caryn Cast, a local Brooklyn designer, to paint a vibrant, eye-catching mural for the parking lot wall. It was of green dinosaurs donning top hats and jeweled earrings, eating food and drinking pints.

We ran Bulletin Market most weekends from April 2016 through December 2016. We worked seven-day weeks and essentially threw a major outdoor event every Saturday and Sunday of that year. We were depleted, but our brands, for the most part, were making good money. They were selling product. They were connecting with new brands and other entrepreneurs. We ran Bulletin Market for nine straight months because it was *working.* We hadn't found our holy grail business or product or service quite yet, but we were making real money and getting closer, inch by inch. It was working well enough that we needed to hire more help. We needed to build out a small but effective team to bring Bulletin Market to life.

HOW TO BUILD YOUR LITTLE LEAGUE TEAM

Once you've found a viable business idea, how are you supposed to run a business if you have no funding and can't pay anyone anything? Half of starting and running a company is being delusional enough to think it'll work. The other half is *making* it work. In order to get from step one to step two, you need people around you who will support your delusion and work hard to bring it to life. This is where hardworking interns, the gig economy, and good friends come in.

There are certain tasks that will require face time with members of what I'm going to call your Birth Team and other jobs that you can tackle with remote help. This is the team you assemble early on to get the thing off the ground and out of the womb. For Bulletin, that meant three school-credit interns, one Upwork helper, and about five superclose friends, at any given time. The peeps on your Birth Team may stay for the long haul, or maybe they're just there to grab a bit of experience. The key here is nailing down what the core, key parts of your business are and what tasks you need to crank on ASAP. Then build your Birth Team roles around those tasks. The most important part of the early days is momentum: to the best of your ability and resources, you need someone touching and tackling those tasks at all times. It looked different for Bulletin than it will for you. By the time we were running Bulletin Market, we had an Upwork helper scraping websites for brand names and e-mails. Our intern Juee was then e-mailing brands, pitching them on renting a booth. Nadira, another intern, was running inexpensive digital ads to promote the market and working to get us listed on Facebook, Yelp, and Google. Elle, another intern who eventually became one of our full-time graphic designers, was creating all of our promotional materials for the markets: fliers, vinyl banners, Facebook Events, Instagram posts, wheat-paste campaigns, and more. I was managing Juee and closing brands, refining our pitch around the markets, securing press, and nurturing our new brand community with e-mails, calls, events, and surveys. Alana was finding a lawyer, negotiating our pop-up leases, forming our LLC, setting up our bank account, and strategizing ways to improve and optimize the entire business. This was the Bulletin Birth Team, and we hovered at around six to seven people for most of 2016. It was our first year running Bulletin full-time, and we had an army of part-time women who worked hard for us, like it was a little bit theirs, too.

The tricky part (obviously) is forming a team when you simply don't have funds. That's why resources like Fiverr, Upwork, and Task Rabbit exist. We use Upwork a lot. It's a marketplace where you can hire experienced freelancers within your budget and collect project proposals from your potential hires. Need a developer to write code that scrapes Yelp for thousands of restaurant names? There's someone new on Upwork who will do it for $20 an hour, and they say it'll take them only an hour and a half. There's someone else who will do it for $60 an hour, and they've done 234 identical jobs before. The Upwork crew does a fair amount of vetting so you don't have to, like running skill tests for technical work and providing a Job Success Score for each freelancer. It's an absolutely brilliant way to get foundational work done that doesn't necessarily require face time: building databases, writing website copy, doing SEO tagging for your site, launching basic customer service, bookkeeping, graphic design. It can take your Birth Team from a handful of local supporters to a gaggle of remote champions who will work to fill the holes in your business. The freelancers on Upwork do short-term work but can morph into long-term teams or be on-call for recurring projects. So even if you have only $20 a week to spend on your side hustle, you can put that money to serious work. All you have to do is scope out those mission-critical tasks, the ones that need constant momentum, and decide which task your $20 goes toward first.

Finding interns for school credit or pure experience is another doable, cost-effective way to find smart, hardworking teammates. When I was an intern, I was eager to get my hands dirty, learn about new, intriguing industries, make connections, and feel out whether or not I liked the type of work I was doing. Our interns felt the same way. But it is absolutely critical that you understand your interns' program parameters, school guidelines, and your local laws around unpaid labor. It is more critical, however, that you understand and recognize that unpaid internships, whether for school credit or not, reinforce the growing wealth gap in America and disproportionately harm BIPOC students and young adults. The data speaks volumes. Unpaid internships give white, affluent students an edge—for life. According to the Economic Policy Institute, "average wealth for white families is seven times higher than average wealth for Black families" and "median white wealth is twelve times higher than median Black wealth." Prosperity Now and the National Community Reinvestment Coalition share that in 2016, "the wealth of a Latino household was only $6,300 compared to white Americans, who held $140,500." This is an incomplete but powerful snapshot of what the racial wealth gap looks like, and it's easy to grasp how Black and Latinx students are impacted by these inequities. When it comes to student loans, "Black and low-income students borrow more, and more often" compared to their white counterparts and graduate with more student debt. These students cannot afford to take on unpaid internships, while in school or thereafter, despite the glaring reality that this type of work experience gives students a leg up in securing subsequent paid full-time or part-time roles.* When I was at Penn and on financial aid, I was lucky enough to receive a small university stipend for the summer, which put money in my pocket when my internships could not. But not every university has this type of stipend program, and the federal government sure as hell isn't stepping in with grants or any sort of solution to this problem. If you do end up finding a consenting, unpaid intern who is able to receive school credit, a few simple practices can make a world of difference in making sure the internship experience is worthwhile and properly addressing issues around access and career development: pay interns a stipend or hourly wage when you can, compensate with equity if they do good work and stick around awhile, buy or cover lunch every day—doesn't need to be delivery if you yourself are on a budget, something modest will do—and be as active as possible in helping turn your interns' experience into a valuable career catalyst. This is absolutely critical. Be prepared to write recommendations, make post-internship intros and connections, and jump in to help with their job search. Make the time. Interns are not free labor. They are taking a major risk on you and your project, and they deserve your respect, gratitude, and guidance. If you can't compensate financially, you'd better work your ass off to compensate in other ways that will help them grow and help them land a gig that will pay.

---

* Janelle Jones, "How African-Americans have been shortchanged out of the materials to build wealth," Economic Policy Institute, February 13, 2007, epi.org/blog/the-racial-wealth-gap-how-african-americans-have-been-shortchanged-out-of-the-materials-to-build-wealth/.

Mark Huelsman, "The Debt Divide: The Racial and Class Bias Behind the 'New Normal' of Student Borrowing," Demos, May 19, 2015, demos.org/research/debt-divide-racial-and-class-bias-behind-new-normal-student-borrowing.

Danielle Douglas-Gabriel, "Minorities and poor college students are shouldering the most student debt," *Washington Post*, May 19, 2015, washingtonpost.com/news/wonk/wp/2015/05/19/minorities-and-poor-college-students-are-shouldering-the-most-student-debt/.

At Bulletin, we pay all our interns, even if they are receiving school credit. As someone who has, multiple times, accepted unpaid internships and had to quit and swap those hours for paid labor, I understand the tension between taking roles that will contribute to your career development and taking jobs that simply pay the bills. Now that we have cash in the bank and sales flowing in, I am relieved we can create internship roles that do both.

As if this all weren't a compelling enough reason to keep an eye on your labor practices, it can also be expensive not to. New York's Department of Labor has a quick fact sheet that outlines what qualifies as a legal school-credit internship, and the ways you, as an employer, need to structure the internship to keep it kosher and avoid costly legal battles. You can google "school credit internship laws" for your state to see if they have something similar or call your local Department of Labor to make sure you have all the details. When I was at Condé Nast in 2013, the publishing behemoth was embroiled in a handful of lawsuits filed by unpaid interns. The interns rightfully flagged that they hadn't been adequately compensated for the type of work they were doing, and Condé ultimately paid out $5.8 million as part of the settlement. That money was split up and sent to interns who worked for Condé over a whopping seven-year period. I've seen companies way smaller than Condé end up in similar sticky situations, so don't go thinking the big kahuna companies are the only ones that can get in hot water. My friend temporarily worked for a new media tech start-up—with a wildly depraved CEO—that employed a gaggle of hopeful, bright-eyed unpaid interns. The CEO behaved heinously time and time again: verbally abusing interns, pitting them against each other, teasing them with promises of equity that never materialized, calling them names, and, at times, speaking disrespectfully to the few female interns in the mix. My friend fled the company ASAP, and a large chunk of the interns reported the start-up and its CEO to their schools. This unnamed scumbag is no longer allowed to recruit interns from any of those universities, and the start-up has gone absolutely nowhere. So yeah, when you fuck up in the world of unpaid internships, ya fuck up pretty hard. It can cost you money, traction, and your reputation.

How do you even find students looking for school-credit or paid internships? When I was younger and looking for paid, unpaid, and school-credit internships, I had no idea where to turn. It was a totally rogue landscape, and listings were all over the map: Craigslist, university listservs, Indeed .com, rando LinkedIn postings. Cut to 2015, and Alana and I were able to sift through a fabulous platform called WayUp to find and vet interns for various roles and responsibilities. Other platforms like Handshake and Internships .com get the job done, too. Another great route is e-mailing the career services department at your alma mater and getting placed on job boards at your former school, or getting an intro to relevant student groups that seem interested in your field. When I was looking for our first handful of Bulletin interns, I asked Penn juniors and seniors if there were any retail groups on campus that I should reach out to. You can tap into groups or communities you were once a part of and see if any younger students are looking for mentorship and work experience. That's how Alison, my first boss, found me. She used our a cappella reunion as a find-an-assistant scavenger hunt. But to make sure you're recruiting creatively and attracting a diverse pool of applicants, be sure to lean on more open platforms like Twitter and Instagram and ask your followers for referrals. Consider reaching out to the career services department not just at your former school, but at institutions outside your network. There are plenty of ways to find passionate interns who will hustle hard for your company, project, or exciting new enterprise. Just remember that you'll be expected to educate, mentor, and nurture whoever you bring on.

Upwork and interns can do consistent, straightforward work that drives real impact, and, if you're lucky, your friends will always be there to give ad hoc support and jump in from time to time. Running Bulletin Market meant weekdays and weekends packed with manual labor. Alana and I were working seven days a week, pitching tents on Saturday mornings at 8 A.M. and collapsing them late into the night. We stayed each day, every day from start to finish on the weekends, baking in the summer sun. Or freezing in the chill of fall. More than once, we got rained out. We had to break down the entire market while it poured and then refund all of the vendors. Alana and I had a ton of friends who would pop by the markets to shop and hang. It was the only way they could spend time with us on Saturdays and Sundays. Seeing the wild workload we had taken on, a fair number of these friends started offering to help out. Sarah, my roommate at the time, offered to oversee the market some afternoons so Alana and I could go for a run, relax, nap, or grab lunch with a friend. Maggie, a close friend (who eventually became a VP at Bulletin!), offered up the same. She ran the show for consecutive weekends the summer we first met, which offered relief I've never forgotten. At our very first pop-up market in 2015, my friend Rae showed up with congratulatory croissants, right when we realized we'd forgotten to buy a speaker for the music. Alana sheepishly asked her to go out and buy a 60-pound speaker from Guitar Center, and she agreed without pause. We asked Rae to keep the receipt . . . so we could return it right after the event. (I mean, we didn't have hundreds of bucks on hand for some $500 speaker! Excuse you! Don't judge!) She came hobbling into the venue forty-five-minutes later, squatting and pushing the speaker toward the outlet as if she were in some competitive tough-mudder tournament. Our closest friends became extensions of our Birth Team, and, to me, that made them like family, and they still feel like family because of the time and love they've given to us and our business. In most cases, these friends didn't get paid by the hour, rack up school credit, or snag resume-boosting experience. They jumped in because they supported us and our delusion, and they believed in us enough to get their hands dirty.

HOW TO MAINTAIN FRIENDSHIPS,
AND WHEN TO DESTROY THEM

More often than not, once you take a big risk and try to do something entre-preneurial, many of your close friends and family may exude skepticism or even ill will. In many cases, this skepticism comes from a good place: your people don't want you to risk it all and fall on your face or reach a point where you find yourself unstable. And in reality, building something from nothing often does have an impact—whether major or minor, good or bad—on your bank account, mental health, and career path.

But it's important to separate critical feedback and loving concern from pure judgment and straight-up negativity. It's one of these unspoken experiences I think a lot of entrepreneurial people go through: you end up shedding a few friends who feel slighted by your lack of availability, or can't jive with your new, "messy" lifestyle, or simply don't believe in you.

Whether you're launching a new business, going back to school, forging an entirely new career path, or working on a major new side project, you're gunna be busy. That, and you may become more frugal with your spend-ing to maintain a healthy bank account while you take certain career risks. Sometimes—at least, in my experience—these changes can lead to bizarre dynamics in even the most stable friendships. A lot of my closest friends started to hit their financial stride, so to speak, the year I quit Contently, committed to Bulletin full-time, and began working at a bar to pay for groceries and rent. I had no health insurance (don't do this!), no salary, and minimal free time. They were in secure, full-time day jobs and many were finally leveling up from entry-level salaries. I was extremely proud of all my friends and knew firsthand how gratifying it felt to get a raise, secure a pro-motion, and have real disposable income. I remember meeting with my tax guy in 2016 and he was absolutely mind-fucked by my 2015 income gains: I had gone from a $30K annual salary at Condé and weekend babysitting cash to reporting income in the six figures. Similar transformations were happening all around me, but I was regressing financially *and* working like crazy! It was like I had backpedaled to my fresh-outta-college lifestyle, one where I was tallying every expense and working through the weekend. That meant I couldn't go to most birthday dinners or meet up for drinks. And I couldn't really make special time for those closest to me. If I wanted to hang with friends on the weekend, they'd either have to come to Bulletin Market or wait until 9 P.M. on Sundays, when we were finally done breaking down all the tents and tables. And if we could make 9 P.M. work, I always tried to arrange a hangout that didn't require spending much money. It was this weird, warped world where I had very little to offer my friends and maintaining the friendship hinged on my schedule and my budget. It made me feel guilty and insecure at times, like everything was on my terms.

Some friends were fully onboard and just kind of respected my situation, which was amazing. And many went above and beyond to make sure we had face time. My close friends Paige and Jana popped by Bulletin Market almost every weekend just to eat, hang, gossip, and catch up. They would make it part of their Sunday ritual and bring me a coffee, eager to see what new vendors were posted up in the parking lot we'd turned into a shopping bazaar. Rae would invite me to tons of activities on the off chance I was free, never letting any of my polite "I can'ts" stop her from trying to include me the next time. The incredible thing about incredible friends is that they provide a way to keep you accountable to your work and your vision. As we touched on earlier, starting something and building something require completely different mind-sets. When you're launching something from nothing—barring having any superearly investors or advisors with equity—you don't really have anyone to answer to except yourself and your business partner, if you've got one. It's kind of like having homework that no one's going to grade or being in a class that's pass/fail. As we all know firsthand, that lack of accountability can often leave you with tiny, open holes in your motivation that get clogged with sheer laziness or fatigue. And if you do have a business partner, it's important that one of you is pushing full-steam-ahead at all times. If you're both weighed down simultaneously, the company has no champion, no one screaming for it to exist from within.

While I had a reliable group of friends that supported me and were eager to keep me accountable, others weren't as readily accepting of how Bulletin affected all areas of my life. They'd get kind of passive-aggressive when I had to bail on plans because a market ran late and I was exhausted or get outwardly uncomfortable when I'd ask to only pay for my portion of a meal, rather than split the total evenly (How absurd! To only pay for what you ordered! Ridiculous!). Usually, these were friends who weren't majorly tuned into Bulletin, acquainted with the markets, or interested in how things were going with me or the business. I don't consider myself a people pleaser, but I couldn't help feeling this internal voice tug at me every time I heard: "Just split the bill evenly, don't be annoying," "Just buy something off their registry," "Just buy the ticket, we want you to come." There were instances when I caved and listened to this voice, instead of listening to my gut, and spent more than I knew I should. Or more than I knew I had. And I always regretted it. I was somehow embarrassed about my situation, even though it was one I had knowingly chosen. Even though spending is a personal choice and maybe I shouldn't have been cajoled by those friends in the first place.

While I understood where certain friends' frustrations were coming from, I knew it would be a long while until I could inhabit these friend-ships the way I had pre-Bulletin. I knew it would be years until I could make a generous salary and enjoy stress-free leisure time. And I knew that would only even happen if Bulletin worked, whatever that meant. For me and Alana, Bulletin had to come first. That's what my gut always told me. Not only because it was new and fragile and growing, but because it could offer a boomerang back to stability in the event we found a viable, scalable business model. Once you take a huge career risk, it's up to you whether there's payoff or not. I don't think appeasing tuned-out, unsupportive friends or romantic partners contributes to that payoff. And it took me a while to figure that out and say "no" or "I can't" with zero discomfort or shame. I stopped caving to my internal voice, my shame, my embarrassment, stopped trying to defend my choices.

There is obviously a fair amount of nuance here, and it's up to you to discern who your true supporters are, who is worth making sacrifices for, and when to make commitments you know you'll need to keep. I am by *no* means telling you to cancel every plan, refuse every wedding invitation, and use work as a blanket excuse for letting people down. It's 100 percent in your best interest to tune out your detractors, but also to invest in your advocates. You will need a support system to get through the rough patches. So, when you're faced with invitations, financial commitments, or opportunities with friends, ask yourself: Has this person been generally supportive in my career change? Does this person make me feel good about myself and my choices thus far? Do I feel in my gut that they want me to succeed? I found that the answers to these questions have been a really solid guide in identifying who is in my support circle and which friends I should invest time and energy into when I'm running low on both.

SMALL THINGS MATTER

The people you surround yourself with during trying, exciting, and ambitious times are the ones who will define your sense of fulfillment and success. As we covered in this chapter, your first steps to launching and building a business are (1) finding a good idea to work on, (2) building a team, and (3) creating an environment and finding a peer group where you can work hard, commit, and thrive. Think about your core team as a group of astronauts trying to haul your rocket's ass all the way to the moon. Everyone should be laser-focused, bought in, and treated with the utmost gratitude.

If you've done some serious due diligence and pinned down a good business idea, the journey will feel deeply rewarding for you and everyone involved. You need enough market research and evidence of product-market fit to bring energy and excitement to your work every day. It will be your armor when the going gets tough and shit's not working how you thought it would. It's what will keep your team afloat when things break, they're over-worked, or when your Birth Team evolves and changes. Having salty people on your Birth Team, Debbie Downers in your DMs, or bitchy, self-involved friends can throw you off course and ruin this thrilling start to your start-up. Fuck those people. If you take your project, new business, or company seriously, so should your inner circle. So, please, ditch all toxic voices. Walk away from anyone who sees your hustle as a personal affront to their expensive birthday dinner. And nurture the friends who motivate you to feel accountable and cheer you on from the sidelines. Whether you're starting a business or navigating a career shift, the outcome is directly correlated with how hard you work and how much faith you have in yourself. No one in your circle should be trying to actively rob you of that faith. It's simply too precious.

TAKEAWAYS!

BE WITH BELIEVERS.

DON'T LET THE H8TERS GET YOU DOWN.

LEARN TO DECIPHER CRITICAL FEEDBACK FROM IGNORANT GARBAGE.

HALF OF STARTING AND RUNNING A COMPANY IS BEING DELUSIONAL ENOUGH TO THINK IT'LL WORK. THE OTHER HALF IS *MAKING IT* WORK.

WHO HELPED YOU WEATHER THE EARLY DAYS?

ALEXIS ROSENBAUM
ROSEBUD

Having a solid support network has been absolutely key to building Rosebud. I don't have a co-founder, but my husband has been, through and through, my true partner. He tells me all the time that he doesn't believe in anyone as much as he believes in me; he carries me to bed when I'm too tired; he forces me to stop working when it's time for a break. He always tells me, You can do this. You're already doing it. I stand by you. When you're an entrepreneur and taking this risk there's so much going on, that's so important to hear. I have two sisters I talk to every single day; I would even go so far as to say we are accountability partners. We challenge one another and keep one another in check. They'll always talk me down from being super paranoid and remind me that, as women, we have such a distorted view of everything. Sometimes you really are just doing great, and everything is fine. My mom has run her own business for decades and is my total hype woman. She gets after it! She always tells me there's no problem I can't solve. My brother and dad are also super supportive in their own way, too. They have a hard time understanding how I do it all and have a different vision of success than I do, but they seem to marvel at my level of intensity.

I've lived in New Jersey for only two years but have met multiple women who have now become friends, and I talk things through with them. One of my most cutthroat friends here will just tell it like it is. I was unhappy with my PR team and was like, How do I have this conversation, I hate confrontation! and she reminded me that I've been paying them for a service, and I deserve to be a bit of a pain in the ass. It's nice to have that coaching and that reassurance. I am the most self-critical person, and I am constantly working on that. Sometimes my mind is not very nice to me. My internal support team—I know they have my back and want me to see myself how they see me, if that makes sense.

LILLIAN TUNG
FUR

When you start your company, you are going through so much mental hardship, twenty-four hours a day. You are literally doing everything yourself. I think of Fur as my first child. And like a child, as the business grows, she gains independence and a pair of legs, and you can start to delegate. But we started Fur in 2015 and I gave birth to my actual first child in 2016. We didn't have employees yet, when I was pregnant with morning sickness I could work from home, I could go to my doctor's appointments. But once I actually had the baby it started getting much harder. Fur was so young, and I didn't want to leave Laura in the lurch with the business. I took only six weeks off after giving birth. I had this tension inside me, I didn't want the baby to suffer, but I also didn't want Laura and Fur to suffer. I always regretted that and did it differently with my second child. I took off three months the second time. But both times, Laura was so supportive. She had her own child a bit later and it was like, now she knows. She knows what it's like—it takes a lot of time and effort and headspace.

It has been so nice to go through these huge milestones together. Until you go through them, you don't really understand them and the level of support needed, and how different it feels. My husband was and is extremely supportive of Fur. My family lives in New York, everyone helped with the baby. Other people in my life thought I was basically becoming a stay-at-home mom when I launched Fur, like it was this fun side project to keep me busy when the kids go to school. I definitely noticed this huge misconception that you can have it all, and an even greater myth that you can have it all when you're the business owner, because it offers more flexibility and people think you can "own" what your life will be like. I feel like Instagram always played into that, where everyone's like, Oh, here's Lillian with her daughter just hanging out on a summer Friday. But you only have twenty-four hours in a day and things are going to have to give. You aren't necessarily going to start your own thing and find more free time or better work-life balance. There are three priorities in my life: my children, Fur, and my husband. Sometimes it changes! Fur, then my children, then my husband. But ultimately, I am juggling all three, and when you are the business owner, you feel every burden even more, but the support feels even more meaningful, too.

**CYO NYSTROM
QUIM**

Right now, Quim is just the two of us, Rachel Washtien and me, full-time. For what we need right now, we have a part-time marketing exec giving us a few hours a week to help understand our tech stack and build out our dashboard to track different marketing metrics. We have a part-time sales rep who does about ten hours of work a week. We've been able to stay small internally because we immediately hired an amazing design firm and a great distribution company. We know our blind spots and the gaps in our skills, and we wanted to find the best people right away to fill those gaps and do those jobs. Some are internal and some are external partners, but this is everyone we need right now.

As far as my support network, my family, my fiancé, and my friends have always stressed to me that the things worth doing in life will always be risky, and it is worth taking that risk even if you fail. My mom ran her own businesses and that lifestyle really inspired me and shaped me growing up. I registered that it was this specific way to "do" your life that would be more stressful and risky at times, but also offer more freedom and flexibility than anything else. You can design your life the way you want to live it. That's been with me since I was a child. Living in San Francisco, too, all these people are starting companies and some had failed, some had done well. In my close friend group, I have tons of friends who have started their own projects to varying degrees of success. Some of their projects ended poorly, but we were all and still are in this culture of "let's go for it."

Of course, there is a lot of privilege in all of this and in my community. Even if you don't have something like a trust fund, there is an understanding among my friend group that if you start a project and you can't pay rent, you can move home with your parents in the Bay Area. There is this security, this safety you have to acknowledge and recognize in the community and in yourself. If you have $250K in student debt or don't have family in the United States, a model support system isn't necessarily enough. It is harder to start a company from scratch with those conditions and considerations. I recognize that I have had a huge support network and people modeling this risk-taking and entrepreneurship my whole life. When I was putting my fundraising deck together, I could talk to five other young founders who had recently done the exact same thing. I feel really grateful that's the case, and that I have so many people believing in me and cheering me on.

JESSICA TSE
NOTTE

It is so important to believe in your girlfriends. As a founder, I learned that sometimes your friends can see things more clearly than you can while you're still in the earliest stages of the unknown. For me, that support helped more than anything. I kept Notte such a secret for a while. I told everyone I had an idea I was working on, but didn't share much else. I had nothing to show for it yet, so I felt a bit weird talking about my business. A close friend checked in with me at one point and asked me what I was up to and what I was working on since leaving my job in trend forecasting. I shared more details than I usually do about Notte and was so hesitant the whole time.

The next day she went online and found my website on her own, and she bought something. The site wasn't even done yet. I got a notification in my e-mail that order number 0001 had come through—it was here! I didn't know what was happening. I noticed it was her and I told her I could have given her samples! But she refused. She said, No, I really want to support you. She started wearing the things she bought and tagging my account on Instagram. Soon, a lot of my old co-workers started ordering from me. I was like, Oh my God. This is real now. I felt like I was going to cry, it felt so amazing. If it wasn't for her or for my friends who started ordering I would have continued to make excuses about postponing the launch, like, let's tweak this, let's wait for that. I don't know how long I would have waited without them.

CHAPTER THREE

WHO DO YOU THINK YOU ARE?

There's one glaring hurdle that, once I faced it, made running weekend-long pop-up markets for ten months straight and fundraising as a female founder feel like a piece of cake. It didn't require physical strain or game theory or endless hours of number-crunching. It was an internal, psychological hurdle that, I've now learned, many women experience when they do something entrepreneurial or off the beaten path.

Between 2015 and 2016, I could not, for the life of me, use the word "founder" as an identifier. In 2015, I was working on Bulletin part-time, so it felt like this half-baked, little-known secret I wasn't ready to share. In 2016, while building the company full-time, it felt like this rough draft I was agonizing over but didn't want to submit for review. Time and time again, I shrank from any talk about building Bulletin or what it really was or how I was involved. It was this totally taboo topic, and I'd freeze in anxiety anytime someone asked that direct, age-old question: "So what do you do?" When I'd show up at parties or meet new people—even at our own co-working space!—I used to clumsily tiptoe around anything Bulletin-related and the fact that I was a co-founder. I'd say something like, "Oh, um . . . I work for this . . . retail company. What about you?" I downplayed my role and rushed through all work-related small talk. While we were at Contently and doing it part-time, I don't think I uttered a word about Bulletin to most of the people I knew. I only shared our newsletter and website with my closest friends, and even then, it was the most nerve-wracking experience.

So now you know that I used to straight-up talk about Bulletin as if I were a part-time employee or even, in my most anxious moments, spew some wild nonsense that I was in-between jobs. When I flash back to each encounter—and they return very vividly—my body is overcome with this icky sense of shame. It's the same sharp tummy tingle I get when I think about regrettable college hookups or reflect on some dumb thing I said in an important meeting. I have interrogated that shame, and I finally think I understand where it comes from, and why so many women feel it.

In my experience, a lot of my flubbing and downplaying and equivocating about Bulletin was driven by fear. I played a rotating roster of doomsday outcomes in my head. If I were honest about my relationship with Bulletin, I'd expose myself to more established people who would immediately size me up and start asking intricate questions about our business. I was utterly convinced that people would sniff out ways to trick me or put me down. What if this person is a retail guru and scoffs at our marketing strategy? What if this dude has his own digital publication and shits all over ours? Despite being the one in the weeds reading every retail thought-leadership piece, talking to brands every day, I always assumed I was too stupid—or too green, too young, too naive—to defend my company and my work. We didn't launch Bulletin as a pair of retail experts having come from Nike or Amazon or Glossier. And who knows? Maybe that will bite us in the ass someday. But not every founder comes from the industry they are disrupting, and yet, no amount of self-education or fanatical research made me feel smart enough. It didn't matter if I was meeting a friend's mom, an old schoolmate, or a stranger, the task of explaining Bulletin would immediately make me feel unintelligent and small.

I was equally afraid of not being taken seriously. If the first fear was being interrogated to smithereens, there was a close tie for second: getting laughed at, and hearing the poorly cloaked version of "that's cute." I still can't decide which is worse. This one scene from *Legally Blonde* always comes to mind. It's the one where Warner and Elle are discussing the coveted Harvard Law internships and he ever-so-gently tells her, "You'll never get the grades for one of those spots. You're not smart enough, Sweetie." The venom spills out through a genuine, tender smile. He seems truly worried that she simply doesn't have what it takes. (We learn later in the film that Elle got into Harvard on her own merit, while Warner got rejected, and Rich Daddy had to place a desperate call to get him in. So, fuck you, Warren! *You* weren't smart enough, Sweetie!) Moving on. The fear of being belittled—whether subtly or in plain sight—was enough to make me impulsively belittle myself. If I acted like I was just temporarily at Bulletin or played down my role as a key decision maker, I could talk about the business vaguely and distance myself from responses and replies that might make me shrink. No one could hurt me. No one could cut it down if they didn't know about it. I used to watch *Legally Blonde* and think, She just shouldn't have told him about the internship in the first place. He wouldn't have had any ammo to hurt her, and she could've avoided the heartbreak.

> THE FEAR OF BEING BELITTLED—WHETHER SUBTLY OR IN PLAIN SIGHT—WAS ENOUGH TO MAKE ME IMPULSIVELY BELITTLE MYSELF.

Getting scoffed at, feeling patronized, or being underestimated can be heartbreaking. If you asked a random woman to recall a time she's been patronized, she would surely have a colorful story to share. And another for when she's been scoffed at. And yet another for when she felt underestimated. It happens all the fucking time. We've been told our whole lives that we are inferior. And if not told, it's what we are shown: by gendered politics, the pay gap, the low number of female CEOs and the lackadaisical treatment of sexual assault on college campuses and in the workplace. We absorb a reality where women are "dumber," "weaker," and less important than men. It weighs us down and drowns us. So, when a woman sees a moment in the sun and the opportunity to showcase her potential—a career goal, a financial win, a brilliant idea—she is coming up for air. And to be scoffed at, patronized, or underestimated feels like active suffocation when you're already treading water.

That's where my fear comes from. I was afraid of the pain that comes with feeling unintelligent and undeserving. I was afraid to start confidently talking about my company, only to be put down or challenged. But looking back, I recognize that these fears were 100 percent irrational. I assumed people were out to be malicious or that they cared enough to "dig in" to my business. But my fears overshadowed the most obvious thing about human behavior: no one really gives a fuck about you. Okay, I'll clarify. What I mean to say is that in most cases, yes, your parents, friends, and partners care about you a lot. But more often than not, people are more curious than critical. I find that most people are hyperconcerned about their own livelihood, future, commitments, happiness, and don't want to expend a ton of mental energy challenging your start-up idea or your business plan. If anything, most people are impressed by the sheer courage it takes to launch something from scratch. Of course, you may have risk-averse family members who challenge the viability of your business idea or a romantic partner demanding consistency and financial stability. And we'll get there—those are real, valid relationships and real, necessary conversations. But the majority of the people who'd ask, "What do you do?"—acquaintances, friends of friends, former co-workers—are not about to go Shark Tank on your ass. More likely than not, they'll be a little bit jealous you're running your own shit, applaud you for being so enterprising, and think more highly of you than they did before. Like, if someone told you they were starting a candle company, would you think to yourself, "Wow. That person is highly unqualified. This idea is so stale. I think I should let them know"? Would you laugh at them? No. Just no. You'd probably think something short and sweet, like, "Oh. That's cool. I've never made a candle. I wish I were craftier. Should I take a pottery class?"

HELLO, I'M IMPOSTOR SYNDROME.
I'LL MAKE MYSELF COMFORTABLE.

While I do think women are more susceptible to experiencing fear and uncertainty in the early stages of an entrepreneurial venture, feelings of incompetence, impending doom, and even fraudulence run rampant within the tech community and can plague absolutely anyone, regardless of gender. This deep insecurity is called impostor syndrome or impostor phenomenon, terminology coined by veteran clinical psychologist and professor Dr. Pauline Rose Clance and her research partner Dr. Suzanne Imes. Clance and Imes first studied a group of college-age women and female faculty members around the United States, noticing that despite their accomplishments, accolades, grades, and other signifiers of success and intelligence, the women in the group felt a deep sense of incompetence and assigned their achievements to luck or some sort of fluke. Impostor syndrome names that nagging voice in your head that worries you won't repeat your success, believes you are undeserving of your success, and agonizes over being "found out" as a swindler or, per its namesake, an "impostor." After unearthing the depths of impostor syndrome and how it affects women, Doctors Clance and Imes and others went on to study the phenomenon across all genders, races, religions, and communities. They studied people across various occupations, incomes, and levels of education. The conclusion? Everyone feels like an impostor. This phenomenon is universal, though evidence shows that impostorism may be more prevalent among underrepresented groups and minorities and have a larger negative effect on their mental health. It makes sense. If you struggle to find representation in your field or industry, you might internalize that you don't belong there. So female founders of color, and founders of color period, may experience more severe negative self-talk and a deeper sense of "intellectual phoniness."

I've seen entrepreneurs struggle with impostorism no matter the stage of their company: pre-seed, seed, privately held, or on the Dow—it doesn't matter. I think founders are distinctly susceptible to chronic, unrelenting impostor syndrome because of how easy it is to overemphasize the broken parts of your company, while undervaluing the things that are working. But even as Bulletin evolved and we amassed cold, hard evidence that our idea was working—I still felt like a fraud. It felt weird to own or internalize our success when, behind the scenes, I knew we still had so much to figure out. And there was a shit ton that flat-out wasn't working. We faced issues as the team kept growing, some of the brands weren't selling well at all, we were understaffed across all departments, we were overworked.

WHEN A WOMAN SEES A MOMENT IN THE SUN AND THE OPPORTUNITY TO SHOWCASE HER POTENTIAL—A CAREER GOAL, A FINANCIAL WIN, A BRILLIANT IDEA—SHE IS COMING UP FOR AIR. AND TO BE SCOFFED AT, PATRONIZED, OR UNDERESTIMATED FEELS LIKE ACTIVE SUFFOCATION WHEN YOU'RE ALREADY TREADING WATER.

The list of things that *isn't* working will always outweigh the list of shit that *is* working in your mind. If you're doing your job right, then your company will grow, and then break, and then grow, and then break again, and you'll never reach a true homeostasis where everything is 100 percent figured out, 100 percent seamless, and 100 percent successful. That's the nature of a start-up, but for founders, this endless optimization cycle can make you feel like you're keeping some dirty secret. So, when friends, family, acquaintances, or industry folks congratulate you on a milestone or ask about your company, all you can think about is how fucked things are, instead of appreciating or taking pride in your wins.

Even external validation doesn't help. We were written up in the *New York Times*, I was awarded *Forbes'* 30 Under 30, Alana and I were named two of the Most Creative People in Business by *Fast Company*, I got a fucking book deal. Sometimes, accolades can make impostor syndrome even worse. You suddenly feel exposed, like you're keeping the dirty secret from thousands of people now, not just your industry or your inner circle. Feeling overhyped, overwhelmed, and on the brink of failure at all times can cause serious anxiety, depression, debilitating stress, and low self-esteem. I've been there. I'm there now, writing about impostor syndrome while still feeling my own healthy dose of impostor syndrome. How very meta.

GET OVER IT AND PURSUE THE SPOTLIGHT

But here's the thing: if you let those feelings pile up and define your experience as a founder, or your experience taking any risk for that matter, then you're setting yourself up to fail. You can actually hurt the growth of your business by keeping mum about your company and your work, because opportunities can only come when you make your hustle known. Impostor syndrome can cause you to shrink and make you less vocal and forthcoming about your goals and ideas. But after speaking with the entrepreneurs behind our Bulletin brands and interviewing dozens of other founders, it's clear that their businesses benefited as soon as they put the lid on their impostorism, came into their own, and started actively promoting their hustle. A huge part of running a business is meeting people who can help make it better: finding mentors, talking to customers, hiring experts, and making valuable connections. You can't do that if you're hiding your dreams in the shadows.

As soon as Alana and I embraced our roles at Bulletin, we became better business owners. By the end of 2016, our first year building the business full-time, we were more confident as founders, and more comfortable tying our professional identities to Bulletin. We were able to start dreaming. We were able to start networking. We were able to put Bulletin out there and start collecting feedback, first impressions, and constructive criticism about the business model. We were able to meet brands that wanted to sell with us ("Oh cool! I know a girl who embroiders pithy stuff on denim jackets. Can I connect you?"). We were able to meet our first investors ("Sounds interesting. I know this guy Nick who runs a fund out of Brooklyn. Maybe you guys should get coffee or something?"). And we were able to build brand awareness.

WHEN SOMEONE ASKS, WHAT DO YOU DO? THINK OF IT AS AN OPPORTUNITY, NOT A CHALLENGE.

Your hustle needs to be put on display in order for your business to grow and in order to find people who will support you and champion you. No one will give a fuck about your side project, solo gig, or start-up if they don't even know it exists. You never know who you'll meet or how they can help you, so when someone asks, What do you do? think of it as an opportunity, not a challenge. Remember that most people are more curious than critical and that the more confidence you bring to the conversation, the stronger the outcome. As women, we're taught to be modest and polite. Or, if you're like me, you fear the ramifications of promoting your hustle: getting patronized, being laughed at, or feeling underestimated.

But by waiting for permission to show off a bit, or letting those fears take over, you're actually screwing yourself over. Don't wait for your product to be perfect or worry you'll be "outed" because your company isn't perfect. Don't wait for your company to be funded or flush with cash—talking up your hustle may help you meet your first investor or someone who knows someone who *knows* an investor. Your Instagram page doesn't have to have ten thousand followers for you or your brand to be considered legit. Every major brand, influencer, celebrity, and business had zero followers at some point, too.

YOUR SUCCESS WILL NOT COME FROM NEGATIVE SELF-TALK, OR SHEEPISHNESS, OR SHAME. IT WILL COME FROM GIVING ALL THOSE THINGS A STIFF-ASS MIDDLE FINGER, AS BEST YOU CAN, AND PUTTING YOUR PROJECT, CAREER SHIFT, RISKY SOLO MOVE, OR NEW COMPANY AT THE CENTER OF YOUR ENTIRE WORLD WITH CONFIDENCE AND CONVICTION.

There are a plethora of ways you can overcome impostor syndrome or silence negative self-talk: log your accomplishments in a journal, stop comparing yourself to others, avoid social media accounts that make you feel inadequate, form a circle of like-minded doers who will applaud your wins, hash out your feelings of inferiority with a therapist, parent, or partner, and simply realize the validity of what you are feeling. This shit runs deep! Internalize the fact that you are not alone, and that *everyone*— even the founders or people you idolize—experiences the same nagging sense of complete and total incompetence. Your success will not come from negative self-talk, or sheepishness, or shame. It will come from giving all those things a stiff-ass middle finger, as best you can, and putting your project, career shift, risky solo move, or new company at the center of your entire world with confidence and conviction. That decision will determine how many opportunities fall into your lap, how any helpful people you meet, and ultimately, how far your new adventure will go.

TAKEAWAYS!

TELL YOURSELF, THEN TELL THE WORLD.

EMBRACE THE LABOR OF EXPLAINING YOUR BUSINESS.

PEOPLE ARE MORE CURIOUS THAN CRITICAL.

NO ONE WILL GIVE A FUCK ABOUT YOUR SIDE HUSTLE IF THEY DON'T EVEN KNOW IT EXISTS.

YOUR HUSTLE NEEDS TO BE PUT ON DISPLAY IN ORDER FOR YOUR BUSINESS TO GROW AND IN ORDER TO FIND PEOPLE WHO WILL SUPPORT YOU AND CHAMPION YOU.

HOW HAVE YOU DEALT WITH IMPOSTOR SYNDROME?

ALEXIS ROSENBAUM

ROSEBUD

I am extremely critical of myself—the most critical—and it isn't a healthy level of criticism. I am constantly working on that. I tend to be so critical because I want to constantly improve my business and improve myself as a human being. The intentions are good, but sometimes it feels like my inner thoughts are trying to take me down: You're never going to be as big as you think you are. Who do you think you are? You're no different than anyone in the CBD space, Alexis, you aren't special.

It is not necessarily easy, but I think female founders have to work hard to change their self-talk. I try to reroute toward thoughts like, You are good at what you do. You are worthy. You are successful. You are doing your best. I know this sounds supercorny, but sometimes I'll have full-blown pep talks with myself out loud in the car or look at myself in the mirror and talk to my ego like it's this separate entity. I'll tell it to leave me alone and that it needs to stop feeding me these ridiculous measurements of success. As a female founder, in this space especially, I feel like there is this silent pressure to do it all: I have to work out and be healthy and eat well and learn new hobbies and take care of my skin. I'm also supposed to be beautiful and be charming and be nice. I'm just trying to work through those negative thoughts and crazy, self-imposed expectations day by day. It is really hard, but I'm trying to challenge myself. It's a mental game.

VALERIE WRAY
125 COLLECTION

I was waiting for society to tell me, It's okay to be out there with your businesses. I was looking for some sort of sign or some sort of moment to validate everything, I guess. But you shouldn't wait for society to tell you it's okay. It's okay simply because you exist. And if you don't tell people you exist, they'll never know. The more you tell people about your business, the more opportunities you'll get. Even though we were doing it part-time and had other jobs. We just got comfortable and excited talking about the brand and started bringing our candles with us wherever we went. At one point, we met Tiffany Haddish's makeup artist and gave her a custom candle that said, "She Ready." Tiffany ended up Instagramming the candle. That's how it happens!

JASMINE MANS
DESIGNER, POET, AND FOUNDER

The hardest thing hasn't been the money or the designs or selling people on the product; it has been believing in myself and believing I am right in the things I am saying and thinking. It's so scary, you feel like you're on the brink of failure all the time. But I've learned that sometimes, you don't want to believe you're a mastermind. I've spent so much time thinking, Someone has to be smarter than me, I need someone to educate me on how to do this and where to take it. But it's like, no—you can be bold. You can have mastery. You know what you're doing. I've had people in my own inner circle say, I want to keep you grounded. You know, you're lucky to be in the door. Don't ask for anything, have no expectations. I've also been in spaces where I have asked for more, and I get, You're lucky to be here because you're Black, your products are new. Who wants a Black entrepreneur in this space? Because of those experiences, I am forced to ask myself if I'm lucky, or if I'm smart. If I'm lucky, it can all go away. But if I'm smart, there is an energy and knowledge fueling this mastery, this thing that I have.

The people in my inner circle who told me that I was just lucky didn't know things about my business or this space. But we expect people who are older to be more educated, and we seek comfort from older people telling us what to do. I sought comfort in specific people: wealthy people I knew and respected, educators, professors. But they had no idea about my brand, the people who love it, the audience who buys my merchandise. I wanted or felt like I needed someone to be smarter than me, but now I realize I have all the tools.

**MEAGAN LONG
GOTEYA**

I work really hard, I know I'm smart, I am confident, and I do believe in myself as a boss and a good business owner. But when the time comes where I have these big moments of success, I feel undeserving. All the other days working toward that goal, I felt more sure of myself. But when the big moment happens, I feel like a fraud. When I actually achieve the goal, I start to crash. We've received a huge wholesale order right after launching, we were asked to participate in a certain cool event or a celebrity or influencer wears our glasses, and each time I'm like, This is so crazy. Why is this happening to me?

I think part of why I react this way is bigger than just myself and my experience. Men have been using capitalism to exclude women from certain spaces—women sense they aren't supposed to start or run a business. We have an internalized fear, like, We shouldn't be here. It is a man's thing to own a business. We were made to feel scared, like a woman couldn't do it. Where I'm from, in the South, it is this shocking thing that I have my own business. It is treated like this radical act. I think encouraging more women to become business owners is really important, because we shouldn't be intimidated out of starting a business, and we shouldn't feel like frauds once we run them.

**JESSICA TSE
NOTTE**

When I started my own jewelry line, I didn't know who I was anymore. I had spent years as a successful trend director at a trend forecasting company. As an established director, I would go to showrooms or trade shows or events and I always had this platform to validate me—people knew who I was and knew the company. I was there for more than seven years. But with building and running Notte, I felt lost for a long period of time. It was such a strange feeling, almost like I went from being someone to being no one, to being nothing. I was like, Okay, I am not a trend director anymore. So, what am I? I'm building this brand, but I have nothing to show for it yet, so am I really a business owner? Can I even call myself that? It was uncomfortable to meet people or catch up with old friends and worry they'd think I wasn't working anymore or that I didn't know what was next. I knew my parents were worried about me. I had a true identity crisis.

CYO NYSTROM
QUIM

My self-perception has ebbed and flowed a lot while running Quim. I have negative voices in my head, but they are a lot quieter than they used to be. I've tried to develop a toolkit for how to deal with those voices that isn't superpunitive to myself. I am trying to be more compassionate about where I'm at and where the company is on its journey. My impostor syndrome was at its peak while I was straddling two jobs at once—my full-time head of sales job and getting my own business off the ground. I wasn't doing either to the best of my ability, and I was working day in and day out for these incredible tech founders who were running this successful cannabis company, and I was like, You can't be them. You can't do what they do. Who do you think you are? I was comparing myself to three male technical founders and another entrepreneur who had started three to four successful companies already. I was watching how they addressed certain business challenges and was so intimidated.

But once I inched toward doing Quim full-time, I realized how silly it was to compare. I was starting a completely different businesses with different needs and considerations, and over time I started to feel more and more validation. When I eventually went full-time with Quim, everyone told me I was a crazy person. As we've hit certain milestones or achieve certain highs, I feel like, Fuck—I am unstoppable. There's this feeling of, I did it—look at me now. And while those moments are amazing, those moments alone are never enough to fight off the bad voices that still live in my head. Those voices will never go entirely silent. But I've learned how to have compassion for myself and my darker thoughts in my low moments, rather than stressing over why I can't silence my negative thoughts or make them go away.

CHAPTER FOUR

THE LEAP OF FAITH

Impostor syndrome can make it particularly difficult to assess when and if it makes sense to take your side hustle full-time. Making that call was one of the riskiest and murkiest parts of our Bulletin journey. And I think that goes for most founders, entrepreneurs, and businesses owners: there's no "good time" to go full throttle on a risky venture, and there's definitely no universal playbook for how to do it. People ask me, When should I quit my job to give this a real shot? or bring up a chicken-or-egg dilemma: Will my side hustle only thrive once I dive in full-time, or should I go full-time once my side hustle starts thriving?

There is no formula for when to go full-time or some objective diagnosis that you or your business are "ready" to make the transition. It's an extremely personal decision that rides on the state of your finances, your mental health, your risk appetite, your support system, the type of lifestyle you'd like to lead, and other factors. Every business owner will have to account for completely different variables. For example, I didn't have mouths to feed. I wasn't married, so I didn't have a spouse or their expectations to consider. My mom was an entrepreneur, so I didn't have to worry about parental disapproval. And yet there are so many psychological and emotional factors I wish I had weighed more heavily when deciding to tackle Bulletin full-time, and I think a few of those considerations definitely apply to everyone.

When Alana and I started Bulletin as a side business in 2015, she dreamed of peeling off from Contently to do it full-time, but I wasn't on the same page. I was allergic to the idea of falling backward: my income, job security, and peace of mind would all take a major hit. By the end of that year, I had been promoted a third time, locked in a six-figure salary, and relocated to my home base in Los Angeles (near my mamma!) to help run West Coast sales. When I moved to LA mere months after launching Bulletin 1.0, I promised Alana I'd continue interviewing designers and writing articles. But let's call a spade a spade: I had just moved across the country to double down on my employment at Contently and take on even more responsibility within *that* company.

Sometimes, I think back and wonder wtf she thought of me during this weird, in-limbo era. Because even though I'd said yes to this shared pipe dream—I would have given anything to write for Bulletin on a full-time salary—I wasn't sold on leaving my cushy income, beautiful new apartment, and the financial stability I'd lacked for so much of my childhood. I was still tethered to Contently, in large part, because of ca$h money. Plain and simple. I had been working since I was fifteen, making baby bucks as a barista, nanny, hostess, store clerk. In college and upon graduating, I used to budget for every single thing that I ate. I kept a spending log of everything I bought— groceries, toiletries, socks, MetroCards, even blackout-drunk munchies down to the cent. I would get giddy over an extra $5 tip. I ate $4 Lean Cuisines and dollar pizza for dinner night after night after night. I shared a bedroom with a seven-year-old. I slept on a mattress in the middle of the kitchen of the first NYC apartment I shared with my best friend, Jana.

I never in my life envisioned $13K commission checks hitting my bank account. Or a corporate credit card to expense fancy dinners with new clients. At Condé Nast, I worked seven days a week to support myself: Monday through Friday in the office, Saturday through Sunday babysitting uptown. At Contently, I worked five days a week, kept completely reasonable hours, and made more money than I knew what to do with. It was the first time I ever felt financial relief in my adult life and walking away from that felt heavy and damn near impossible.

So much of my early adulthood was rife with financial insecurity and committing to Bulletin full-time was pretty much synonymous with inviting that insecurity back into my life. And now, on the other side of the line, I know that I was *absolutely* right. A deep sense of fear and uncertainty kicked in the first week we began working on Bulletin full-time. And I felt that way for many years. Because for most people, pursuing a new business full-time is objectively risky, and financially, it's a serious gamble. As a founder, when you make the jump, you will put money on the line and leave money on the table: you will lose a consistent salary *and* spend personal funds on your business.

So, if simply reading this gives you anxiety or has you mumbling *fuck no*— that's okay. I felt the exact same way, and, in fact, leaned into my keep-stable-job, make-money plan as some sort of shield when Bulletin really started to pick up. It's completely fine if you aren't ready yet. The most important thing is to be honest with yourself about where you are emotionally and what you really want going forward. Think about the reality of your current situation: maybe starting a full-time business right this very second isn't the right move because you don't feel financially stable enough yet. Maybe this is something you start planning for and decide you'll make the leap in two years.

I didn't want my concerns about money to overshadow the opportunity. I wanted to challenge myself and build something from scratch. I wanted to overcome my hesitations about money and tackle them head on, rather than letting them silently control me. I went to the root cause of my fear and I took proactive steps to feel differently about it. I am a problem solver by nature. I have a constant impulse to analyze and fix and troubleshoot. In my mind, money was a one-dimensional issue I could solve by . . . having more of it.

So as soon as I sniffed out that Alana wanted to go full-time, I started stashing all of my Contently commission checks. I knew her plans by August 2015, when she brought up applying to Y Combinator, a well-known accelerator program that hosts companies for a start-up bootcamp. With YC on my radar, my Q3 and Q4 commission money went straight to my savings account. I was conservative in spending my biweekly paychecks, too. While I was making more money than ever, I saved and budgeted just as obsessively as I had when I was making $30,000 a year. At the time, I wasn't absolutely positive I'd end up leaving Contently and pursuing Bulletin seriously, but I wanted to give Future Me the option to weigh Bulletin as a real career opportunity down the line. I knew I wouldn't be able to make an objective, rational decision if my emotions were clouded by money-related stress and insecurity. Having a financial safety net could give me more flexibility in mapping out my future and let me build up the courage to "go backward" and quit Contently if that was what I wanted.

I WANTED TO GIVE FUTURE ME THE OPTION TO WEIGH BULLETIN AS A REAL CAREER OPPORTUNITY DOWN THE LINE.

Which is why the state of your finances is probably the number one factor you should consider when deciding to make your part-time project your main thang. I want to say its hustle or work ethic or passion, but I really do believe having some sort of financial cushion—an amount that you are personally comfortable with that helps *you* feel protected—will help you maximize those other inputs. If you want to give your project, business, or start-up idea a real shot, you need substantial runway. "Runway" is how long you have to build the company or execute the project given your current cash flow and burn rate. That is, if you have $20,000 in the bank, you make $1,000 a month, and it costs you $3,000 per month to run your company, you have ten months of runway. Meaning, you will run out of cash and have to close up shop unless you decrease your burn rate and/or increase your monthly profit.

The state of your personal finances is critical for two reasons. First, as a founder or small business owner, you will very likely be funneling your own cash into the business, especially early on. Alana and I fronted cash for things like tables for our pop-up markets, shipping on e-commerce orders, or Ubers to and from meetings. You'll either be fronting money on necessary expenses and recouping it over time when your business begins to generate enough revenue, or you'll be paying for necessary expenses and won't ever see that cash again if the biz goes belly-up. Of course, a lot of this is nuanced and depends on how you fund the business: if you take out a bank loan, you may avoid injecting personal funds into the biz. If you manage to raise funding superearly on, you may manage to avoid spending your own money. But most likely, you'll be forced to watch dollars disappear from your account in the name of product development, marketing, trademarks, copyrights, hiring, research, and more. Having a financial safety net gives you more time to build your company and refine your business model. It gives you more opportunity to try to reduce your burn rate or find ways to increase revenue. It's simple math, really, but the more money you have in the bank, the longer you have to screw up, learn, and evolve.

LAUNCHING A FULL-TIME BUSINESS CAN BE PAINFULLY STRESSFUL: YOU HAVE A LIMITED AMOUNT OF TIME TO MAKE IT WORK, YOU HAVE TO ALLOCATE RESOURCES PROPERLY, AND YOU HAVE TO ADJUST QUICKLY WHEN YOU FAIL OR FUCK UP. BEING BROKE OR FINANCIALLY UNSTABLE DURING THOSE HIGH-STRESS PERIODS CAN REDUCE THE QUALITY OF YOUR DECISION-MAKING AND FURTHER COMPOUND AN ALREADY SHITTY SITUATION.

What's reason number two? Runway aside, I think having a healthy amount of financial cushion helps preserve your mental health as a business owner or founder. Launching a full-time business can be painfully stressful: you have a limited amount of time to make it work, you have to allocate resources properly, and you have to adjust quickly when you fail or fuck up. Being broke or financially unstable during those high-stress periods can reduce the quality of your decision-making and further compound an already shitty situation. How can you adequately think through ways to improve your business model or attract more customers if you're unable to make rent for the second month in a row? How can you even fund those improvements if you're superlow on cash? Financial instability can be distracting, psychologically taxing, and in many cases, all-consuming. Three terrifying things you *do not* want to deal with when getting a company off the ground. I know because despite saving up strategically and planning ahead, money issues came up early for me, and they threw me for a wild ride.

By mid-2016, I had jumped into doing Bulletin full-time, and my savings were dwindling. We didn't pay ourselves a salary and reinvested any market revenue back into the business. So that small financial cushion was very necessary—it helped cover our rent, groceries, and any other expenses that popped up. But even though we spent conservatively, I was still bleeding cash, and it made me anxious to watch my savings disappear. I knew what I was getting myself into because—as I've already quipped—almost every founder puts money on the line and leaves money on the table. But once we pressed the buzzer and time started tickin', my inner money monster started wreaking havoc on my sense of security and peace of mind. I had prepared, at least logistically, for these intense first few months sans salary. But I hadn't prepared emotionally or mentally and went into immediate fix-it mode when the anxiety became too overwhelming.

I got a job as a waitress-slash-bartender at a spot called Videology, which was right up the street from my apartment in South Williamsburg, Brooklyn. I would put in a full eight hours at Bulletin, and then pull a night shift at the bar from 6 P.M. until midnight three or four times a week. Needless to say, I was a hot. Ass. Mess. I wasn't earning enough money to actually replenish my losses. I was just working at Videology to help offset those losses and *feel* like I was doing something about my shrinking bank account. The decision to bartend was driven by pure anxiety, and those fourteen-hour days left me foggy, fatigued, and worn down. I wasn't at 100 percent in either world: with Bulletin, I started to feel nervous and resentful. Instead of proactively thinking through ways to scale the market business model—i.e., doing some good old problem-solving—I would wallow in my feelings of uncertainty and indulge in negative self-talk about money, both mine and Bulletin's: We won't last another month like this. The markets aren't actually scalable. I'm losing

$2,000 every month. We spent too much money on our rebrand. I'm gunna be totally broke by the end of the year. I was overworked and overwhelmed. My brain struggled to think positively and proactively, but I felt trapped in my own nightmare. I didn't have the mental breathing room to think through ways of optimizing our business and making more money. I was stuck in a mental loop that squarely focused on the fact that I was losing cash every day, every week, every month.

DON'T JUST CALCULATE THE AMOUNT OF SAVINGS YOU'LL NEED TO FEEL SECURE OR BUDGET OUT YOUR PERSONAL AND COMPANY SPENDING WEEK BY WEEK. TAKE SOME TIME TO THINK THROUGH YOUR FEELINGS AROUND MONEY, HOW IT AFFECTS YOUR MOOD, HOW IT AFFECTS YOUR HAPPINESS, AND HOW MUCH IT FACTORS INTO YOUR DECISION-MAKING, SENSE OF SECURITY, AND SENSE OF SELF.

After five months juggling both Bulletin and Videology, I decided to abandon my bar gig and take my life back. I had not successfully quieted my money woes or magically restocked my savings. I kind of just started to realize how burnt out I was. I was working night shifts at Videology to "do something" about my dwindling finances, but *no* amount of hours spent at Videology would change the root of my insecurity and neurosis around money. This relationship is something every burgeoning business owner or start-up hopeful should think long and hard about before going full-time. Don't just calculate the amount of savings you'll need to feel secure or budget out your personal and company spending week by week. Take some time to think through your feelings around money, how it affects your mood, how it affects your happiness, and how much it factors into your decision-making, sense of security, and sense of self. On paper, I did everything right: I saved up, spent meticulously, and even layered in a *new* side hustle to offset spending for my freshly *full-time* hustle. I was proactive and responsible. But because of my family history and, therefore, a gut instinct to catastrophize, I still felt reckless, anxious, and on the brink of total financial ruin all the time. I had prepared myself financially, but not psychologically. You have to do both.

Step one: make sure you have enough money in the bank to sustain yourself and your business. Optimize for time. The longer you have to get your business up and running, the more of a buffer for screwing up and learning. Without my personal savings, 2016 would have been an even more tumultuous year. I can't imagine how it would have felt to watch our digital magazine flop, knowing all the while I had no cash to my name. Or how I would have survived such a sharp pivot—the future of Bulletin in total limbo—without nervously checking Wells Fargo and seeing some fallback money in the bank. I don't think I would have made it out the other side. You are signing up for a lifestyle that's rife with surprises and setbacks. And they always come in hot. They'll come in piping—scorching—if you have to juggle both business and personal money emergencies simultaneously.

Once you've sussed out how much you should save, take some serious time to investigate your feelings and instincts around money, and how they may affect your mental health as a first-time founder. Talk to other business owners or founders in your field and ask about financial hiccups and demands they faced in the early days. It will help you put yourself in their shoes and assess how you might react to similar fires. This is something I wish I had done, rather than assuming savings in the bank was synonymous with financial security. How would you feel if you got sued for a few thousand dollars? How would you feel if you tanked a substantial sum for a subpar rebrand? How would you feel if you needed to front $1,000 to file important paperwork? How do you cope with money-related stress, and what are its triggers? If you can't get a grip on your relationship with money, feelings of financial insecurity may impede your ability to see your business clearly, scale your product, make thoughtful decisions, and give it your all.

ONCE YOU'VE SUSSED OUT HOW MUCH YOU SHOULD SAVE, TAKE SOME SERIOUS TIME TO INVESTIGATE YOUR FEELINGS AND INSTINCTS AROUND MONEY, AND HOW THEY MAY AFFECT YOUR MENTAL HEALTH AS A FIRST-TIME FOUNDER.

Do I regret going full-time when I did? Despite bouts of financial distress and early months with minimal traction, the answer is no. When we eventually quit Contently in January 2016, we had no idea how the hell Bulletin would make money long-term or what scale it would reach. We had savings, an idea, and a lot of chutzpah. But how did I ultimately make my decision? Where did I find the courage? How did I know when to quit my stable job and take that leap of faith? Well, to start, let's get on the same page. I feel like a lot of people think "leap of faith" equals "believing you'll succeed." But that's not actually true for me or for most of the female entrepreneurs I know. I didn't pull the plug on Contently because I knew Bulletin would work out. You will never have that foresight—I still don't have it, even today. I finally left Contently because after a year of brooding and internal back-and-forth, I came to terms with the fact that I was unhappy. I realized I'd be more fulfilled making less money but doing work I loved. And that's when my faith kicked in. That's what *my* faith looked like.

Leaping. Let's unpack it for a sec. You are literally star-jumping your ass away from the known and into the unknown. Maybe you're reading this book and you're just like me back in 2015. You have a full-time gig that's stable, but it's left you unfulfilled. You have a pipe dream, side project, or part-time business you want to make your main event. Your safety isn't at risk where you are right now: you have a consistent paycheck, hopefully some health benefits, and clarity around your role and responsibilities. You have shelter, food, friends, a routine. Nobody's telling you to, asking you to, or even demanding that you jump. If you're thinking of leaving, that's great! But you could easily turn your tush around, make a reservation at your favorite restaurant, order a fat beer, and LOL at the thought of kissing your normal life goodbye. This happens to a ton of people. They have an idea for a business or career transition, but they accept the reality that their current full-time job and true passion do not and will never intersect. A banker wants to be a musician. A store clerk wants to be a designer. A hotel manager wants to become a restaurateur. They measure the height and distance of the leap, realize they may not make it, turn around, and curl back up to their comfortable life. Not everyone is eyeing a transition from full-time, stable job to steady side hustle, though. Maybe you're jobless and collecting unemployment. Or maybe you're patching together part-time gigs just to break even every month. I've been there. Either way, when you're just scraping by, it can be difficult or outright impossible to envision a reality where you wake up every day and get to work on your pipe dream, pocketing cash all the while. And for good reason.

MY FEELING OF FAITH IS FAR LESS ABOUT THE PROSPECT OF MY SUCCESS AND MORE ABOUT THE PROSPECT OF MY HAPPINESS.

There's a real audacity, a delusion, that comes with actually leaping. With abandoning everything you know and have—with zero external coercion—to live a life of real risk and uncertainty. You can leap and immediately fall into the abyss. You can make it halfway only to have external forces fuck up your success—a larger player rips you off, a business partner turns against you. Or, you can land. You must have the guts and fearlessness to say, I don't care what's coming. Bring it on.

And yet, it takes more than a bold come-what-may attitude to leave your current lifestyle behind. And this is where faith comes in. Faith, as I know it, does not mean "I believe in myself." It does not mean "I trust I'll succeed," or "I'm hyperconfident this will work." My feeling of faith is far less about the prospect of my success and more about the prospect of my happiness.

When you have a passion or a dream, it often hurts to do anything else. As 2016 inched closer and I gave Bulletin more and more of my time, I started to feel that pain quite acutely. Throwing myself into work began to feel inauthentic and icky, like I was betraying a key part of who I was by putting Bulletin editorial on the back burner in favor of repetitive sales calls. It hurt me to abandon my writing. It hurt me to spend eight hours of every day on sales pitches, hawking a software and service I didn't really care about. It hurt me to reconnect with old high school or college friends who *were* in editorial or other creative fields. I would get jealous and sad, realizing I'd prioritized a stable salary over professional and personal fulfillment. I'm not saying creative fields are the shit and everything else sucks. It's just that I yearned to be creative—professionally—and that life seemed totally foreign to me because of the choices I had made over time. It hurt me to look at my career trajectory as a sales executive and see how incongruent it was with the path I envisioned as a child or an eager teen. The me I was in the middle of building was light-years away from the me I wanted to be. The work I was doing was light-years away from the work I wanted to do. Maybe you know what that feels like. I simply reached a critical inflection point where the pain of those realizations outweighed the seductiveness of comfort, consistency, and cash.

THE ME I WAS IN THE MIDDLE OF BUILDING WAS LIGHT-YEARS AWAY FROM THE ME I WANTED TO BE. THE WORK I WAS DOING WAS LIGHT-YEARS AWAY FROM THE WORK I WANTED TO DO. MAYBE YOU KNOW WHAT THAT FEELS LIKE. I SIMPLY REACHED A CRITICAL INFLECTION POINT WHERE THE PAIN OF THOSE REALIZATIONS OUTWEIGHED THE SEDUCTIVENESS OF COMFORT, CONSISTENCY, AND CASH.

I developed this itching sense that no matter what, I'd be happier and more fulfilled as a struggling entrepreneur who was writing every day than as a successful salesperson who wasn't. I didn't know if Bulletin was scalable or marketable or poised to succeed, but I knew it offered me the opportunity to start building the right me. And that was my feeling of faith. Not a premonition that I'd make tons of money or launch a booming business. But rather a gut instinct that despite potential hardship, struggle, and chaos, leaping toward Bulletin and away from my comfortable life would bring me a larger sense of joy than any commission check or promotion ever could. Faith, for me, is knowing that you're being true to yourself. Even if it costs you.

I DIDN'T KNOW IF BULLETIN WAS SCALABLE OR MARKETABLE OR POISED TO SUCCEED, BUT I KNEW IT OFFERED ME THE OPPORTUNITY TO START BUILDING THE RIGHT ME.

WHEN WE JUMPED

All that said, I would be total piece of work if I didn't discuss a major financial catalyst that motived me and Alana to make Bulletin our daily grind. As I mentioned earlier, Alana voiced her interest in applying to Y Combinator, a prestigious start-up accelerator in Silicon Valley, in late 2015. At the time, Y Combinator was accepting applications for two different programs: YC, the core batch program, which offers $150,000 in funding in exchange for 7 percent of your company, and YC Fellowship, which no longer exists but promised $20,000 in exchange for upward of 2 percent ownership. Alana wanted us to apply because a few alums from her school had done the core batch program, and it seemed to have a huge impact in validating and growing their businesses.

We put together an application for our Etsy 2.0 business, an editorial e-commerce site featuring the coolest emerging designers. We had made $4,000 in total sales by then and had fifty brands listing products. We were a rinky-dink e-commerce site with beautiful photos and long-form editorial.

We saw the application process as a challenge and a learning experience. It was the first time we had to succinctly and convincingly describe our business, the market size, our traction, our vision, and how we'd allocate any funding. It was also the first time we were prompted to identify as "entrepreneurs."

The application asked us who the founders were, what our equity split was, and what our titles were within the company. In filling out the application, we started to think bigger. We started to take ourselves more seriously. But most important, we started to really believe in ourselves and what we were capable of building. We weren't technical founders building something form-fit for a surefire YC application, but we had worked hard and built up a stable community of brands, (some) revenue, and modest growth in site visitors, sales, and engagement month over month. We didn't *expect* to get into YC—we knew it was a long shot. But the application process in and of itself felt like a pivotal moment: it was our first real go at introducing Bulletin to the tech world, and our first time digesting just how much progress we were actually making. YC could have skimmed our application and rejected us outright, and we still would have extracted value from the entire process. Many shared Google docs, phone calls, FaceTime sessions, and endless edits later, we hit submit.

We didn't get rejected outright, and YC read through our entire application. They were intrigued, which meant Alana and I got invited for a face-to-face interview in Mountain View, California. Alana called me right when she got the invitation e-mail. I was working out of the Contently San Francisco office that day, got her call, and we both started screaming. I jogged from my desk to the mediocre salad place across the street saying "oh my God" over and over again to a vat of wilting lettuce. We had a shot. We had an open door. We were going to pitch our fuckin' hearts out.

Shortly after, we were both in Mountain View for our ten-minute interview slot. As we drove to the meeting, we were blasting the song "Confident" by Demi Lovato and I got super carried away both dance-driving and shriek-ing, I almost rear-ended a dude on the freeway. Alana always drives now. We pulled up to the YC campus and braced ourselves for the big moment. We had packed a single bottle of beer on our way out, just in case we had crazy pre-interview jitters and wanted to sip down our nerves. We twisted it open and hid the bottle in a pair of leopard-print pajama pants we had tossed in the car. We didn't want any YC partners or other interviewees to see us drinking beer, in a car, at 11:30 in the morning.

The time came to shoot our shot, so we locked the car and power walked toward the building. The rest is a blackout. For both of us. Not because of the three sips of beer, but because we were so overcome with nerves and adrenaline that I think it overpowered our ability to form cohesive memories. We had a rapid-fire, ten-minute interview with three YC partners who asked questions we had prepared for and others we had not. There's plenty of lore and literature around the YC interview process. If you want to know more, google around and you'll definitely get the scoop. It's a quick 'n' dirty, intim-idating interrogation that leaves you feeling excited (because you survived!) and frustrated (because you think it could have gone better).

And then, we waited. YC calls you if you get in, and e-mails you if you don't. They have a famously competitive acceptance rate, around 1.5 per-cent each year, and we knew our chances were slim. We were at Alana's friends' place trying to eat pizza and *not* act like we were dying with sus-pense. It was almost midnight when we got the e-mail. We saw it pop up on Alana's iPhone screen and impulsively fell to the ground. We both hov-ered over it and read through every single word aloud. While we didn't get accepted to YC's core batch program, we did secure a spot in their Fellow-ship pilot, which meant $20,000 in funding and access to the incubator's network of entrepreneurs, partners, mentors, and investors. We were in complete and total shock. One stipulation of the program and receiving the money was that you had to be working on your start-up full-time. This actually came up in our interview, and while we were still fully employed at Contently, Alana and I both instinctively lied (oops) and gave a clumsy "yes" when the partners asked if we were doing Bulletin full-time. But now, it was go-time. The fork in the road was actually here. We had a decision to make: take the check and quit our cushy jobs, or stay gainfully employed and keep chipping away at Bulletin in our spare time.

We had to decide by December. I had just moved to California three months earlier to help build out Contently's West Coast presence. Remember, we had started Bulletin as a fun side project, or so I thought. I wasn't supercozy with the idea of doing it full-time, and Contently was my real (and paying) employer. I did what was asked and expected of me, so I moved, and signed a one-year lease on an apartment. I moved my entire life across the country. Some of my shit was still in boxes when I decided to move back to New York.

I'll never forget that December, sitting next to Alana a few weeks after that watershed night in San Francisco. I was in New York for a quick holiday trip, and we were riding the last ferry from Manhattan back to Brooklyn, where she lived. It was chilly, and we had just put on a little pop-up to promote the magazine during peak gifting season. The moment on the ferry is so crystal clear, and one of the few conversations that I truly think changed the course of my life. We were chatting about the Y Combinator opportunity, all the things we'd give up if we went full-time, and how insane it was that this door had even opened. We casually rattled off how we'd spend the $20K and what parts of the business we wanted to invest in. We were sitting alone in our section downstairs. Alana gave me a coy but serious look, like, Are we gunna do this? Are we doing this? And we both just smiled in silence, looking at each other. My friend, this incredible woman, wanted to take this journey together. She wanted to take the biggest risk of her career—of her life up to that point—and her eyes were inviting me in. I had been saving up and stashing cash. I was miserable as a sales executive. I wanted to write. I wanted to grow. And really, I just wanted to be happy.

That week, I packed up my life in California, found a subletter, and officially became Bulletin employee number two. Together, we took the $20K from Y Combinator and quit our jobs. We had no idea what was coming.

MONEY MATTERS

While there is no set answer for when to quit your job or bring your side hustle full-time, there are a handful of signals that will indicate that it's time. One huge signal is how you feel about your full-time job or current career, and whether you would be personally satisfied keeping your side hustle on the side indefinitely or not. If your side hustle is supplementing some deep lack of fulfillment with your full-time job then, at some breaking point, your misery might outweigh your fear of financial insecurity. That's what happened to me and many others I know. So, it kind of boils down to, How unhappy are you? and What are you willing to do about it?

You will also see financial signals that will help indicate when it's time to take the leap. One signal may be reaching a certain dollar amount in your savings or getting a bank loan approved. Another may be receiving some sort of grant or early-stage funding or getting into an accelerator program with investment dollars attached. The cold, hard reality is you'll need money to feed yourself—and potentially others; you'll need money to support your business; you'll need money to pay rent or your mortgage; you'll need money to pay for health insurance . . . the list goes on. Don't jump ship until you have enough money—an amount to cover the above, yes, but also, an amount that makes you feel safe and secure. Set a number—a savings goal, a fundraising goal, a Kickstarter goal, a personal loan total—and make moves to go full-time once you hit it.

Lastly, your business may tell you when it's time to start giving it your all. This wasn't our catalyst, but it might be yours. Your side hustle may grow quickly and start revealing opportunities for more monetization. But in order to capture those opportunities, you may need to invest more time in your business or project. You may run an influencer marketing side hustle that generates a lot of buzz and gets an influx of interested new clients after a supersuccessful campaign. Or maybe you run a stationery brand on the side and a major, national chain wants to collaborate on a few designs after finding you on Instagram. You may be reading this and think I'm crazy, but this has happened to so many people I know and to brands that we've worked with. They put time, effort, and patience into their side project and gained recognition over time. That recognition then snowballed into opportunity, and they were finally able to ditch their jobs and start their dream careers.

Going full-time with your pipe dream—no matter your current employment situation—is not a necessary step to starting a business, nor is it the right step for everyone. I come from a white middle-class family and attended an Ivy League university. I secured a reasonably high-paying second job after graduating and had time to save and strategically plan for my big leap. In short, I had the resources to pick myself up should I hit rock bottom after running with Bulletin full-time. My mom had an apartment in LA and room for me in her bed and made enough money to make sure I had shelter and food had everything gone to total shit. I still have that safety net. But in reality, that's a luxury many people don't have. Understanding your own financial situation, as well as your fiscal responsibilities, is key. You can be a badass self-starter no matter how you divvy up your time, and realizing your dream—whether or not that's creating a business—can be accomplished *with or without* a day job. In fact, many of the women who sell with Bulletin still work full-time jobs or juggle multiple part-time roles and run their businesses on the side. We work with an elementary school teacher who makes jewelry after work and on the weekends and sells in multiple stores around the country. We've sold embroidery from an incredible needlepoint artist who is, remarkably, a full-time attorney. Kiara Sheé, who runs merchandising for Bulletin, is also an illustrator and influencer who does freelance design work and sells her own jewelry and prints. Alana and I juggled two jobs for a year and accomplished a lot with Bulletin even while working 9 to 6 somewhere else.

> IF YOU'D FEEL MORE FINANCIALLY AND MENTALLY STABLE KEEPING YOUR PROJECTS SUPPLEMENTAL, THEN DO THAT. KEEP JUGGLING. KEEP HUSTLING. KEEP WORKING. BECAUSE EVEN IF YOU'RE DOING IT PART-TIME, YOU ARE STILL A STYLIST. AN ACCOUNTANT. AN EDITOR. A BRAND.

Sometimes, the financial risk of going full-time with your passion or side project is just too risky given other obligations, restrictions, or situations in your life. You don't have the option of prioritizing your happiness or meeting a certain dollar amount in your savings account. And that's okay. Because you are still remarkable for having a side hustle in the first place and refusing to define yourself or your trajectory by your full-time job or paid part-time work alone. You are proactively nurturing a version of you that feels more fulfilling and using precious, delicious free time to work. To build something that's yours. Maybe you're a caregiver who does part-time styling or accounting, or a college student with a small-but-lucrative essay editing service, or a dental assistant with an Etsy shop. If you'd feel more financially and mentally stable keeping your projects supplemental, then do that. Keep juggling. Keep hustling. Keep working. Because even if you're doing it part-time, you are still a stylist. An accountant. An editor. A brand. Your main gig does not define you, and you're an entrepreneur all the same.

I REALIZED I'D BE MORE FULFILLED MAKING LESS MONEY BUT DOING WORK I LOVED. AND THAT'S WHEN MY FAITH KICKED IN. THAT'S WHAT MY FAITH LOOKED LIKE.

TALK TO ME ABOUT GOING FULL-TIME

JEN ZEANO
JEN ZEANO DESIGNS

I got a degree in psychology—nothing related to business or anything. I tried working in the field, but I absolutely hated it. I hated having a boss and the whole 9-to-5 routine. I was just miserable going to work every day. There was no room for creativity. There was nothing within the field that I tried and enjoyed. I worked retail for four to five years through college, and I hated that, too. I thought because it was retail and I had a crappy schedule that that was why I didn't like it, but it turns out that level of structure just wasn't for me, regardless of the industry. One day, I took a trip to Disney World and I was so purely happy that I just didn't want to go back to work. When I got back from the trip that Monday, I walked into work and I quit. My boss was like, "Did you get another job?" and I said, "No, I don't have one lined up." She asked me if I knew what I wanted to do next, and I told her, "No, but I'm never going to be happy here. This isn't what I'm supposed to be doing with my life."

My wife had just gotten a job with her degree, so it was okay if I didn't work for a little bit. I just took a few days to think about it, and realized I didn't want to apply for another job. I needed to figure something out. That's when I started Jen Zeano Designs. I hadn't launched a brand before or anything, but I had to make JZD work because I wasn't working. I thought about what I enjoyed doing most, and how I could use my voice as the main platform for the business. That's what inspired me to make JZD a Latina empowerment brand.

My wife and I live in a border town and 90 percent of the population is Latinx. We saw how Latinx people got treated differently and noticed there is way less Latinx empowerment in cities that are farther away from the border. So, I wanted to start an online brand and platform to help spread Latina magic throughout the world. Even now, I still have doubts. There are times I feel like I have no idea what I'm doing. But when I look back, I am proud of my decision. I was either going to make JZD work or be in a job I hated for the rest of my life.

You have to go through hard times to know you don't want to go back to that. I knew the type of job I would have been stuck with with my psychology degree. I knew what I would have spent the rest of my life doing, instead of doing what I loved or making a greater impact. That has always been my motivator when I get discouraged. Sometimes I feel like quitting because we had a slow week. But to me, it has always been: make it work, or go back to something you don't want to be doing.

JANINE LEE
FLOSS GLOSS

When I graduated back in 2010, I took a fashion internship and immediately realized I didn't want to contribute to that industry. Traveling to India was very devastating, and I just felt like if I was going to source something or sell something, I want to know where it's coming from. Fashion—that whole world was not for me. I started bartending until I found something else. My co-founder, Aretha, and I were doing a ton of fun nail art stuff on Tumblr at the same time, before Tumblr was big.

We had our own site, flossgloss.tumblr.com, and we really wanted to get on Fuck Ya Nail Art. My dad saw it and was like, "You need a real website," so we bought a GoDaddy URL. We were kind of like, "Are we a business now?" And in my head, I was like, Fuck, yeah! We are! My dad could see how excited I was and just how much I was putting into my own nail art and little custom polishes and asked what Aretha and I wanted to do. And I almost impulsively decided we should do it full-time. It was 2011.

I called Aretha, and I told her we should just go for it and do this, we should design our own bottle, formally start making our own polishes, and launch our own line. She was superdown. My dad floated me $500 to get a business license in California. I was twenty-two at the time—I was like, I love this, this is so amazing, I'm starting a business! We were still waiting tables and bartending the whole time at night and working on Floss Gloss during the day. We did a ton of stuff through LegalZoom, I started taking business school classes online, googling vendors and manufacturers.

Getting funding and finding manufacturers was so overwhelming, and we needed cash up front to make the first batch of product. We did a small friends and family round and raised $80,000. It was literally the bare minimum we needed to cover cost of goods and PR—we didn't want to be some small-fry Frankenpolish. We were here to play. We started doing Floss Gloss full-time at that point and busted our asses to make press connections and get the first batch out there. We felt like dedicating our all to it was the only way to give it a real shot and seize that first major opportunity with debuting the line.

LEILA KASHANI
ALLEYOOP

I used to work in marketing and product development at a toy company. I was tasked with finding white space and creating and marketing interesting products for kids. I launched lots of successful products and brands in my career. During one meeting with a buyer, I realized in the middle of the presentation that she was staring at my armpit: I had only shaved one underarm and probably looked ridiculous, waving my hands around talking up this new doll I had created and cared so much about. This actually wasn't a new problem for me, either. Before working at this toy company, I had spent years in brand marketing and traveled the country all the time, leaving home superearly and getting back late at night. Existing makeup tools and other personal care products weren't made with this type of constant travel in mind.

In generations past, most women were packing carry-ons for thirty days at a time, not thirty hours. Given my background in developing and creating toys and in marketing brands, I knew I had the experience to create new beauty and body care products specifically made for women on the go. My first prototype was a portable razor meant for missed spots and touch-ups. I brought my prototype to work and my boss at the toy company saw it and asked if she could try it. I told her she could, and within a couple weeks, Ulta Beauty e-mailed me. I thought it was a prank because it happened on April Fools' Day. My boss had shared the prototype with them and they wanted to take it nationwide. I was still working full-time at the toy company, but I knew if I took the Ulta deal I had to leave. I thought, Here is your opportunity to become the entrepreneur you've always wanted to be.

Ulta wanted to go live in six months, so I decided to quit and launch my own brand. I had no idea what I was getting myself into. I immediately had to meet with factories and designers and find help with all the moving parts: the functionality, formulation, the blades. I was really shocked by a rocky start. I was a senior level employee at this toy company and had created successful products before—everyone at the company and all of our partners respected me and took me seriously. Starting my brand as a small, one-woman show was a completely different experience. I struggled to find partners who would take me seriously.

In hindsight, I wish I hadn't gone full-time as soon as I did, and I wish I hadn't done it explicitly for the Ulta deal, even though the deal was incredible and got us so much exposure. I launched a product before I really built and launched my brand. I wish I had built the brand first. I had such a short window of time to finalize the deal with Ulta, get the final product launched, pick a name, put the name on the products, and get the razor on the floor. We ended up with an initial brand name I wasn't really excited about, but I had put all my eggs into this basket and quit my job, so I had to move forward.

I took the Ulta opportunity as this shining star, and it is so easy to jump in when someone says they want and believe in you. But I made that more important than thinking about what was best, what was most sustainable, and what that opportunity would lead me to next. I was young and had my blinders on. Looking back, I wonder if I should have said no and not jumped in as quickly until I felt really good about where I was at, did a bit more testing, and had more time to put pen to paper around the brand identity and positioning. I also don't know that I would have leapt into things full force like that if I'd had kids, like I do now. I don't know that I would have done the same thing. At the time, I thought, What's the worst that can happen? I can go back to work and get a corporate job. I can move in with my parents. I didn't overthink it, I just focused on the end result and where I wanted to be, versus where I was. I was able to push through.

Now, people ask what it's like to run my own business. I'm like, I cry myself to sleep sometimes and it's a scary place to be. When I made the jump, I wasn't thinking about the risks and the implications, I wasn't thinking about the leases you sign or the failed products you'll develop. But as you grow the company, you start to realize that your risk and your awareness of it grow, too.

MEENA HARRIS
PHENOMENAL WOMAN
ACTION CAMPAIGN

I'm the founder and CEO of Phenomenal Woman, and I'm also the head of strategy and leadership at Uber. It can be challenging to juggle everything, and it's a choice that I've made. The job at Uber actually came out of a tech tour I did with Phenomenal Woman when I was running the brand full-time. I ran the brand full-time for nine months, and I couldn't turn it off in my head. I couldn't stop thinking about how to improve it and how to grow it. I knew I couldn't get away from it; we had accomplished so much in that short period and I knew even more opportunities were coming our way. But I am all about constantly iterating, even in terms of my journey, and I was ready to wind down the intensity of my involvement but keep building the brand brick by brick. I wasn't looking to go back into tech, but I had a bunch of really good friends and mentors telling me to at least think about the Uber offer.

I took the job because I felt like it would be a massive learning opportunity. I came into Uber at a difficult period and I was eager to contribute and provide a fresh perspective. I work on projects at Uber that help advance women in the workplace and build diversity and inclusion within the company. I'm taking the risk of not building my company full-time right now, but I feel like I'm earning a mini-MBA because of my exposure to Uber, and I have everything I could have imagined in a leadership role: I get to be creative and innovative, and I have autonomy.

RANDI SELTZER
ROCKAWAY GYPSEA

I'm a full-time teacher and if you had told me years before launching that I'd have my own jewelry business, I would have been like, I don't know how to *make* jewelry. I've always been a creative person. I'm the girl who juggles three or four part-time jobs because I like to do a lot and try new things. I didn't know what I wanted to be. I ended up becoming a teacher, but I did a ton of crafty and creative stuff on the side, like bedazzling cereal boxes and turning them into working clocks, or starting a dating blog.

There was this wedding dress project I launched called Trashed in the Dress. I hosted events for women where they could get wasted in their wedding dresses. You know, you never really get to wear it after that one time, so I figured it might be fun. As part of that, I taught myself how to make flower crowns. I wanted the actual crown part to last and look cute once the flowers died, so I taught myself how to hand-stamp from YouTube University, as I call it. I fell in love with hand-stamping, and things took off from there. I made a few bracelets and posted them on Facebook. People saw them and were asking where to buy them, and some of my students said they wanted to buy them, too. I was like, I mean, I can sell you one I guess? And that's how I started having a jewelry business.

I've been able to grow Rockaway Gypsea at my own pace. I added new products slowly here and there. I'd learn how to make new things and if people bought them, I worked harder and produced even more. If people didn't buy them, I just ditched 'em. It's definitely a struggle, juggling a full-time job and a side hustle. I have to give myself working hours for Rockaway Gypsea during the week, and if I don't, it means I have to work double on the weekends to meet the deadlines I've set for myself.

I try not to bite off more than I can chew, but that's been a learning process. For a while, I promised two-day shipping on my Etsy page to try to make more money and get more customers. But then I tried doing it, and I was like, Fuck this. I'm not Amazon. So, I changed it back to a time frame that's more manageable for me, and yes, it means I get fewer sales, but it's my part-time hustle. I don't want to be working until 11 P.M. to get some two-day order out. I still want to have a life.

I think as women, we spend a lot of time putting other people first or thinking about how what we do affects other people. Rockaway isn't something I do for crazy sales or lots of money, it's something I do for me. Even though it's hard to juggle it all sometimes, this business has improved my quality of life. I am working on this business that I made, I am selling products that I made, and I've created this brand that is so fulfilling for me.

MICHELLE ALFONSO
INSTAGRANDMAW

I launched my card company Instagrandmaw while I was in school, so I had to figure out how to do my schoolwork and graduate and run this business on the side. I worked a lot of retail jobs while I was in school, which was superexhausting for me. I was only twenty-two when I first got started. I really wanted people to see my work, but I didn't know how to put it out there.

I'm an illustrator, and I would always try out these illustrated portraits of rappers. I remember Valentine's Day was coming up, and I was in this weird life period where I didn't really know who I wanted to be or what I wanted to do. I thought it might be fun to just put the portraits on greeting cards. Like, I would have been so happy to receive a Valentine's card with Tupac on it.

And it didn't seem like there were any hip-hop themed cards out there, so I figured it might work.

I started on Etsy when I was doing it part-time and had to figure out everything from scratch. I didn't even know what mail service to use to send out orders! I was so clueless. I had never made a physical product with my illustrations before so there was a lot of trial and error. I literally googled "what size is greeting card"! But I felt like it was important to just put my work out there, and I feel like with anything, you can never go in fully prepared and you have to be open to learning as you go. I didn't come from an entrepreneurial family; I'm actually the first in my family to really own a business and do something like this.

I gained a few wholesale clients, like Urban Outfitters, through Etsy, which was huge for me. I ended up launching my own website to make the brand feel more official. By the time I graduated, I decided I wanted to spend more of my time on my actual work and realized I would be more useful and effective in making the business happen if I went all in. I wanted people to feel like I was giving it my everything. It's a really tricky decision, though.

Having gone full-time with Instagrandmaw, I know what it's like to work superhard and see money come in but realize it isn't enough to pay the bills. The entire brand has been self-financed—I basically put whatever I make through sales back into the business. And I'm still definitely figuring that piece out. I have a few other illustration clients unrelated to Instagrandmaw, but it's happening. I'm a full-time illustrator! Even when it's difficult for me to get the resources I need for the business, I'm not discouraged.

ALEXANDRA FINE
DAME

I started Dame after I was fired, just dabbling here and there, while I was searching for a new job. Getting fired was really hard on me—it felt like how it felt getting an STD for the first time. I was so ashamed, so embarrassed, and I never thought this would happen to me because I work so hard, and I think I'm great! But I started talking to lots of other people and, as it turns out, many people get fired at one point or another for a million different reasons. I was living at home again with my parents, and I realized how much I loved working on Dame. I started to work on it more and more, and it kind of became my new direction. At some point I remember saying, I'm going to give this six months and I'm not going to look for another job while I build Dame. I want to see how far I can go and if Dame doesn't work out, I'll start looking again. My mom was so stressed about it, her whole vibe was like, Um, are you sure? I knew what I was doing was crazy, at least statistically, but I didn't realize just how crazy it was at the time. I could have done a lot more work on and calculations against how much money I needed to sustain myself long-term, how I was going to grow properly to hit a certain amount in revenue. In a way, though, being a bit naive really benefited me. It let me be delusional, look at my competitors and ask, Why not me? I can do this better.

To go all in, I think you need equal parts confidence, delusion, and a dose of reality.

CHAPTER FIVE

TAKING MONEY AND MAKING MONEY

*Raising a bunch of money, and raising way more than you
need, it ends up stunting people's actual growth as businesses.
It destroys businesses. It's like, look, you know, you plant a seed,
it needs some water, but if you just pour a whole fucking bucket
of water on it's going to kill it.*

—JASON FRIED, *CEO of Basecamp**

One of the most important and strategic choices you will have to make when launching your business is how you're going to fund it. The way you finance your venture directly informs how it will grow, how big it will be, and how quickly you need to get there. But it also dictates your lifestyle: how much free time you have, the amount of stress-inducing cortisol pumping through your veins, how hands-on you get to be with certain aspects of your business. Every entrepreneur, whether running their company full-time or part-time, needs to strategically think through how they want to finance their business.

There are plenty of ways to fund your venture—ranging from getting a personal loan to raising a seed round to bootstrapping or crowdfunding. The brands in our network have done everything from launching an iFund-Women campaign to raising a friends-and-family seed round to refusing any and all outside investment altogether. The reason there is so much variation is that how you *take* money should reflect how you *make* money, and your financing strategy will differ depending on what you're building, how much it costs to run your business, and, most important, how much you want to control your company and its future.

---

* Eric Johnson, "'Venture capital money kills more businesses than it helps,' says Basecamp CEO Jason Fried," *Recode*, January 23, 2019, recode.net/2019/1/23/18193685/venture-capital-money-kills-business-basecamp-ceo-jason-fried.

THE WAY YOU FINANCE YOUR VENTURE DIRECTLY INFORMS HOW IT WILL GROW, HOW BIG IT WILL BE, AND HOW QUICKLY YOU NEED TO GET THERE.

Early on, back in 2016, Alana and I stumbled into the world of venture capital. In taking Y Combinator's $20,000 as part of their Fellowship program, we signed away our right to grow a small or mid-size business. We took money from a seed accelerator that only has eyes for venture gains, meaning, in an ideal world, Bulletin would eventually become a one-billion-dollar unicorn—an Uber, Airbnb, Facebook, or Slack. I meet a lot of people who ask, How can I raise a seed round? or How do I get VC money to start my business? I immediately reply with, Well, why do you *want* VC money? *Why* are you raising a seed round? The answers I get often worry me, because they remind me of how *I* would have replied back in 2016: We need the money to launch the product, We want to start paying our team, We aren't generating revenue yet, We need money for marketing, It seems like there's a lot of capital out there, my friend just closed his pre-seed in, like, *two weeks!* These answers always indicate to me that the person doesn't understand the critical connection between her fundraising strategy and the future of her business. If you're raising a seed round or exploring venture funding as an option, you need to know what you're signing up for. You're *not* signing up to get quick cash for your marketing campaign or money to make a key hire. You're *not* signing up for a local, mid-size business that makes a couple million in annual revenue and hums along, year after year. You're *not* signing up for a few years of grunt work and a smooth, guaranteed exit. You are signing up to chase a wild, taxing, delicious dream—in some cases, for years on end—that generates gobs of cold, hard cash for your investors and might even change the world. Because the way you finance your company determines what the company becomes. But at age twenty-four, as a first-time founder lookin' at a crisp $20,000 for the taking, this never even crossed my mind.

I had no idea what venture capital money was before getting accepted to Y Combinator Fellowship and accepting our first $20,000 check. So, if it's this murky, confusing, buzzy term for you, that's okay. That's allowed. Because we've been there. Put simply, venture capital is money invested in a risky project that has high growth potential. Every single word in this sentence is extremely important. But if I were under duress and had to pick just one . . . okay, maybe two . . . I'd pluck "growth potential" from the lineup. Because venture capital is a high-risk, high-reward game. It's kind of like gambling. VC's have set funds—or pools of money—that they use to invest in a portfolio of companies. They get this money from LPs, or limited partners, who come from all over the place. Some LPs are just straight-up rich people, some are pension funds, some are university endowments. LPs exist behind the scenes, and VCs court them or build relationships with them in order to create these funds. It's kind of like going to a Las Vegas casino with $1,000 in your pocket that you've crowdsourced from a few friends, but those friends are expecting you to come back from Vegas with $100,000 to divvy up among them all. They don't tell you how to spend the $1,000—it's up to you to figure out if you're going to play poker, blackjack, craps, roulette. You're the VC, your friends are the LPs, and the pressure's fucking on. VCs take a percentage of profits generated through acquisitions and IPOs from their portfolio companies—this is called a carry. So, you have some skin in the game, too, and it's on you to make that Vegas trip worth it to both pay out your friends and make some money for yourself.

I HAD NO IDEA WHAT VENTURE CAPITAL MONEY WAS.

This pressure means VCs need to invest thoughtfully and strategically, and use market trends, data, personal references, and their gut to determine which companies and founders they should invest in. VC partners infuse multiple companies with cash every year, knowing full well that not all of them will garner the returns they and their LPs are looking for. But if even one makes it big—if they chance upon a Stitch Fix or Zoom—they've done their job. All it takes is one major exit or, ideally, a few major exits, to give LPs the returns they demand and VCs the carry, or commission, they rely on as compensation. VCs are typically looking for a ten-times-or-greater return on their investment, so if a start-up can't convince VC partners that it can scale and deliver those gains, the chances of its getting funded are relatively slim.

WHY AND WHEN TO GROW FAST

Remember when I warned that the way you finance your company determines what the company will become? If you take on VC money, you should understand VC expectations and LP expectations, and how those directly affect the way you and your company will live and breathe. Even if there's a lot of VC money out there for the taking (known in Silicon Valley as "dry powder"), that doesn't mean you should take it. So how do you know if you *need* it? This is a tricky question, and I am by no means an expert. But the answer to this question is usually buried somewhere in a pile of:

- What are you building?
- Can it scale rapidly and efficiently?
- How large is the market you're going after?
- How does your business make money?
- What is your profit margin?

I sat down with our first institutional investor—aka an actual expert—to talk this stuff over. Nick Chirls hails from an early-stage fund called Notation Capital, and they led our pre-seed round back in late 2016, after we had been bootstrapping Bulletin Market for over a year. During our convo, there was a certain assessment framework that became immediately clear: you should only take venture money if you're creating a new market or disrupting a large market, and therefore won't be profitable for a long time. But what does it mean to "create" a new market or "disrupt" a large market?

Airbnb is a great example of a company that created a new market. Staying in strangers' homes sounded absolutely bonkers before Airbnb created a platform that normalized and legitimized that behavior. They were the first company to build a product that connected local hosts and paying guests: they set the pricing structure, outlined the terms of engagement, and quite literally birthed a brand-new industry. Henry Ford, the inventor and proliferator of the modern car, once (allegedly) mused, "If I had asked people what they wanted, they would have said 'faster horses.'" Airbnb is the modern car. It was a brand-new, revolutionary, never-before-seen innovation that required a shift in human behavior.

Glossier, on the other hand, is a huge market disruptor. Makeup existed way before Emily Weiss founded Glossier, and the company's products are not all revolutionary in and of themselves. Putting makeup on and using skincare products are not new behaviors, either, but Weiss was disruptive in how she motivated customers to purchase. At the time, Glossier's use of community-sourced feedback to create and launch products and their deployment of social media and influencer marketing over traditional channels completely disrupted how beauty brands were typically launched and marketed. She created a new playbook for product development and beauty marketing in a space saturated by older, traditional brands that were stagnant and slow to innovate. Where legacy makeup brands were continuing to spend ad dollars on decaying magazine placements or annoying banner ads, Glossier was saturating Instagram with user-generated content. Where Chanel was hiring famous actresses and models to star in their campaigns, Glossier was putting real girls front and center.

Both Airbnb and Glossier are billion-dollar companies that took on gobs and gobs of VC funding. One created a brand-new market and shaped a new user behavior, and the other disrupted an already-billion-dollar market by leveraging existing user behavior for commercial gain. Both required a massive injection of cash up front—and along the way—to hire employees, build the product, improve the technology, market the brand, cover legal and operational costs . . . the list goes on. It's an "if you build it, they will come" execution that requires VC funding to become and stay commercially viable. You can't build and scale Airbnb or Glossier with a small bank loan. If your company isn't creating a new market or disrupting a multibillion-dollar market in this way, VC funding might not be part of your story.

So, what happens if you take venture money, when you really shouldn't have? What happens if venture money bites you in the ass? This happens all. the. time. I have read endless articles about companies that imploded after a seed, Series A, or even later stage round, because they grew too fast or grew too soon, or both! They had to lay off staff, shutter parts of the business, sell off assets, or close up shop entirely. Just look at WeWork, Airware, or Jawbone. Often, because VCs demand rocket-fuel growth to see ROI (return on investment), start-ups scale earlier than they should, and faster than they should, to meet these expectations. Every company, Bulletin included, is susceptible to this type of pressure. Just a week before writing this paragraph, a fellow Y Combinator company in our batch that had raised capital from a slew of prestigious investors and firms announced that they were shutting down. They failed, as they put it in their blog post, due to high customer churn and a lack of product-market fit amid fast-paced growth. In layperson's terms, that means they weren't able to keep customers because they built the wrong product and spent too much money, too quickly. With that news, the prospect of this type of failure—fueled by VC money—hit closer to home than ever. These founders were smart and charismatic and had studied their customer in intricate detail. They didn't piss their money away on anything fancy or gaudy or unnecessary, and they took themselves and their vision quite seriously. From what I've seen, though, that isn't enough to keep you afloat. Typically, these failures happen because companies don't have product-market fit despite pursuing a large, billion-dollar market or they *do* have product-market fit in a market that's simply too small.

IF YOU HAVE VC MONEY BUT DON'T HAVE PRODUCT-MARKET FIT, YOU ARE SIGNING UP TO SCALE SOMETHING NO ONE WANTS.

But wait, sorry . . . WTF is product-market fit again?, you're sitting here, asking quietly. Well, astute readers with good memory (love you guys!*) will remember from Chapter 2 that product-market fit (PMF) basically means making something that people want. As Andy Rachleff, co-founder of Benchmark Capital, puts it, having product-market fit means you are "addressing a market that really wants your product—the dogs are eating the dog food."* For many companies who go venture, they haven't found PMF yet. Meaning they haven't formed a product or service that anyone really wants or needs. But, for whatever reason, they scale anyway. This lack of PMF can happen for a multitude of reasons: the company hasn't cracked the business model yet, they haven't priced the product correctly, they aren't addressing a real pain point . . . the list goes on. But the core issue is plain and simple: if you have VC money but don't have product-market fit, you are signing up to scale something no one wants.

So, what does this actually look like? Let's use a hypothetical, VC-backed software company as an example. Let's name it Supersize Industries. Supersize Industries makes enterprise software for mid-stage companies. They raised a $500,000 seed round to build out the tech, hire a small team, and service its first eight clients. Five of the eight clients churn, or peace out, within the first year because the product is too expensive. All five churned clients say the software was somewhat useful, but the product offering did

---

* Tren Griffin, "12 Things about Product-Market Fit," Andreesen Horowitz, https://al6z .com/2017/02/18/12-things-about-product-market-fit/.

not justify the cost. Luckily, Supersize Industries just signed up twenty new clients (good job, guys!) so at least things are lookin' up. Supersize Industries needs more money to service these new clients and add even more features to the platform, which they think will help justify the platform's price tag. They raise a $4 million Series A to hire a few more engineers to build out these features and more salespeople to pitch the platform and secure more dollars on deal$. The salespeople are pitching the product left and right and taking home fat commission checks for every company they sign up. The marketing team is pouring gobs of cash into acquisition marketing like Google Adwords. But then, six months in, eleven of those twenty new clients don't renew! They all say the platform is too expensive and isn't delivering enough value! The Supersize Industries executive team scrambles to rework their pricing structure and decides to add even *more* features to the platform to increase a sense of perceived value in the product.

But Supersize is in a real pickle: They've spent tons of money on marketing a product that doesn't stick, they've hired a shit ton of salespeople to sell a product that doesn't stick, they've layered in a ton of features that feel like bells and whistles on top of a product that doesn't stick, and they're losing customers within months of signing them up. They have three months of runway—that is, cash in the bank—left, and while the product is as robust as it's ever been, no one wants to buy it. That Series A was the absolute worst thing to happen to Supersize Industries. They used those ten new clients as a faulty signal for product-market fit, they didn't properly investigate their churn issue early on, and having the Series A cash allowed them to throw money at Band-Aid solutions.

What could they have done differently? Well, it's hard to say. We're talking about a totally fictitious company, after all. But I'm left wondering: back when they were seed stage, three of their first eight clients stuck around, while the others abandoned the platform. It may have been wise to spend time digging deeper into those three customers and their loyalty, rather than investing in a marathon sales cycle to close more accounts to justify the Series A.

THE VENTURE TRAP

If you read the juicy hypothetical above and wondered, But wait, where are the company's investors in all this? Aren't they kind of to blame here, too? Glad you're paying attention. And the answer is kind of tricky. Investors do varying degrees of due diligence when deciding to invest in a company. When I've asked investors point-blank about failed tech IPOs or block-buster start-up failures, they've straight-up said to my face: If a company is hot enough and hyped enough, many investors don't do any sort of due diligence. *They just want to get in on the deal.* I should mention these have been male investors commenting on white-founded, male-founded compa-nies—from what I've seen, heard, read, and personally experienced, female founders have to shell out gigatons of data to get any funding. Ditto for minority founders.

> FROM WHAT I'VE SEEN, HEARD, READ, AND PERSONALLY EXPERIENCED, FEMALE FOUNDERS HAVE TO SHELL OUT GIGATONS OF DATA TO GET ANY FUNDING.

But I digress. You'd think a VC or any type of investor knows the ins and outs of the company they're funding (regardless of the founder's gender or race!) and has done some surgery on the business model and the business plan. In reality, it totally varies from investor to investor, company to company, and deal to deal. That, and every new funding stage requires a deeper and deeper dive into the business. For example, during early fundraising rounds like pre-seed and seed, investors are more focused on the founders, the idea, and the market size than quarterly profit and loss statements or even customer retention. They may not ask you for any raw revenue documentation, like exports directly from your payment processor. They'll take your deck and financial model—that's enough. But often, investors do *way* more digging into your raw data, your churn, and your projections once you hit Series A financing onward.

When you raise a Series A, most (read: smart) funds will set up a literal war room to digest all of your customer or user data, expenses, revenue, and more. At least, investors did that with Bulletin. I haven't gone so far as to assign the fake Supersize Industries with fake Series A investors and a fake diligence process—I have more riveting things to think about!—but in our hypothetical scenario, it seems like the investors are somewhat to blame for their misguided assessment of the health and longevity of the Supsersize software. Whoever led their fictional Series A probably took those twenty hot new customers at face value, when perhaps they shouldn't have. If the founders pitched a convincing story that their churn problems were over, new customers were thrilled, and the business was growing faster than ever, the Series A investors may have been sold and therefore were remiss is overlooking a few glaring red flags. And this isn't some rare occurrence. *This happens all the time.*

That's because a big part of raising venture money—for better or for worse—ties back to storytelling and optics. That means face value is the name of the game. There are countless instances of companies that have raised venture money on faulty or cherry-picked data, beautiful branding, Big Name advisors, or exaggerated numbers. Just look at Fyre Festival or Theranos. In both instances, the founder was able to manipulate intelligent, discerning investors into throwing money at an arguably fraudulent, but optically impressive company. Billy McFarland, founder of Fyre Media, used glossy social media marketing, world-renowned influencers, and the cachet (can we call it that?) of Ja Rule to scam investors out of $27 million. Elizabeth Holmes, Theranos CEO and founder, leveraged famous, well-respected advisors, a Stanford education, a Steve Jobsian black turtleneck, and incessant press and media coverage to scam investors out of more than one billion dollars! These are extremely extreme cases, but they serve to illustrate a point. Because venture capitalists are placing a bet when they invest in companies, they are, at times, easily allured by certain signals that this bet might actually work out: a revolutionary, grand vision, a supercompelling founder, a masterful salesperson. It's almost as if venture investors *want* to see this flawless, thriving company with zero warts, zero weak spots, zero issues. It's the type of company that gets them excited and makes them feel good about parting with their LPs' cash.

This dynamic is only exacerbated when you look at things from the founder's angle. Getting venture money is hypercompetitive and notoriously difficult. Even getting in the room with a VC or angel investor is no small feat. So, you only got one shot, one opportunity—to quote Eminem—to dazzle your audience and walk away with a check. You're obviously going to focus on the parts of your business that *are* thriving and avoid mention of certain dark spots or roadblocks to massive scale. As one investor once put it to me, "Pitch the sizzle reel." It's literally a performance. And it's a selective performance by nature. Founders position their company and traction with a carefully phrased and highly produced deck. They're granted thirty-minute meetings to vie for $300,000 checks. The entire system is set up so that optics run the show, and that means that, sometimes, investors truly overlook red flags about a company's profitability, scalability, or path to product-market fit. Or, and more frighteningly, they aren't even looking at those things in the first place.

Sometimes, start-ups don't have product-market fit but take venture cash anyway, like Supersize Industries, and other times, start-ups do have product-market fit, but the market's too small. This means that despite a beloved product, organic traction, solid customer retention, and healthy unit economics, the company will still fail under the thumb of venture scale. Why? Well, simply because there's a hard stop to how big the company can grow with its current customer base, and that ceiling means investors won't get the returns they're gunning for. I think this is one of the most tragic ways in which VC money can utterly ruin an otherwise incredible company. Because while venture money can help make real magic happen— it can help you acquire customers, perfect your targeting, invest in luxe ad creative—it *cannot* expand a market. That type of magic just isn't possible.

But so often, start-ups see a shiny billion-dollar valuation at the end of some fundraising tunnel and sacrifice slow, deliberate growth in a limited market for the validation, resources, and cachet that comes with VC funding. They are then left with the insane pressure to scale, grow, expand, and acquire more and more customers, when in reality, the market's tapped out or poised to be. In the most heartbreaking cases, start-ups notice this ceiling and then change their product or service to target a much larger customer base. When this happens, companies often abandon the values, identity, quality, and the ingredients that made them so successful in the first place. They cave to investor pressure and seek even more scale and often lose their most loyal customers in the process, or shut down entirely. Often, the founders end up running a company they might not even recognize anymore.

> BECAUSE WHILE VENTURE MONEY CAN HELP MAKE REAL MAGIC HAPPEN—IT CAN HELP YOU ACQUIRE CUSTOMERS, PERFECT YOUR TARGETING, INVEST IN LUXE AD CREATIVE—IT CANNOT *EXPAND A MARKET.*

Sophia Amoruso's first venture, Nasty Gal, raised tens of millions in venture funding after an impressive era of rapid growth and bootstrapping, only to file for bankruptcy and sell for around $20 million. The vintage-apparel and lifestyle brand grew from an eBay store and Myspace community to a full-fledged venture-backed retailer in just a few years. In 2012, the injection of $49 million into the business at a $350 million post-money valuation prompted a company-wide effort toward growth over profitability, and the tactics they used to achieve growth were at odds with the company's authentic, organic persona. Soon, a massive retailer offered Amoruso $450 million for her empire, but she declined due to investor influence. Mind you, this was six years into the biz, one year after Sophia had hit $28 million in annual sales with no paid digital marketing and no VC cash. Her pre-VC story proves that a smaller market is not a bad thing. Growing organically is not a bad thing. Owning a small corner of the market will not necessarily kill your business; form-fitting your company to a larger, yet unfamiliar market and the hyper-growth–minded investors on your cap table just might, though. Post-Nasty Gal and her second venture, Girlboss, Sophia launched her fully bootstrapped company Business Class, which offers a thorough two hundred-page course on launching and scaling a business from scratch, and a networking app for community members called the Lounge. She has no investors to answer to, she's focused on profitability, and, as I write this, the Class is full.

IN MY EXPERIENCE, FOUNDERS SHARE THE SAME, SOMEWHAT DANGEROUS, PERCEPTION OF VC MONEY: THEY VIEW IT AS SOME SORT OF VALIDATION OR STAMP OF APPROVAL, RATHER THAN AS A CRITICAL DECISION THAT WILL INFORM THE FUTURE OF THEIR BUSINESS AND, AS MENTIONED, LIFESTYLE.

The future of your company is in your hands, at least for now, and I can only hope that speaking candidly and openly about the downsides of venture funding have made you a bit more critical of that approach. In my experience, founders share the same, somewhat dangerous, perception of VC money: they view it as some sort of validation or stamp of approval, rather than as a critical decision that will inform the future of their business and, as mentioned, lifestyle. And I don't blame them! Successfully raising venture money *feels* really good! I've done it—and it's a fucking doozy! But successfully raising money is *not* synonymous with having a successful business.

After Alana and I raised our Series A, countless fellow founders and entrepreneur hopefuls seemed to fawn as if we had won a prize or received a badge of honor. They acted like we had it made. And don't get me wrong—two young women taking their seed stage start-up through a successful Series A fundraise is an impressive milestone, one other women should aspire to reach, and celebrate once they do. In 2018, only 2 percent of venture funding went to female-founded companies, so of course, being a part of that minuscule sliver meant we popped champagne and sent cheers throughout the office once the wire with the money hit our account. Of course, going through a successful fundraise is a feat for any founder, and serves as a testament to the founder's storytelling acumen, sales skills, networking juju, and growth thus far. But even so, while raising a Series A feels, in some sense, like reaching the top of Mount Everest, it should also feel like a serious, no-looking-back blood pact with your employees, investors, and fellow founders. Yes, you can only raise funding if you've hit certain growth benchmarks, have a certain degree of product-market fit, and can project future hockey-stick growth in revenue, customers, and users. But you aren't successful, as defined by venture capitalists, until that hockey-stick growth starts, and doesn't stop. Signing on for the Series A (1) cemented our commitment to growing rapidly, and (2) put us under even more pressure to build a business that met our investors' expectations. You are only successful if you do those two things, so, if anything, raising money doesn't mean you're suddenly successful, it means you're making a promise to succeed. Closing a round—whether pre-seed, seed, Series A, or beyond—can serve as a benchmark that you have real indicators of potential success, but feeling like you've made it once your round closes is probably the least responsible feeling you can feel. Once your money's in the bank, you should have a raging, hot, 120-degree fire under your ass. You've just borrowed a ton of money, given up equity or ownership stake in your company, and promised a ton of people that eventually, they'll get back ten times what they put in. If the idea of that commitment doesn't make you feel anxious, energized, and accountable, then you should *not*— I repeat—should *not* take on VC funding. VC funding is an obligation, not a reward.

YOU SHOULD HAVE A RAGING, HOT, 120-DEGREE FIRE UNDER YOUR ASS.

HOW TO GROW SLOW

For those launching a side hustle while bearing the load of a full-time job, you might want to grow slower and more organically to start, if your product category or service offering allows for it. Nick, my investor and resident financing expert, agrees. Revenue financing, as he puts it, is the best way to finance your business because you get to keep control of your future growth and "the cash is just as green." This approach is what a lot of brands in the Bulletin network decided to do when they first launched. Rather than taking out a bank loan, vying for pre-seed funding, or crowdfunding from the jump, they essentially made product in small batches, sold it for a profit, and continued to steadily reinvest their earnings back into their business. Many companies start this way and continue on this path, because it keeps you in the driver's seat and you can grow at your own pace.

Not every company can do this—it entirely depends on what you are building and how much it costs to get started. But for low-cost side hustles you're cool growing over time, this approach helps mitigate certain risks and allows you to firm up what you're building before you scale. This is how Bulletin brands like Instagrandmaw and Made Au Gold all started and continue to operate to this day. They began with a single product category or design, monetized it, reaped a profit, and used those margins to produce more product or test a new category or design. Lea launched Made Au Gold by designing wedding invitations and menus on Etsy and selling her templates as PDFs. She didn't even have enough money to print the menus on quality paper for her customers. Within a few months, she sold enough PDFs to turn a profit, took those earnings, and immediately bought fancy paper to physically print on as a next step. After she turned a profit selling printed menus and other designs, she used her earnings to buy a gold foil press to test embossed designs on her site. Repeating this process over and over, Lea eventually started manufacturing pins, making accessories, and dabbling in apparel. The grow-as-you-earn approach helped Lea minimize the risks associated with producing inventory. She didn't design and manufacture a ton of product up front in the hopes it would sell; instead, she used sales data and customer feedback to inform what she produced and when.

As you can see, this process is much slower and requires patience, and, in most cases, a stable stream of income from some other job or another form of financial stability for a period of time. This approach also only tends to work for certain product categories that have lower up-front costs for production. For example, Janine from Floss Gloss *needed* to raise a small friends and family round, or, alternatively, could have taken out a personal or business loan, because it costs a shit ton of money to produce market-ready nail polish. Way more money than it costs to produce greeting cards or prints, in the cases of Instagrandmaw and Made Au Gold, or hand-stamp bracelets, like Randi from Rockaway Gypsea. For Janine, this rinse-and-repeat reinvestment cycle was out of the question, because she had to meet certain production minimums with her manufacturer and pay for proper packaging, a slew of legal expenses, and paperwork specific to her product category. There are certain types of services and products that will require you to source funds you do not yet have in order to get things off the ground: you might need to buy equipment, hire a manufacturer, or pay for various cycles of product development. That's where crowdfunding, personal loans, business loans, and business lines of credit come in.

A FULLY REALIZED, CROWDSOURCED CAMPAIGN CAN BOTH GET YOU THE CASH YOU NEED AND PROVIDE EVIDENCE OF PRODUCT-MARKET FIT. IT'S AN IMMEDIATE, LUCRATIVE WAY TO TEST INTEREST IN YOUR PRODUCT AND BUILD A COMMUNITY OF EARLY TESTERS AND PASSIONATE SUPPORTERS WHO WILL SPREAD YOUR BRAND GOSPEL.

One of my favorite brands on the planet, Dame Products, crowdsourced its first wave of capital from a very successful Indiegogo campaign that launched in 2014, and CEO Alex Fine is still a huge proponent of this straight-to-the-people approach. She was such a fan of crowdfunding that in 2016, Dame took to Kickstarter to raise money for their second industry-disrupting vibrator. A fully realized, crowdsourced campaign can both get you the cash you need *and* provide evidence of product-market fit. It's an immediate, lucrative way to test interest in your product and build a community of early testers and passionate supporters who will spread your brand gospel.

A ton of other major household name brands have launched on Kickstarter, Indiegogo, or iFundWomen and either proceeded with venture funding after the fact or chugged along and used those donations and their brand revenue to drive their business forward. Companies like Brooklinen, Oculus (now tepidly owned by Facebook), the card game Exploding Kittens, and Ministry of Supply all launched on Kickstarter. There are other crowdfunding platforms you can go to: Patreon, Ulule, and Republic are also growing in popularity. Note that most of these platforms do take a percentage of your funds as compensation for helpin' you get there (they deserve it, tbh), so you should factor that in to the total amount you'd like to raise. There are nuances to each platform, and they all have different requirements and commissions, but they share the common mission of democratizing access to funds and building early networks and communities that care about your product. Another major differentiator is that some allow flexible funding, meaning you can cash out even if you don't hit your fundraising goal, while others are all-or-nothing.

There are some downsides to crowdfunding, too. In many cases, companies have to quickly deliver on the promises they've made when crowdfunding, whether that's launching a service within a certain time frame or manufacturing and delivering a product within a guaranteed window. By going public with your product or service before it has launched, you are also making your idea susceptible to copycatting and straight-up stealing. Before you move forward with a crowdsourced campaign, I'd suggest cold e-mailing, DMing, or LinkedIn messaging other founders who have done it successfully to understand the pros and cons. We'll get into cold outreach and networking in a bit, but you should always connect with other entrepreneurs who have gone down your path before you to help avoid pitfalls you might not see coming.

BUSINESS LOANS MIGHT MAKE SENSE IF YOU HAVE TO FINANCE A LARGE UP-FRONT COST LIKE BUYING EQUIPMENT, MANUFACTURING SOMETHING, SOURCING INVENTORY, HIRING A SECOND-IN-COMMAND, OR PAYING FOR A RETAIL SPACE OR WAREHOUSE.

Other more traditional approaches to financing the launch of your business include business loans, business lines of credit, and personal loans. When it comes to business loans, LendingClub and FundingCircle are digital platforms that offer a more seamless and transparent alternative to getting a loan from your local bank. In most cases, these loan applications are faster, you receive the loan within a week or less, and once funded, the platform provides a plethora of resources and account management. Business loans might make sense if you have to finance a large up-front cost like buying equipment, manufacturing something, sourcing inventory, hiring a second-in-command, or paying for a retail space or warehouse. With a term loan like this, you are getting a large sum of money up front—an amount up to $500,000 is typically available—and then repaying in installments, usually on a monthly basis. And of course, you're incurring interest until you pay it back in full. In most cases, lenders will require some sort of collateral to make sure you're incentivized to repay. That means if you fuck up and don't pay back the loan, the lender can take ownership of your collateral and sell it to help recoup their losses. This type of loan is called a secured loan, and because there's collateral in the mix, you get a lower interest rate. If you're not offering up collateral, it's considered an unsecured loan, and you'll pay a higher interest rate on your borrowed cash.

A business line of credit is kind of different and functions more like a credit card. If you go this route, you'll be given a line of credit—usually a lower amount than a term loan—and you can use as much or as little cash as you need and on a more flexible basis. These usually max out at $150,000 and the lender doesn't require any sort of collateral in the event you default or don't pay your balance. And, unlike a term loan, you don't get a $150,00 lump sum all at once, so you only pay interest on what you actually borrow. That means that even though $150,000 is available, if you only borrow $10,000, that's the amount you'll accrue interest on, not the $150,000. It operates just like a credit card in that, functionally, you borrow money and repay the balance, and you'll accrue more interest the longer you take to pay it back. But, once you repay the balance, you can borrow that money all over again. So, if you borrow $10,000 on a $150,000 line, you'll still have $140,000 at your disposal. And as soon as you repay the $10K, you'll have $150,000 all over again.

This option works for businesses that need to manage cash flow or borrow money on an ad hoc or flexible basis. For example, certain retail stores will use a business line of credit to pay for inventory, staffing, or maintenance during a quiet month in Q3, knowing full well they'll have a boom during the holidays in Q4 and be able to pay it back in full. There are tons of lenders out there—Kabbage, traditional banks, Fundbox, OnDeck, BlueVine. They all require different credit scores, annual revenue, and years in business in order to approve you for a line of credit.

PERSONAL LOANS ENTER THE FRAME WHEN YOU DON'T HAVE A BOOMING, MONEY-GENERATING SIDE HUSTLE OR BUSINESS YET, YOU NEED A SMALLER AMOUNT OF MONEY TO GET STARTED, AND YOU DON'T HAVE BUSINESS COLLATERAL TO SECURE A BUSINESS LOAN.

Personal loans, on the other hand, are anchored against your own personal credit score and you typically won't need to offer up collateral to borrow money. That, and you don't need to submit your company's annual revenue or cash flow as part of the approval process. Personal loans enter the frame when you don't have a booming, money-generating side hustle or business yet, you need a smaller amount of money to get started, and you don't have business collateral to secure a business loan. Basically, if you are just launching your biz or side hustle and you have zero business credentials or traction, you might consider a personal loan to snag the tiny bit of cash you need to get the ball rolling. Personal loans typically work for people with really strong personal credit scores, little debt, and substantial income, and those three factors will get you a fab interest rate that isn't superhigh. So, if you need only $5,000 to about $20,000 to get your business up and running, a personal loan might make more sense. In fact, you may even be boxed out of getting a business loan because the amount is so low. The only thing to keep in mind here is that personal loans leave you, as the individual, liable for any defaults and late payments. That means if you don't pay back a personal loan, your lender can sue you (real talk!) and your personal credit score gets dinged. With business loans, on the other hand, your start-up or company is the liable party, and you as the individual are way more protected.

Ultimately, though, the wisest thing you can do is keep your personal and business finances totally separate and try to build up credit for your business. So sure, consider taking out a personal loan to jump-start your business or side hustle if you don't have revenue or momentum yet, but be sure to switch to a business line of credit or term loan as soon as your business starts thriving and you actually qualify. You'll wanna separate church and state as soon as you can to reduce your personal liability in the event your business fails or you struggle to repay borrowed cash on time.

GOT RISK ON MY LEFT, AND RISK ON MY RIGHT

The way you finance your business has a direct impact on who owns your company and how much they own, and, therefore, on who has the power to make supercritical choices that guide your company's growth. For example, venture capital is synonymous with equity financing. Meaning venture capitalists—whether angel investors or institutional firms—are giving you money in exchange for equity, or ownership, in your company. Typically, these venture capitalists offer up a certain amount of cash in exchange for a certain percentage-stake in your company. That calculation is anchored to your company's valuation, or how much it's worth.

VENTURE CAPITALISTS—WHETHER ANGEL INVESTORS OR INSTITUTIONAL FIRMS—ARE GIVING YOU MONEY IN EXCHANGE FOR EQUITY, OR OWNERSHIP, IN YOUR COMPANY.

Calculating your valuation is no straightforward or clear-cut feat: you need to set a pre-revenue valuation if you aren't making money yet and a post-revenue valuation if you are, determine if you own tech or an innovative product that ups your valuation, and consider market risks that might ding your valuation. You should set your valuation based on your traction and earnings thus far, but leverage future growth and expected earnings to increase that number. A valuation is less reflective of your company's current performance, and more reflective of what's to come. It's a true science, and often, investor feedback will inform you if your valuation is too ridiculously high or in a sweet spot based on market data, comparable companies in your space, and frankly, instincts. Ultimately, though, the most important thing to know is that when you take VC money, you are automatically handing over shares, or units of ownership, in your company, and that level of ownership depends entirely on how much your company is worth.

WITH VENTURE CAPITAL, YOU ARE STRAIGHT-UP RELINQUISHING FULL OWNERSHIP OF YOUR BUSINESS TO GET THE CASH YOU NEED TO MAKE IT SUCCESSFUL.

Need an example? Say you are raising $1 million in venture financing at a $5 million pre-revenue valuation. This is how you'd calculate just how much of your company you're giving up: $1,000,000 (money invested) / $5,000,000 (valuation) + $1,000,000 (money invested). This comes out to about 17 percent. And remember, this 17 percent cuts into your percentage, too. The more pie you give away, the less pie there is for you to eat! And with each round of fundraising: pre-seed into seed, seed into Series A, Series A into Series B, you lose more and more ownership. Ultimately, VCs are taking a huge risk by funneling money into your company at any stage, so they want—and deserve—a large piece of the pie in the event each slice is worth millions or billions someday. And in many cases, VCs also demand a board seat or decision-making power to help guarantee that risk pays off and increase the likelihood of a profitable outcome.

With venture capital, you are straight-up relinquishing full ownership of your business to get the cash you need to make it successful. This is why, as we discussed earlier, many companies take on equity financing and fail. They let other people into the board room and give decision-making power to outsiders—investors with less industry knowledge and/or selfish, money-hungry motives—and these new players make choices that blow the company to shreds. They force rapid, chaotic growth; install shitty, disconnected leaders; or dilute the product to target a larger market, completely ruining what made it special. These are horror stories, sure, but there are also major upsides to VC ownership and involvement if you get into bed with the right people. VC money isn't always a brutal deal with the devil. Good investors, board members, and co-owners can help you hire magnificent, brilliant leaders, work to improve the product dramatically, and scale the business beyond your wildest dreams. Just remember that VC money is not free, and giving up ownership can be an expensive, and potentially company-ruining, decision.

VC MONEY ISN'T ALWAYS A BRUTAL DEAL WITH THE DEVIL. GOOD INVESTORS, BOARD MEMBERS, AND CO-OWNERS CAN HELP YOU HIRE MAGNIFICENT, BRILLIANT LEADERS, WORK TO IMPROVE THE PRODUCT DRAMATICALLY, AND SCALE THE BUSINESS BEYOND YOUR WILDEST DREAMS.

With personal loans, business loans, and business lines of credit, you are not giving up ownership stake in your company, but if you're putting up collateral to lower your interest rate or as a stipulation of your loan, you're definitely putting your ass on the line. By putting up collateral, you're basically allowing your lender to seize valuable business assets (or personal assets, if it's a personal loan) in the event you can't pay back what you've borrowed.

This creates a different type of performance pressure than VCs do: if you're doing well, you've got nothing to worry about, but if your business slumps or you fail entirely, you'll automatically lose stuff with monetary value, whether it be property, equipment, inventory, your savings, stock, or other investments. These types of losses can be a huge financial burden, for yourself and/or your business, and be extremely debilitating to your credit score and ability to borrow money in the future. With VC funding, though, if you fail, you just . . . fail. In most cases—unless fraud's involved—VCs don't require that you pay back their investment if your company falls apart. If the end is nigh but you still have cash in the bank, your investors might ask you to return whatever's left over. But you kind of walk away unscathed financially, and your credit score, personal assets, and business assets stay intact.

Crowdfunding is similar, in that if the company ultimately fails, you aren't required to pay back your supporters, your credit score isn't affected, and you don't hand over remaining assets to Kickstarter or IndieGogo. That's not to say crowdfunding is some free pass to free money: the Federal Trade Commission has been cracking down on fraudulent campaigns, and you're susceptible to a lawsuit if you literally never deliver the product or spend all the money on shit unrelated to your company. Sure, your crowdsourced supporters are accepting a certain level of inherent risk when backing your project, just like VCs are when they throw hundreds of thousands into an unproven product or service. And as a backer, it's not that easy to win a lawsuit against a crowdfunded creator or entrepreneur. But, regardless, as a crowdsourced project, you're expected to deliver on your promises, and if you don't, and your backer can prove bad faith, you or your business might be personally liable. You're not giving up any equity or ownership when you crowdfund, and you're not putting up collateral like you would with a term loan, but you are making yourself vulnerable to lawsuits and legal drama in a worst-case-scenario outcome.

In many cases, you'll have to finance your business based on what's actually available to you. You may not qualify for a personal or business loan. You may not be able to execute a successful crowdsourced campaign. You may go out for VC funding and leave empty-handed.

DON'T DO WHAT'S EASY, DON'T PURSUE WHAT'S POPULAR, AND DON'T PICK THE QUICKEST SOURCE OF CASH.

But before you pick a path, think long and hard about what type of financing makes sense in the first place, and then tackle that approach with intention and determination. Don't raise VC funding just because you know other founders who have done it successfully. As we've discussed, you have no idea what life is like on the other side of that decision, or if those founders regret it or not. Don't take out a personal loan just because you can. And use various resources like online loan marketplaces, advisors, and other entrepreneurs to research and review your smartest option. Remember, the way you finance your company determines what the company becomes, and it also dictates your level of personal financial risk and reward. Your financing strategy is one of the most critical decisions you'll make in jump-starting your side hustle or launching a full-blown business. Don't do what's easy, don't pursue what's popular, and don't pick the quickest source of cash. Do what's smart. Your company's future depends on it.

VENTURE SPEAK, TRANSLATED

Friends and family round: In some cases, entrepreneurs will pursue financing from close friends or family members who believe in their business idea and are willing to write checks that will help get it off the ground. Raising a friends and family round is obviously contingent upon having a high-net-worth network or a network of supporters who have money they are willing to invest without seeing immediate returns. This round usually predates any pre-seed, seed, or other venture financing, functions as the company's first formal fundraise, and is often the riskiest round to join as an investor. Typically, friends and family are investing in you as a person and a potentially successful business owner and in the viability of the idea. But at this stage there is usually little evidence of product-market fit, and in many cases, there is no product or service yet whatsoever. In this round, you are still giving up equity and dispersing shares in the company to those who invest, so it is a form of venture financing.

Pre-seed financing/seed funding: The entire concept of institutional pre-seed and seed financing was born super recently. So just know that. Before about 2008 (and the financial crisis) most companies jumped right into a Series A, then B, then C. Series A funding used to be the first and earliest check, and basically was what seed funding is now. So, now what is it? Seed funding is sandwiched somewhere between your first angel checks and your Series A. And, depending on the sandwich, you might have a first layer of pre-seed topped with an even thicker layer of seed cash. Pre-seed always comes first and is typically a smaller round that backs sharp founders, a good idea, and a bit of traction. These checks typically max out at $20,000, but honestly, fundraising is such a fluid, confusing beast of a thing, some people are raising

$2 million pre-seed rounds now. Angel investors can be part of your pre-seed round. Pre-seed predates your formal seed round, where, most of the time, you've found some evidence of product-market fit, you need resources to grow and keep testing, and the team has proven they aren't clueless. Seed rounds are, on average, up to $3 million, and angels can also be part of your seed round! So, what's the *real* difference between pre-seed and seed? Basically, how early they are investing, and how much cash they're putting in. Seed or early stage investing has always existed, it's just splitting off into narrower lanes now. Pre-seed is earliest, and seed is . . . just slightly later.

Angel investors and angel funding: Angels investors are called angels for a reason. These are usually wealthy individuals who believe in your business idea and your potential as a founder. Angels are often former successful entrepreneurs themselves, or other rich people who are plugged into or interested in the start-up space. Sometimes there is a mentorship element at play, wherein angels explicitly invest in companies where they have domain expertise so they can be helpful to the founders. Angel investors invest their own money in your company, unlike venture capitalists, who source cash from an institutional fund they've pooled from LPs, or limited partners.

Incubator/accelerator: An incubator or accelerator is a company that typically provides resources, funding, guidance, mentorship, and workspace in exchange for equity in your company. Incubators help you focus on building out your idea, while accelerators help you focus on scaling your idea. In most cases, companies have to apply to these programs and the incubators and accelerators only work with a limited number of start-ups. These programs are typically for earlier stage companies looking to raise a pre-seed or seed round, and they take a pretty significant equity stake given how hands on they are at such a risky, early moment in the company's evolution. Incubators and accelerators can serve as a badge of approval, almost, for potential angels or institutional investors. It indicates that other, more experienced players have vetted the idea and had a hand in the idea's refinement. Y Combinator, Tech Stars, and other programs actually culminate in a "Demo Day," or a day to directly pitch these institutional and angel investors. For this reason, many start-ups join incubators or accelerators as a means of kick-starting their fundraising process.

Runway: Runway is synonymous with "how long you have until you run out of cash." This is typically measured in months, and founders calculate their runway by tallying how much money they spend in a given month, also known as your "burn." For example, if your company is not profitable, burns through $100,000 per month, and you have $800,000 in the bank, you have about seven or eight months of runway, or months until your company runs out of cold, hard cash. If you're a smaller company with $10,000 in the bank and a $1,000 monthly burn, the same rules apply. The term is superrelevant when you're fundraising. Investors are usually skittish about investing in a company with limited runway, so it is usually wise to kick off a raise when you've got money in the bank. That, and if you're taking money in exchange for equity, you don't want to overcalculate your runway and risk taking on more cash than you need. Because, as we know, taking more money means you're giving up more equity. On the flip side, you don't want to raise too little money because you'll need enough time to build the right product and scale. The term is equally relevant while you're operating. You need to know—at any given time—how much money you have on hand, how much you're making, how much you're spending, and what your runway looks like.

Valuation: Your company's valuation is essentially the estimation of what it's worth, and that estimation requires both art and science. These calculations work to determine the fair market value of your company, and you need a set valuation in order to do any sort of equity financing or work with VCs. Early on, during seed and pre-seed stage investing, it is ridiculously hard to calculate an actual valuation. You and your investors will look to similar companies, market trends, and your revenue projections to hodgepodge a number together. So, in early financing stages, valuation speaks less to how much the company is actually worth, and more to how much equity an investor gets for his or her investment. That is, if an investor puts $10K into a company with a $1 million valuation, she gets a 1 percent equity stake in the company. If you keep growing and fundraising, your valuation will (most likely) increase over time.

Venture capital and venture capitalists: Venture capital describes the high-risk, high-reward financing that venture capitalists inject into early stage start-ups in exchange for equity—or ownership—in the company. Venture capital is literally synonymous with the term "risk capital," because this type of investment is not guaranteed the ten-times return most VCs are looking for, and actually, there's no real return guarantee at all for investors. For example, a venture capitalist could pour millions into a business, only to watch it implode in three-years' time. In most cases, the company doesn't have to pay the VC that money back, and VCs are forced to completely write off the investment. That's why venture funding is kind of like gambling: venture capitalists, whether big firms or individual angel investors, usually invest in a portfolio of companies every year, hoping one hits a home run. They are looking for the next Shopify or Venmo, but most companies go belly-up on their path toward world domination.

To help stabilize those investments and prevent these portfolio companies from going belly-up, venture capitalists often get involved in the start-ups they've given money to, whether that means joining a start-up's board of directors, providing ongoing mentorship and resources, or helping start-ups with recruiting the right talent. The most important thing to know is that venture capitalists are looking for highly scalable start-ups. They are not looking for moderate growth and slow expansion over decades, they want rapid scale—as soon as humanly possible, if not sooner. If a VC is not convinced that your business idea fits that profile or has the potential to yield massive, ten-times-plus returns, you will have a hard time securing venture capital funding.

LPs, or limited partners: Venture capital firms raise funds from LPs, or limited partners. VCs then invest those LP dollars into start-ups looking for cash. LPs exist behind the scenes and trust the general partners at VC firms to make them richer.

Product-market fit: This term was coined by Marc Andreessen, and it refers to a company that is "in a good market with a product that can satisfy that market."* It is often considered the first step in building a successful company. If you have product-market fit, your customers are satisfied with your product or service, spreading the word about it and referring other customers to it organically, and you're going after a large market with real demand for what you've built.

---

* Marc Andreessen, "The PMARCA Guide to Startups: Part 4, The only thing that matters," Pmarchive, June 25, 2007, pmarchive.com/guide_to_startups_part4.html.

Equity: Equity is the same thing as ownership. With start-ups, it is usually calculated by looking at the number of shares, or units of ownership, a person has been given or has purchased. Shares are usually assigned a price (we won't go into when and how; it's complicated) and often, investors buy them to own part of your company, while start-up employees get the chance to accrue a fixed number of shares over time as part of their compensation package. Whoever has the most equity, or number of shares, has the highest level of ownership in the company. When companies start, the founders usually have full or majority ownership. As start-ups grow and scale through Series A, B, C, and beyond, though, many founders lose their majority stake as investors buy up more and more shares and take on more and more equity.

Cap table: If you have done any kind of equity financing or raised money in exchange for shares in your company, then you have what's called a capitalization table, or a cap table for short. Your cap table is a data set that outlines who has shares in the company, how much those shares are worth, what percentage of the company those folks own, and the total market value of the company itself.

Series A financing: Series A financing comes after pre-seed and seed stage financing, and usually comes into play once a company has built a viable product, found a viable business model, and is ready to scale and acquire even more customers. Unlike most pre-seed and seed investors, Series A investors usually demand a board seat and/or controlling interest in the company. Series A financing is typically followed by Series B, Series C, Series D financing, and beyond, each of which bring a greater infusion of capital and require you to relinquish more and more control of your company.

RAISING MONEY DOESN'T MEAN YOU'RE SUDDENLY SUCCESSFUL, IT MEANS YOU'RE MAKING A PROMISE TO SUCCEED.

HOW DID YOU FINANCE YOUR COMPANY?

JASMINE MANS
DESIGNER, POET, AND FOUNDER

I was looking for a high-margin, low-risk product. So, I started with a coffee mug. I purchased 75 of them for $200. It guaranteed a low investment with a high return. After all, something that costs us $2 may sell for $25 or $30. As a poet, I was taking money from my poetry career and reinvesting it in merchandise, because I knew, if I did this show and made $2,000, I can make $200 worth of products, take those products on tour, and make $3,000 to $4,000. I felt like, as long as I am an artist and I am performing, I can pull this off. Since then, I've made investments and had hypotheses that have paid off and others that haven't. I've come to learn how to deal with failure and to understand which financial risks I can take, and which financial risks might plummet the company. When you take any risk, know up front if you can and how you can recover. Don't take a hit that you can't survive.

Black women haven't been taught about risk or to invest in ourselves; a lot of Black entrepreneurs like myself will hold back on a risk where our white peers wouldn't. I've learned to educate myself on where I can get a loan, where and when I can take chances with money. I think it's very important to take risks if you want someone to believe in and invest in your brand or product. I tell other young entrepreneurs or friends to take the risks we expect others to take. It shows you take your business seriously. And when you get a positive outcome from the risk, like making your money back or making more money, it positively influences you to take more risks and try new things.

Now I sell shirts, jackets, tote bags, and more than just the mugs. I understood that people would buy the mug, some would buy a $30 shirt, and maybe someone won't buy the T-shirt, but they'll want a $5 poster. Someone will buy a $150 jacket, and if not, they might want the $15 tote. All of these different customers at different income levels want to invest in your product, but do you have the different products and prices for those people to invest in? Something as simple as trying to reach or accommodate more people can make you more money.

JACLYN FU
PEPPER

We deliberately decided to get on Kickstarter instead of raising from VC investors. On Kickstarter, we were able to truly test demand. We would see our customers preordering and supporting us, and we wanted that customer feedback and test of how many people needed this product. If we didn't hit our Kickstarter goal, then we knew there wasn't enough demand for it, so why waste the time and resources on this idea? Exceeding our goal was real validation that we should use these funds and reinvest them into the company 100 percent, and it let us jump-start our company without having to lose equity.

There is definitely a science to running a successful crowdfunding campaign, and we talked to tons of other founders about their experiences, good and bad. We realized that a lot of unsuccessful campaigns didn't gain traction because they only started promoting the campaign or the business once the campaign went live. You need to launch and start promoting ahead of time. You can't have this "if we launch, they will come" mentality.

We were always building Pepper as a community and a brand from the start, so we were able to do a lot of storytelling with our customers and with the press beforehand.

Months and months before our launch we started building up our e-mail list and social channels. We wanted to build hype around the Kickstarter campaign and get women really interested in finding a solution to this problem. By the time we launched the campaign, we had over one thousand people on our mailing list who were eager to learn more about and buy this product. We spent months sending personal e-mails to our friends and acquaintances, posting Pepper to our personal social accounts, asking our network for help spreading the word, connecting with press. We then did a second round of press once we launched. We were fully funded within the first ten hours of our campaign.

CYO NYSTROM
QUIM

We bootstrapped Quim for as long as we could, and then we eventually began our fundraising process. When you're in that process, you meet dozens of dozens of people, some of whom are like, This is amazing. I'd love to invest. And then the time comes to make it formal and you're like, Hey! Remember me? and it can fizzle. They'll say, Maybe at a later stage or It isn't the right time for me. It can be really hard to know what's real and what's lip service. I thought I'd finish fundraising in two months. When we first started, we were taking feedback from people who had not fundraised. Don't get fundraising advice from people who have not fundraised.

When our deck was done and we were ready, we went to networking events, pitched at some cannabis competitions, and we got little bites over time: a $25,000 check here, a $30,000 check there. One time Rachel and I drove hours into the mountains to collect a $50,000 check. We grew the business to a certain point and are now back in the fundraising game, though the deal terms and dynamics are totally different now. Quim is a much less risky investment than it was early on, because we've been working on it for longer, we have an established brand, we sell in places like Urban Outfitters. We've gone from taking $25,000 checks from random dudes in Florida to working with more strategic partners who have experience in the space.

We haven't taken venture money yet, though. I would say anyone who has or is considering investing in us is more of an angel investor offering mentorship or an angel investor that sees a lot of opportunity. They see us as "Viagra for women" and are willing to allocate some money.

It is important to stretch your money for as long as you can, because the farther you go, the stronger and more self-sufficient you'll be. Being able to say no or turn down a deal with bad terms is the most important and empowering thing in the world. You have to be able to walk away from that money and still have faith in your company.

JAMIKA MARTIN ROSEN

When I first took an entrepreneurship course, it was about entrepreneurial accounting and finance. At the beginning of the course, other students kept mentioning "equity," and I didn't know what that was. We finally reviewed equity in class and I was like, People give you money and you don't have to pay it back?! I was shocked by the entire concept. I did an accelerator next and ended up talking to a ton of VCs and investors, but no one in that group really had any revenue or real traction. I always remembered hearing and learning through that period how hard raising capital was, and how it was kind of like a full-time job. I started making ROSEN products and considered raising capital, but I felt like, No, this is what I need to be doing full-time—I need to be building my brand. I'm still learning about convertible notes, or how to set a valuation, and at the time, it felt even more daunting. I just wanted to build. So I decided to keep building and financing the business myself.

It was a continuous and slow chug along, just making a little bit of money here and there to put back into the company when I could. I didn't pay myself. I used all my money to order ingredients, labels, get my packaging together, and just did that over and over again. We've grown almost every single quarter since I started. Now I'm asking, Do I want to raise money? Do I want to consider it? But now, I'm so far into bootstrapping—and look how far I've gotten! So many people said I wouldn't be able to do it, but I did. My biggest advice to anyone bootstrapping is that as soon as you're making solid money—maybe five figures a month—try to bring someone in who can help you manage and understand your cash flow, and help with budgeting. If you go the bootstrapping route, you're definitely signing up for some stress. Week to week, you may not be able to pay this person or that person, or you may have to skip paying yourself to get ingredients. Those things can pile up. Sometimes you'll feel like, I don't know if I can keep doing this. But I kept going, and I made it happen.

CHAPTER SIX

THE BUSINESS YOU START WON'T BE THE BUSINESS YOU RUN

"**P**ivot" is a complex word. When people explain the power of a smart pivot, they flick the word around like it's this lightweight, teeny fairy that just visits your company one day and solves all your problems with some magic wand. When people explain the outcome of a bad pivot, they automatically lace the word with a dark, ominous undertone, like it's this dirty money-sucking devil that barged into your office and destroyed your company from the inside out. While the word carries some complex emotional baggage, the dictionary definition of a "pivot" is actually pretty simple. And the number of successful companies who have gone through a pivot is pretty damn high.

If you're running a company or a brand, a pivot is a major strategy shift, a new, unrelated product focus, or a radical change to your business model. And, as you could probably tell from my melodramatic intro, pivots can make or break your company. It's true. But most companies have had to pivot at some point: companies aren't born with some bulletproof playbook, and volatile markets and cultural shifts mean the playbook they *do* have is always changing, anyway. Sometimes, you'll have to brace yourself. And other times, you'll be 82 percent sure you're making the right decision (and that's you maxing out!).

It's a common phenomenon, clearly, but the thought of a pivot can be extremely daunting. So, let's take off the kid gloves. If we unpack the word, we're really talking about a scary, usually risky, mostly unproven change to your business that could end it or save it. So how do you know when to go for it? How do you do it successfully? And can you just have the "save your business" part of the menu, please?

Pivoting should be a product of looking, listening, and learning, not thinking. In most cases, you shouldn't force-feed your company a change it didn't ask for. You should be giving your company the opportunity to evolve after signs and signals indicate the status quo just isn't working anymore. Learn to spot those signals, first and foremost, and pivots will come from a place of education and knowledge, rather than a place of fear and uncertainty.

Remember when we shuttered the Bulletin "magazine" to launch Bulletin Market, the pop-up series that helped brands sell offline? While the markets worked in isolation, they didn't scale, and there were signs and signals that made it superobvious. The markets required a boatload of time, physical labor, setup, breakdown, and promotion. We were working seven days a week, and we didn't have the womanpower or money to run multiple, concurrent markets in one weekend. We were helping only thirty brands a week in one location, and even *that* was a grind. We would get rained out on certain weekends and have to reimburse all the brands. We would be stuck in 100-degree July heat at an outdoor market, desperate for foot traffic, a lemonade, a portable face fan—*anything*. The porta-potty company would forget to service our lot, and we'd end up running a stinky, poopy-hot market for two days straight. We also had zero data on which brands and products sold well, because every brand ran their own point-of-sale. That meant we had no idea if sales were growing, shrinking, or stagnant weekend to weekend, month to month. In fact, aside from foot traffic and press hits, we couldn't really measure anything. And if you can't measure something, then you can't really improve it.

THE PORTA-POTTY COMPANY WOULD FORGET TO SERVICE OUR LOT, AND WE'D END UP RUNNING A STINKY, POOPY-HOT MARKET FOR TWO DAYS STRAIGHT.

We couldn't control the Bulletin brand identity, either, because we had so many different types of brands sharing space, branding their booths, and selling a wildly diverse selection of products. By nature, it wasn't as curated as our precious editorial marketplace. This model wasn't something we wanted to copy and paste across multiple locations, nor did that feel like the responsible thing to do, despite it being lucrative. So, while this pivot taught us a lot about experiential retail, community-building, PR, and more, toward the end of 2016, it started to become obvious that this wasn't our final iteration. We had to find a way to offer the same service to our brands and the same experience for our shoppers in a way that was revenue-generating, but also repeatable and sustainable.

That's when we opened our first store. The location kind of fell into our lap, with a local Williamsburg realtor sending Alana a quick text that the landlord was looking for a commercial tenant ASAP—had we ever considered a permanent storefront? At first, we scoffed: "that's a crazy commitment," "we don't know how to run a store," "that's expensive," "this feels like it's going too fast." But then, we realized that a permanent storefront actually solved a lot of our problems: we could move our operation indoors (thank God), we could control the point-of-sale and thus, all the data, we could more heavily curate the brands and products, and we could track, improve, and even replicate the model. We wouldn't be beholden to volatile weather, tucked under flimsy Amazon tents that swayed in the wind and broke in the rain. We'd be in a nook of our own, a space we could design and control. With a beautiful storefront on one of the busiest blocks in the neighborhood, by golly, we could build a brand! And slowly but surely, brick by brick, that's exactly what we did.

We opened our first storefront on North Seventh and Wythe Ave in late 2016. The landlord gave us a a relative steal on rent, and thirty brands were eager to take the next step in our Bulletin journey and agreed to join the store. We called it the "WeWork of retail," because just like companies pay to co-work in a WeWork-operated building, brands were paying to co-retail in a Bulletin-operated store. We did a giant IKEA run to get shelves and tables, painted the walls, treated the floor, and called up Shopify to get point-of-sale hardware. Our move toward brick-and-mortar stores opening and running was a major pivot, a permanent (and indoor) evolution. We still charged brands a fee for space, but this time, it was per month, not per weekend. And rather than letting brands keep 100 percent of sales, we would keep 30 percent and paid brands 70 percent. Instead of the business owners having to physically be at the market to sell their goods, we would hire staff to oversee the entire store experience. Which meant that instead of brands running the point-of-sale, we would handle every single transaction.

As with the markets, we didn't own the inventory. Typically, a store pays for inventory at wholesale prices, and then sells it to customers at its designated retail value. They have to pay to earn. But we hosted all of our inventory on consignment, meaning, we housed the inventory, but we paid for a product only once it sold. And the brands, who loved the direct customer feedback and visibility into real-time sales from running their own point-of-sale at Bulletin Market, loved to know what sold and what didn't. So, we provided them with a real-time sales dashboard to track product performance by the minute. All of the elements were the same; we were just taking on more of the workload and more of the risk, which meant our compensation structure had to shift slightly in our favor. Because we had more control of the shopping experience, we could measure our success, and we could evolve and iterate quickly; we were confident that if the store model worked, it would be our ticket to scale. If we could run a profitable store, we'd have a real playbook: launch store, make money, rinse, and repeat.

When you pivot, you are bound to end up running two businesses at once: your former flame and your new honey. In 2016, we spent three months running a digital marketplace, nine months running a weekend pop-up, and two months running a full-time store. That's fourteen months total, meaning, there was obviously overlap. We built and launched our Williamsburg store in less than two weeks, and by November, she was up and running. Come December, we were running back-to-back Bulletin Holiday Markets that hosted more than eighty brands each.

Why would we dare try to run a new store and massive market series at the same time? Well, we wanted to work with as many brands as possible during their (and our) most lucrative season, and frankly, a part of me thinks we were slightly worried the store model might not work. When you make a pivot—big or small—you may rationally understand that it's a sound, smart business decision, but emotionally, you might not be convinced it'll work. You may be scared of the unknown.

Because we were straddling the old and the new, December was a bitch of a month. We were in our first major retail season in a store not even a month old, and we were hosting the largest, most popular market of our career. It was multitasking at its most extreme. I don't regret it, but I often wonder if we would have learned store-related lessons earlier if we had given 145 Wythe our full attention from the start. I wonder if we would've had stronger sell-through in that first busy season had we not been juggling a back-to-back weekend event. On the other hand, we were gearing up to apply to Y Combinator again, and the market revenue made for a standout application. We were planning on opening a second store, too, so the market served as great lead generation and gave us hundreds of brands to consider for that new space.

THE MORE YOU DELAY SINGULAR FOCUS ON YOUR NEW STRATEGY, THE LESS LIKELY THAT STRATEGY IS TO SUCCEED.

In our case, there were a handful of passable reasons for multitasking, but I would caution against it. The worst thing you can do is compromise your focus, and your team's focus, and be running two businesses at once. When you pivot, have conviction! Grab that fuckin' metaphorical spear and lead your business into battle with the unknown! Track new metrics, set new goals, reset your team's mind-set, restate your vision, and believe in your judgment. The more you delay singular focus on your new strategy, the less likely that strategy is to succeed.

Having conviction when you pivot can be superhard, though, because, both when it works and when it doesn't, pivoting is emotionally taxing. It can feel like an honest-to-God breakup with your business and, sometimes, it really hurts. You've spent days upon weeks upon months upon years investing in your business. You've dedicated your life to it and built an entire identity around it. You've wrestled with self-doubt and fear just to bring it to life. Often, people pivot with a deep sense of sadness and disappointment, torn up by this sense that they failed to "make it work." It can feel like mourning the loss of something you held a superstrong attachment to, like euthanizing a beloved pet or leaving a childhood home. But there's this glimmer of hope buried beneath all the anguish. There's this sense that you're healing something that's gone rotten. That you're fixing a problem and giving your company a second chance at survival. Because rationally, and in your gut, you know something's wrong.

PIVOTING USUALLY IGNITES A SEVEN-LAYER DIP OF CONFLICTING FEELINGS: GRIEF, ANXIETY, DOUBT, REGRET, OPTIMISM, EXCITEMENT, AND URGENCY.

If your business isn't growing, if you're losing customers over time, if nobody wants to buy or use what you've created, you know it's time to either quit or evolve. Those are the signals you need to be dialed into at all times. Pivoting usually ignites a seven-layer dip of conflicting feelings: grief, anxiety, doubt, regret, optimism, excitement, and urgency. Every single feeling is totally natural. But as best you can, try to avoid getting hung up on the past—on the "what-ifs" and "whys" and "if I'd only done X or Y" thought patterns. Because chances are, there isn't just one missed opportunity or bad decision that drove you to this point.

The need to pivot is a product of multiple miscalculations, missed targets and, honestly, a ton of shit that was probably out of your control. Could we have quickly gotten more customers to the original Bulletin site had we spent all our money on acquisition marketing? Maybe, for a while. But that's not what we did. Could we have organically grown a loyal online audience if we just had some more runway and more time to get them engaged? Sure, it's possible. But we didn't have more of either. You can't dwell on the past or indulge too deeply in your negative self-talk, because you have to trust that you made the best decision you could at the time.

Sometimes, pivoting leads to failure. And you just have to accept that. As I write this, Bulletin is in the middle of yet another pivot. We are launching a wholesale marketplace. It will let stores shop our curated network of brands and diversify the inventory they offer their shoppers. To focus on this marketplace, we shut down our e-commerce site, which accounted for only a small fraction of our business but allowed us to sell to consumers nationwide. Are we crazy? It's definitely possible. But given that our e-commerce sales paled in comparison to our brick-and-mortar numbers, it didn't feel like a blood sacrifice. We wanted to get thousands of brands into stores nationwide, not just hundreds of brands into Bulletin stores across NYC, and this marketplace finally lets us spread our wings.

YOU CAN'T DWELL ON THE PAST OR INDULGE TOO DEEPLY IN YOUR NEGATIVE SELF-TALK, BECAUSE YOU HAVE TO TRUST THAT YOU MADE THE BEST DECISION YOU COULD AT THE TIME.

Meanwhile, am I plagued by complete and total uncertainty? Of course. Do I worry we won't be able to scale and will slowly die until we run out of money? Yeah. Do I feel nauseated with anxiety every single morning? Not every, but some. We're working on it! I'm rattled, because I know that despite my listening and analyzing and doing all the pivoty things right, I simply don't have foresight. And I know it is more likely that we will fail than succeed. That's the math. That's my and Alana's shared reality. Soon, we may come face-to-face with the money-sucking pivot devil that destroys companies from the inside out. He could be right around the corner, waiting to laugh right in our faces.

But this marketplace is the only way we can efficiently scale and help more entrepreneurs build their businesses, which has always been our North Star. So yes, sometimes pivots lead to failure. We may not reach enough retailers or sign up enough brands. We may get overshadowed by a better-funded competitor. We may hit a sudden recession, 2008-style, and lose half of our marketplace overnight. Fact: failure is caused by both obvious misses and buried misfortune waiting to happen. It can burn slow or come in like a wrecking ball. Pivoting is not a guarantee, it's a gamble. So, in the face of potential failure, that hunger for your North Star becomes really important. It's the only thing that will safeguard you from developing a nihilistic, sullen attitude.

I'll admit: it's much easier to write all of this than it is to do it. I don't easily accept the prospect of failure, but I don't trot around with unwavering grit and courage. Frankly, I am triggered, mid-sentence, just thinking through where we are now and how much more we have to accomplish and "do right" in order to get to our North Star. I am constantly trapped in the delta between the Bulletin of Today and the Bulletin of the Future that helps more brands, makes them more money, and makes us more money. It's an uncomfortable place to live—that delta is superdark and extremely lonely.

As a founder or leader in general, you have to make big, swift changes behind a veil of confidence and conviction. And you have to act like a fortune teller when in reality, you have no idea what's to come. Which means you're often dealing with pretty serious feelings entirely solo, or alongside a co-founder who's equally spooked. Privately, I am forever indulging in our aforementioned seven-layer dip of grief, doubt, regret, and all the rest. I wake up with one and go to sleep with the other, or sometimes, a cocktail of three conflicting emotions strikes randomly during the day. It's easy to write about listening to your customers! Avoiding the "what ifs!" Dismissing negative self-talk! That's what #inspo #Instagram #accounts are made of! But you're real people, and I'm a real person. And we all know that in certain periods of upheaval or change, "positive thinking" sounds nice, but it can feel like a foreign concept when the process of pivoting has unearthed deep, dark insecurities about your judgment and your business.

SOMETIMES YOU'RE STUFFED WITH OPTIMISM AND OTHER TIMES YOU WANT TO SHIT YOUR PANTS WITH ANXIETY.

I'm just taking a small aside here to acknowledge that yes, I know accepting failure is a wild concept that entrepreneurs toss around like it's no big deal. I know that if you're mid-pivot, evolving your side hustle, or even making a big, risky shift in your career, sometimes you're stuffed with optimism and other times you want to shit your pants with anxiety. I've been there. Change is scary as fuck. But! I think it's about doing your best to make educated changes, so in your moments of doubt, you can lean on real data and evidence. And it's about gleaning some optimism even when it's hard, because that's what's best for your mental health and your company. Starting the day with a skip in your step will probably make you more productive than starting the day nauseated with doubt. And what's worst case scenario? You fail. And eventually, you get over it.

TAKEAWAYS!

IT'S NOT WHAT YOU WANT, IT'S WHAT PEOPLE NEED.

TAKE WHAT'S BEST AND BUILD ON IT.

CHANGE ISN'T OMINOUS— IT'S PROMISING.

I DON'T
EASILY
ACCEPT THE
PROSPECT OF
FAILURE,
BUT I DON'T
TROT AROUND
WITH
UNWAVERING
GRIT AND
COURAGE.

WHEN DID YOUR BUSINESS CHANGE?

JEN ZEANO

JEN ZEANO DESIGNS

After I introduced my first two or three designs, which really focused on Latina empowerment, I decided to pivot and switch over to English. I thought it would be a good way to broaden my market a bit, but the sales completely stopped. My customers were not into the English shirts, and it was so scary, I thought I would never sell anything again. I still have those shirts—they're on my site and, to this day, they barely sell. I know now that my Latinx market just wasn't interested in this new direction, and it taught me to really lean into what was working and not stray from what I initially set out to do. After that, I had to look at my strategy again. That's when I designed my most popular shirt, the "Latina Power" tee. It is still our number one bestseller. That tee was like a phoenix rising from the ashes, and it got picked up by all these other outlets and got so much social media attention. It just helped us so much. After that major failure with the English shirts, the Latina Power shirt took off and became the definition of our business.

LEILA KASHANI

ALLEYOOP

We launched our portable razor brand Sphynx in Ulta and realized after just a few months on the shelf that, because it was positioned next to the razor aisle, people were using Sphynx as a full razor replacement. We ran into a lot of customer feedback, and people telling us that the product wasn't meant for full shaving. Early on with that, we learned the value of our customer and that customer feedback was everything. You can imagine why you have a problem; you can come up with your own reasons. But start conversations with your customer—find out if you're right.

I had really envisioned a bigger brand that effectively spoke to women on the go, that's who my customer was. I wasn't reaching her as best I could. The problem was, I wasn't getting enough customer feedback because our products were being predominantly sold in retail, more so than direct to the customer. With retail, you don't get to hear from the end customer as often. So, I created a customer Slack group. I e-mailed ten thousand people and almost three thousand agreed to join. I picked two hundred customers, and those people are the ones who helped me create a new brand, Alleyoop.

I had three months to pick my brand name, and six months to get products on the shelf. I didn't have a good feeling about the brand name Sphynx, I never really did. This group helped me with product development, renaming the brand. It was a team effort. I wanted to build a larger brand that was category agnostic, and every product needs to solve a problem. My customers helped me identify those problems and brainstorm products in body care, beauty, and lifestyle. Sphynx was a name that wasn't going to take me to the next step, and that brand was born in a time crunch. I learned that I wanted to build things with intention, with my customers' input, and that's how Alleyoop was born.

POLLY RODRIGUEZ
UNBOUND

Unbound started as a multi-brand subscription box for third-party sex tech and pleasure products. I did all of our customer service for, like, two years. That taught me so much about where the opportunities were in this market. I found out that tons of the products we were selling were poorly made, had no warranties, broke a lot despite being kind of expensive, and the brand marketing was hypersexualized and not superrelatable. I gathered all these nuggets of information that helped me know I could go to market with a business model and product set different from what we were currently doing.

After learning all this, I wanted to pivot and make my own products that were better quality at a lower price. I met a ton of VCs who refused to invest in this new direction because it was an inventory-based business or because my product category was too controversial. We got rejected from accelerators, lost pitch competitions, and got hundreds of investor rejections over the course of two years. I held focus groups, I read all the books, I learned as much as I could. And in reality, you are never going to be 100 percent sure, because you can't tell the future. But you have to believe you are doing your best with the data that you have.

CHAPTER SEVEN

GROW UP AND GLOW-UP

As we've already explored, there are a million little forks in the road on your path to launching a business and building a brand: When do I go full-time with my side hustle? When should I acquire capital for my business? When do I expand my team? There are no textbook answers to these questions, and *your* reality and vision will establish your own personal timeline for many of these tough calls. Another major inflection point? Deciding when it's time to *spend* money to *make* money. Or, in other words, when it's time for your brand glow-up. Most businesses I know, whether self-funded, crowdfunded, or venture-funded, take a scrappy, get-it-done approach when it comes to building an inaugural brand identity, launching a first batch of product, finding an office, or making a debut website. There's absolutely no harm in this—this is exactly what you should do.

You have to start somewhere, and the sooner you make your business and brand a reality, the faster you can listen, learn, iterate, and grow. But in some cases, you may eventually outgrow whatever you start with—your logo, branding, packaging, ingredients, tech stack, website, whatever it is— and a serious refresh will be in order. Alana and I have always been superscrappy. From the early days of Bulletin, we did our best to be resourceful, get creative, and operate on a superlean budget. It became a running joke among the team. Our first employee liked to affectionately call us "janky." Let's Urban Dictionary that gem, shall we?

> **Janky:** adjective used to describe a person, place, or thing which is questionable, fucked up, wrong, strange, broken down, or undesirable.

For the first three years of Bulletin, we would always choose the cheapest, quickest solution over the more expensive, durable option. Which, at times, did result in pretty rough outcomes. Memories that play like a sitcom blooper reel. Our pop-up tents broke *all the time* during Bulletin Market, often falling on vendors (literally. Actually.) or blowing away in the wind. We built our first store in Williamsburg with our bare hands, which meant chipped paint all over the walls, uneven shelves, and permanently dirty floors. I merchandised Williamsburg the day it reopened with bathroom accessories from Bed Bath & Beyond that I had bought at 7 A.M., after leaving the scene of a Bushwick booty call. There's a time and place for affordability, speed, and DIY thinking. But there's also a time and place for brand maturity and development.

In many cases, our focus on "growing fast and breaking things"—a Silicon Valley trope—meant we either got taken advantage of, delivered a subpar product, or spent even more money to Band-Aid our boo-boos. None of these outcomes felt great—in fact, when they happen, you feel like total garbage—but they all served as major red flags and indicated that it was time to invest in a more sustainable, and pricier, approach.

When we opened our first store in Williamsburg in late 2016, for example, we slapped together a team of retail associates within a week's time. We asked around for referrals, posted on Craigslist and Facebook, and even had a few friends running the store from time to time. We had our heads down ordering shelves and units and fixtures, liaising with brands, building a marketing plan, getting our membership billing system in order . . . getting people to run the store seemed like a it would be a straightforward task. In our eyes, there were plenty of students and creatives and actors who would love a part-time job at a cool new retail concept in the heart of Williamsburg. We (very) quickly hired a small batch of retail associates and designated a de facto manager, and we were off to the races. We had interviewed them, collected resumes, and given them the Bulletin spiel. What could go wrong?

I MERCHANDISED WILLIAMSBURG THE DAY IT REOPENED WITH BATHROOM ACCESSORIES FROM BED BATH & BEYOND THAT I HAD BOUGHT AT 7 A.M., AFTER LEAVING THE SCENE OF A BUSHWICK BOOTY CALL.

In the early days of running our stores, employees worked solo shifts. We had one specific employee, an actor, who would clock in and out for full shifts, only to disappear from the store for hours on end. One time, Alana happened to be in Williamsburg for a meeting and walked by our Wythe location at around 2 P.M. and found it closed. The employee was nowhere to be found—no note on the door, no sign of him. A lunch break? An emergency? She decided to give the employee the benefit of the doubt. But then at 5:30 P.M., the store was *still* closed. She saw it with her own eyes, and meanwhile, I'd been sent a barrage of Instagram DMs from disgruntled customers who were hoping to go in and shop and complained the space had been locked up all afternoon. Alana confronted the employee the following day and, after a series of vehement denials, the actor finally admitted to leaving shifts for auditions. Not just once, but often. This struck us as absolutely absurd. While we were in the office working, a part-time employee was pulling the wool over our eyes and taking complete advantage of us. Here we were, a retail-as-a-service company, and our store was *closed* to accommodate a part-time retail staffer's audition schedule. I was absolutely mortified. Not only had we been duped for weeks but, even worse, I felt like we hadn't been fulfilling our promise to the brands *paying* to be in the store.

You may read this and think, But how could you be so irresponsible? Weren't there processes in place to prevent this type of thing? How could you let this happen? We hadn't set up our Nest camera yet, and, a small team of four at the time, we were trying to make too many things happen on too minimal a budget. Certain aspects of the business simply didn't get as much TLC as they needed, and some elements were straight-up jankier than others. Early on, you're looking at a pool of money and playing Hunger Games with how much goes where. At the time, we didn't have the funds to hire a veteran manager who knew how to build and train retail staff, or the budget to pay full-time, in-store employees who were committed to our new retail model and invested in the company's success. Or, perhaps we did, but we allocated it elsewhere, like to developing our retail booking platform or marketing for the new space to get foot traffic and sales.

No matter how you slice and dice it, our initial approach to finding, hiring, and training our retail staff was far from effective. It may have been fast, and it may have been cheap, but it resulted in a shitty store experience for our brands and our customers. In retrospect, it's blatantly easy to see that a rock-solid retail staff would help boost the other two growth levers we had put more of our money into: a great store experience inspires more foot traffic and sales, which then leads to happier brands and more bookings. But at the time, our scrappy, make-it-happen mentality led us to the easiest and quickest solution. You need to be resourceful while staying responsible. And in this case, our resourcefulness actually resulted in irresponsible decision-making, and we lost store sales and precious time because of it. It was shortsighted thinking at its finest.

WE WORKED RIGHT BEHIND OUR PEPPERONI-SLINGIN' NEIGHBORS AT PRINCE STREET PIZZA, WHICH MEANT THE THICK, HOT ODOR OF CURED MEAT WOULD WAFT INTO OUR OFFICE COUNTLESS TIMES A DAY, AT TIMES MAKING US HUNGRY, AND AT TIMES MAKING US NAUSEATED.

By 2017, we had opened our second location in Nolita. After spending months feeling disconnected from our retail staff and the store experience at large, we decided to take proactive steps to help bridge the gap. Once we opened our Nolita location, we moved our six-person team into an apartment-turned-workspace situated right behind our brand-new storefront. That way, we could have a higher touchpoint with the retail team, the products, the visual merchandising, and our customers. It was our first real office—no more coffee shops and co-working spaces. Our storefront landlord gave us a sweet deal on the apartment add-on, so the rent was superreasonable. It felt like a no-brainer.

This was a wise, responsible choice when it came to addressing our desire to be more hands-on with our store environment and our shopper, but it had more questionable ramifications on our workspace and office atmosphere. You see, we went from being six women, snug in a 400-square-foot, low-ceiling apartment, to seven, then eight, then nine. . . . By the end of 2017, there were ten of us vying for even one inch of personal space and, at one point, one of our interns didn't even have a desk. She had to work from the couch. Given the limited space and growing number of working women, the office got dirty and messy with ease. We had a tiny outdoor patio with a door that didn't fully close, and, in the summer, that meant ants would form a battalion and march on in to eat up crumbs and circle sticky surfaces. We'd take turns playing exterminator, ordering ant spray off Amazon Prime and blasting the suckers until they stopped moving (sounds superfun to work at Bulletin, right?). We worked right behind our pepperoni-slingin' neighbors at Prince Street Pizza, which meant the thick, hot odor of cured meat would waft into our office countless times a day, at times making us hungry, and at times making us nauseated.

The entire environment quickly began to compromise our productivity and left our employees wanting more space, less mess, and an office that didn't smell like oily pork nubs. Which I guess was superreasonable. Despite knowing this and experiencing it firsthand, we definitely overstayed our welcome. Finding another low-priced office in downtown Manhattan would be a one-in-a-million chance, which contributed to our staying put. Our team was polite and kept mum about their discomfort—they never outright protested the office environment or even complained. But by mid-2018, it was painfully obvious that not changing offices would be disrespectful to the team, a group of women who worked so hard for Bulletin day in and day out. This would mean a relatively significant spike in our rent, and it definitely took some time to stomach the jump.

Often, when you're in "scrappy" mode and super budget-conscious, it can be hard to assign and internalize value to things that don't directly impact your bottom line. A new office? At two times our current rent? But how will this help us sell more product? How will this help us partner with more brands? But Alana and I had to learn that just because *we* were comfortable with certain working conditions for the sake of our budget, that didn't mean the team wanted to work in a claustrophobic matchbox that smelled like steamy pizza. And your team's sense of security and satisfaction at work should carry the most value, especially if they've been quietly and gracefully roughing it.

OFTEN, WHEN YOU'RE IN "SCRAPPY" MODE AND SUPER BUDGET-CONSCIOUS, IT CAN BE HARD TO ASSIGN AND INTERNALIZE VALUE TO THINGS THAT DON'T DIRECTLY IMPACT YOUR BOTTOM LINE.

INVEST IN YOUR TEAM

Our janky approach to hiring retail staff for our first store and our extended, cramped stay in our Nolita office made one thing abundantly clear: don't skimp out on hiring great people, and once you do hire them, spend thoughtfully, when you can, on helping to improve their work experience. That is, try to avoid full-blown jankiness when it comes to your staff, no matter the stage your company is at. In our slapdash effort to get an initial retail team in place, we inadvertently hired crappy people who didn't take the job seriously. In outgrowing our Nolita office but staying put, we made our team question our judgment and silently stew over when we would make their work experience a priority. There's no hard evidence that it inhibited their performance, but common sense dictates that the happier your team, the better work product you'll get. And the less likely they'll quit.

This advice applies whether you're working with one intern, a team of two, a single contractor, or a full-blown workforce. First: take the time to pick the right person from the start, even if they're a tad pricier. And then make sure they feel respected. If you're an independent maker who needs a graphic designer from time to time for logos or packaging support, think competitively and selectively. Don't just go with a family friend or your first referral. Be patient and find the person who elevates your brand and wants to impress you. Make sure you have their design portfolio, ask them to do a small, one-off project to test their aesthetic, or have them provide a proposal or mood board ahead of signing on the dotted line. If you're contracting a lawyer or accountant to help get your business up and running, don't just go with the cheapest, most convenient option. Do your research, e-mail or DM other founders or successful business owners for referrals, look into local resources that may have vetted directories. It could save you a boatload of time and cash in the long run. There's absolutely nothing worse than spending tons of money to "fix" people or processes that don't work because you skimped the first time around.

Once you've found the right intern, contractor, or first hire, make it a point to pay them on time, give them the tools and resources they need to do a good job, and make their satisfaction a priority. This can be as simple as showing up on time for Zoom calls, if you're remote, vocalizing appreciation when they do a kick-ass job, and collecting candid feedback on how to make your work relationship even stronger. These suggestions sound wildly basic, but once you're in the thick of kick-starting a side project or starting a company, it's easy to see those helping you as gears in a larger machine. You'll get distracted by budget emergencies, ambitions, sudden opportunities, and logistical hiccups. But you can't let these things eclipse a consistent, genuine focus on those helping you, and a commitment to measuring how happy, challenged, and productive they are.

Whether it's setting a monthly alarm on your phone to collect feedback over e-mail or scheduling a biweekly check-in, there are plenty of easy, low-lift ways to try to retain great talent. It costs time and money to vet, re-hire, and train new people—no matter what business you run, how many people you work with, or whether you're still side hustling or have gone full-time. So, while not all glow-ups look alike, I think *every* entrepreneur should glow-up to find and maintain the best talent, if you don't have a first-in-class team already.

PAY FOR WHAT'S ACTUALLY IMPORTANT

Team and talent aside, everyone's glow-up is going to look completely different and every company should invest in what matters most to their business. If you get to the point where you think, If I just had enough money to take this specific piece of my business up a notch, I know it would be a game changer and help us reach our goals. *Do it*. Understand your particular ingredients for success and budget around them.

At Bulletin, for example, we've always had to build and maintain a community. That's why Instagram has always proven such a valuable platform for our brand. It has been the single most effective tool in growing our community of brands, and once we realized we got it right, we tried to get it even better. After a few months of steady momentum in followers and engagement, we decided to contract my friend Mackenzie to help formalize our brand voice and offer a road map to exploding our audience. Mackenzie had just left BuzzFeed after launching and running most of their social channels for almost four years, and she was offering her brand-building services as a part-time consultant. This was in 2017, when Bulletin began focusing on supporting women-owned businesses and scaling the membership model across multiple storefronts. Rachel, an early full-time employee who ran our social media day-to-day, worked with Mackenzie to scope out who our target audience was, what range of content we should own and cover, and how to refine our brand voice on the platform. What should our captions sound like? How long should they be? How frequently should we be posting? Where should we be curating content from? What content should we be producing ourselves?

Mackenzie tackled all of these questions and more, and gave us a thorough, prescriptive presentation with a blueprint that would accelerate growth in followers and engagement. For us, it was extremely rewarding to work with a veteran in the space who could come in, work with our internal team, and build a concrete strategy around a channel we felt was key to our success. With her blueprint in hand, we started to become known for our choice Instagram content and brand voice on the platform. Our Instagram persona inspired people to check out Bulletin stores, visit our website, and motivated brands to apply to sell with us.

That being said, a painfully on-point Instagram strategy isn't immediately necessary for every business. Instagram is a highly oversaturated platform crowded with content, and mastering it takes time, money, patience, and commitment. All of us—as individuals, brand-builders, business owners—dream of the exposure and growth a massive Instagram following could bring. But a massive Instagram following simply isn't relevant to every company and what it's doing. Because of our business model and our focus on building community, paying an expert to get us in tip-top shape made total sense. But if you're running a business that isn't focused on consumer attention and community-building, glowing-up your Instagram may not be the wisest or most effective investment.

As I mentioned earlier, you're always playing Hunger Games with your budget, trying to figure out what to invest in first, and what to hold off on. If, for example, you're launching your own consulting business (like Mackenzie did!), having a huge personal Instagram following or growing a giant audience for your company's Instagram account might seem like a good idea, but it may not actually be a huge help in bringing you business. It might make more sense to invest in a sleek, attention-grabbing website that shows off your work with earlier clients and outlines your skillset and strengths. If you're building a consulting biz from scratch, some serious networking is in order. You need a pool of prospective clients to show that sexy website to!

That means paying to join a bustling co-working community, buying tickets to relevant networking conferences, and attending industry-specific events might make for smarter investments to start.

IT CAN STILL BE REALLY FUCKING SCARY AND ANXIETY-INDUCING TO SPEND MONEY ON STUFF.

Even if you think carefully and strategically about where you glow-up and when, it can still be really fucking scary and anxiety-inducing to spend money on stuff. Whether you're redoing your website from scratch, upping your skincare line's ingredients, revamping your product packaging, or hiring a more expensive developer or designer, it's hard to part with money, even if it feels like the right thing to do. We just moved offices yet again and budgeted for nicer office chairs, a comfier couch, branded notebooks, and other tiny details we've neglected for three years. Even though I'm sitting here telling you to invest in your team and create a pleasant work environment, whatever that looks like or means to you, when Bulletin does it, it still hurts to see that money disappear.

As you decide on certain glow-ups, you need to go into them knowing you won't always be able to pump $15K into something and get $30K back in a certain window of time. Return on that $15K investment may take other, more intangible forms at first. After investing in a major rebrand or new store fixtures, for example, we didn't see a giant uptick in sales immediately, but, in the short term, Bulletin's digital and physical experiences felt more cohesive and more premium. That leaves a lasting impression with anyone who entered our store and anyone who visited our website, and it's a better impression than they would have gotten without the rebrand or better fixtures. If a customer walked into our store seeing cruddy, rundown fixtures, she may still have bought product, but maybe she wouldn't have told as many friends to come check us out. If a customer visits our site and the brand doesn't feel streamlined across every word, every page, every detail, that business owner may not trust us as a platform and partner. These outcomes obviously feel much softer than "spend $15,000 on a rebrand, generate $60,000 more in sales"—but they matter.

A glow-up is always bittersweet, because it will never feel exclusively "good" to spend money. Even for the most necessary, clear-cut glow-ups, you'll likely still feel that tiny pang of, Shit. Okay. Shit. I'm doing this. But think about how delicious it feels to know, deep down, that you're giving your company that fair shot, that you're doing everything you can to help nourish it, improve it, and make it work.

IF IT DOESN'T HELP YOUR GROWTH, PUT THAT CASH BACK IN YOUR WALLET, AND WALK AWAY.

Every glow-up you invest in should be an investment in giving your company a real, undeniable chance to succeed. If a fancy Instagram account doesn't accomplish that, leave it be. If a PR consultant or PR agency doesn't accomplish that, don't hire them. Invest in what makes *your* company tick, don't break down every time you burn a dollar, and if it doesn't help your growth, put that cash back in your wallet, and walk away.

HOW DID YOU UPGRADE YOUR BUSINESS OVER TIME?

JAMIKA MARTIN

ROSEN

We've grown so much this year, I had no choice but to really analyze and upgrade our supply chain. We've gone from me making everything myself with a superold hand mixer in my kitchen to a commercial kitchen and warehouse setup. Next, I plan on hiring a supply chain expert. I'm excited to look back six months from now at this huge trans-formation in our supply chain, product fulfillment, and inventory planning. Because right now, there's obviously apprehension. Unless it's a dire thing like we HAVE to figure this out ASAP or we go under, there's never that same sense of relief when you see the money leave your account. Those non-dire upgrades can always feel a bit scary, but you need to remind yourself that you're investing in growth, even if you don't necessarily see the direct impact and more sales right away.

I've also done upgrades to keep my mental clarity and freedom in check, like hiring an expert to help with cash flow. I didn't want to keep waking up in the middle of the night stressed about cash flow, wondering if we'll have enough in the bank for this ingredient or this or that. I asked myself, If I put this on someone else, what will it open up for ME? And I knew it would help calm that constant anxiety and sleeplessness, but it would also let me focus on other parts of the company that need my critical attention.

JASMINE MANS
DESIGNER, POET, AND FOUNDER

By selling in stores like Bulletin and getting customer feedback, we started to realize our T-shirt fabric wasn't as high quality as it needed to be. After learning this, I wanted to make the product more solid. If we could improve the quality of the shirt and make it even more popular, we could print more, which would help reduce the cost to produce them. I also wanted to find a way to see the product myself and confirm the fabric was in line with the level of quality I wanted for my brand. With this in mind, I just recently pulled all my distribution and hired a new screen-printer in New Jersey. Now, I get to spearhead the production quality and be more in control. I can see the product, see how it's being shipped, and know what it looks like when it reaches my customer.

It was a big, costly change, but I've already found that it's way more fruitful for the company. Now, we have someone who is actually in charge of the product quality. We've grown so much by leaving this automated system—this more personal approach allows us to grow and change and make edits quickly.

JANINE LEE
FLOSS GLOSS

For our first collection in 2012, we had $80K, and we needed to pay our manufacturers, and cover legal and business stuff. We didn't raise nearly as much money as I knew we needed, but I was like, We need a public relations person.

We had fashion girls and Tumblr girls and all these people seeing our nails and asking us where they could buy our colors. That's why the PR investment was specifically important to us—because I knew that if we got in front of the right beauty editors, those conversations would go smooth as butter. So, we wanted PR help, that was for sure, but the people we met in San Francisco were so insane. We finally met this guy from New York and flew out there in August of 2012. He was way expensive, but he seemed like the only one with the Rolodex we needed and the right connections.

We ended up meeting with this beauty editor at *Teen Vogue*—they were doing a roundup of their top ten favorite indie brands. That article happened, and then everything snowballed for us. We got so much press. We had so many people knocking on our door. We ended up moving to New York in 2014. We were just like, This is where it's all going to happen. We are fucking here, let's get it. Moving and spending on that press was one of the smartest investments we've ever made.

JACQUELYN DE JESU
SHHHOWERCAP

One of the first major changes and upgrades I made was redoing the product packaging entirely. I originally launched the Shhhowercap with just a logo and hangtags. We packaged the product that way for about a year. We needed to figure out a way to perfect the packaging so it would look better when it was posted on social media. I wanted it to look great whether it was on a shelf or on someone's Instagram grid, and I thought it was important for the brand itself to be more prominent wherever the product was displayed. For gifting, too, the loose Shhhowercap was challenging to wrap.

Throughout that year, I noticed that it was often a gifted purchase, whether for a friend, a mom, a co-worker. After that first year with just a logo and hangtag, I created the Shhhowercap box that everyone knows and loves today. With the box, the brand is clearly present on the shelf no matter how many SKUs are displayed, and it has a more reliable, consistent aesthetic for when people post it on social media. It's much easier to wrap, so the gifting process became way simpler. It was a complete and total game changer for my business.

**VICTORIA ASHLEY
LAUNDRY DAY**

My first set of pieces were stored in these plastic sleeves. It just didn't elevate the brand. I knew that by changing the packaging, I could change the perception of the product, make it more luxurious, like a keepsake. Every time I buy something, I keep the box it comes in. Even if I don't like the feel of certain packaging or I hate the box, I take note of the way it opens or if there's a paper insert or if it uses a certain texture I haven't seen before.

So when it came time for our first glow-up, our first "new look," it was really important for me to invest in packaging that offered a memorable experience. The product experience starts with the packaging. Now, the PVC sleeve is gone, and we use these beautiful boxes with rich colors and a magnetic closure. It's soft to the touch and has a little window, so you can see the piece before you buy it. It is super retail- and shipping-friendly.

Working on that glow-up and doing a proper launch was so important. I couldn't afford it two years ago, but I wanted to make sure I was doing this right and putting the brand out there in a way I wanted it to be seen. I needed to wait until I had the resources, but I'm proud I got there.

FAKE IT 'TIL YOU MAKE IT

People will take your business *only* as seriously as you do. Here are ten ways to get serious and invest in your success.

1. **Put it on your LinkedIn (trust me)**

   The first thing I tell every aspiring new business owner is to make it LinkedIn official. We already touched on being supervocal and forward about your business's existence and stressed that the sooner you own your idea, the sooner it'll find opportunity. Maybe you're just getting started and feel like it's too soon to broadcast your new biz to the world. You're worried about not being ready or not having enough traction to justify the LinkedIn line item. Whatever it is, turn the volume way down on those negative outbursts. You need your network to know that this business or project or side hustle is real—it's happening!—otherwise, they can't help you. You may mention the company to someone IRL, and they might look you up, only to see your name and whatever your full-time job is. No side hustle or new project in sight.

   Make your company a LinkedIn page, and then put your company name, title, and launch date on your personal account. If your co-workers or bosses find out, remember that it isn't illegal to have a side project (as long as it isn't directly competitive with your full-time employer), and pacify them by stressing it's something you do in your God-given free time. You are the founder of this thing. The owner of this thing. The creator of this thing! You are its mother. Make sure you use any and every opportunity to document that fact.

2. **Do a design upgrade, on the cheap**

Whatever your current design stack looks like, ask yourself, Could this be better? The logo, fonts, packaging, site design, and copy you launch with may not line up with who your customer has turned out to be. After launching, you start to learn *a lot* more about who's buying your product, using your service, and falling in love with your company. It's always worth refining your visual identity now that that knowledge is readily available.

It can be supereasy and relatively affordable to do a quick design glow-up. Make a Pinterest board of brands, pictures, and colors you love that feel spot-on for the vibe and feeling you're trying to evoke with your brand, packaging, website, etc. Then, prioritize what to redesign first. If you run an e-commerce brand, it might be your packaging. If you've started a small agency or consulting firm, maybe it's your website. Set a minimum and maximum budget for your redesign, write instructions for what you're looking to do and change, and then blast platforms like Toptal, Fiverr, Upwork, Dribbble, and 99designs to see if anyone's up for the challenge. You can even create some quick, canned copy and do a series of targeted Instagram DMs to try to recruit freelance designers you love and follow.

If you don't have the funds to do the above, you can download helpful apps like Canva and Planoly (both founded by brilliant women who sought to democratize access to design templates and help entrepreneurs level up their branding). These platforms provide out-of-the-box, sharp templates and color combos for IG Stories, grid posts, presentations, and more. They quite literally put a digital designer at your fingertips.

3. Always bring a business card

If you're going to be courting investors, marketing a crowdfunding campaign, networking with industry peeps, or even interviewing interns, you want to give the most ironclad first impression. A business card does so many things: the fact that you have one shows you are serious about your role, the colors, font, and design offer a window into your company's brand identity. Business cards don't replace connecting on LinkedIn or swapping e-mail information on your phone right then and there. Do that, too.

But if you'd have a business card at a normal, corporate job, you should have one for your side hustle or your new venture. Lean into all the bells and whistles one usually associates with employment. If you do work for it, make a card for it.

4. Leverage influencers' influence

Social proof is a real thing. It's this sick, twisted decision framework that secretly influences us to buy the things other people are buying or validating. It's why Instagram influencer is a real career, why companies exist solely to produce fake Amazon reviews, and why weight-loss-program commercials use a montage of testimonials. You don't have to go ham and hire expensive influencers or pay for fake reviews (we're more honest than that!), but it might be worth thinking about how social proof plays a role in your particular business. A few easy, relevant glow-ups include: launching an Instagram story series of customer praise, starting a loyalty program, adding a reviews plug-in to your site, or filming a client testimonial or two.

What you choose to do depends on your specific business but using social proof in your sales or marketing collateral is a universally useful tactic. In some cases, paying for some crazy-pricey influencer makes no sense. Sometimes, it's just hard to anticipate (and then afterward, measure) how effective influencer campaigns really are. Other times, your most influential customers may not have social media influence at all. At Bulletin, I gave fifty local college students a $30 credit to promote our consumer site over a three-month period. Most had under one thousand Instagram followers. In that same time frame, a major singer with millions of followers organically posted our URL and our store address to her Instagram page. We generated way more in sales from the college student promo than the celebrity mention.

Leveraging influence can be super small-scale and still extremely effective. It's an easy glow-up that builds your brand a halo bedazzled with approval and validation. Figure out who your customer gets inspired by, what type of social proof really motivates them, and then test an affordable, easy way to marry the two.

5. Try some PR microdosing

You're not going to get written up in the *New York Times*, Refinery29, TechCrunch, or the Cut right away. Without a PR team or a serious, full-time commitment to getting national coverage with big name publications, you won't have endless press falling into your lap. While press doesn't always help with sales, growth, or building traction (we'll touch on this later), it *can* be helpful in helping your brand seem more legit, more well-known, and more influential than it actually is because, often, the bigger-name press outlets want to see some sort of coverage or market validation before they put you in print.

PR microdosing means going after smaller, local publications for coverage. It means reaching out to niche Instagram accounts with larger followings than you for a feature, partnership, or story. It isn't running a full-blown press strategy or taking tons of time mass-DMing different accounts, but it is two to three hours a week of focused work. If you are starting up in Austin, target Austin-specific publications.

If you're launching an app or a tech platform, don't e-mail TechCrunch, but send an e-mail to a list of local tech bloggers or publications. DM those bloggers and journalists on Instagram or Twitter if you don't find their e-mail info. If you're starting a business that deals with food or music or fashion, find local media folks who play in those spaces. Don't be superinvasive or creepy, but tell them you're a fan of their coverage, send a link to your site, give a one-sentence description for your business or project, and say you'd like to find a way to connect with their audience.

If you're starting your own agency or consulting firm, for example, find other small, noncompetitive agencies with more reach than you and ask if you can promote or spotlight each other. Someone starting their own paid marketing firm could highlight a branding agency, and vice versa. Get creative with your PR and promotion, but keep it local, manageable, and low stakes. Sometimes, you and your business need to become relevant to a smaller circle of people before your grand debut with the big, bad world.

And a final word: if journalists politely decline your request to connect or don't reply after a second gentle nudge, then fuck off! And leave them alone.

6. Meet fancy people, and then name-drop them

People are human. Sometimes, they want a whiff that you have some wider social and industry validation before they place a bet on you, help you, or give you the time of day. The world is a sick place! But here we are. With this in mind, don't be shy aligning yourself with people or partners that have already given you the stamp of approval. If you've had cursory conversations with bigger names or corresponded with more seasoned brands or businesses, don't keep those experiences to yourself. Mention them offhandedly in your other meetings, when you network with potential clients, or when you're meeting other legit people—even people in other fields.

Perception is reality, and if you got in the door with another, more mature business that offers validation, then yeah, talk about how you opened that door. Let them see that you opened that door. Only worked with other small, up-and-coming businesses? Don't fret. That still counts! If you've done any sort of partnership or collaboration or have clients of any kind, talk about it! It means you're taking yourself seriously and trying to find strategic partners. Oh, and that those strategic partners want you right back.

7. Draft a first-pass business plan

If you're launching an app, you may not know how you really plan to make money yet. If you're starting a brand, you don't know how much of your first collection you'll sell, so it's hard to tell the future. But put a business plan together, even a very rough one, so you have it on-hand in case anyone asks. For all you know, you could meet a potential co-founder at a party. Your friend who's really good at numbers might offer to give it a pass. You may need it to get approved for a loan. Crack open Excel and start modeling out the bare minimum: how much money do you have to work on this, what are some up-front costs to consider, what are different ways to price your product. You can google around to find industry-specific business plans if you don't know how to get started. Microsoft even offers basic Excel templates and industry-specific frameworks in Word and PowerPoint if you want to skim some examples. Yes, I'm serious.

Gathering this information will make you feel more legit, and it'll help you feel more in control. Even if you have a nugget of an idea, put pen to paper around the concept, but try to roughly sketch out the financial piece, too. So, when someone asks for your business plan—and they will—you're never starting from scratch or standing dumbfounded. You've already tossed around a few ideas and have some numbers to share immediately.

8. Throw a deck together

While it totally depends on what you're building and what your business does, having a deck is a major flex. This "deck" is essentially a ten- to fifteen-page presentation you can create in Canva, Keynote, or PowerPoint that tells your story, shares your traction, and sells your business. Nothing too crazy—we aren't talking manifesto—but something short and sweet that defines your company, states what you do, and who you are. If you're a brand producing product, it might make sense to communicate your values or quality standards, what inspired the items or collection, and your background in fashion or design. If you render a service, like consulting, accounting, or copywriting, a brief deck with client testimonials, your background, and your full list of services could work.

Decks serve as a nice follow-up after meeting someone at a networking event, or to share with potential partners or collaborators. Even if you hire an intern, giving them a deck like this makes you seem more important and, ergo, their work seems more important. If you're not a designer and/or you're bad at copywriting, you can hire for both of those weaknesses. If you think you can manage the deck copy, post to Fiverr or Toptal to hire a deck designer at a rate of your choosing. If you need help with copy, post to Upwork or Scripted and submit all the info you need to include and let them work their magic.

9. LLC it

An LLC is a limited liability company, which means the business operates as an independent entity and its owners are not legally liable for the business's debts. It is a popular way for small businesses to formalize their companies. When I managed Bulletin's brand payouts, I always noticed a subtle difference in how I judged entrepreneurs who had incorporated their brands and others who hadn't. While I was close to many entrepreneurs who sold at Bulletin and who I have known many for years, I wasn't always privy to how many people were on their team or whether they ran their business part-time or full-time. That meant that in some cases, I was left to build an impression from afar. When I saw an LLC to pay I subconsciously thought: they have a team, an office, they're an entity. If I saw an individual name to pay I'd think: this is a one-person thing, maybe they're doing it on the side.

These judgments were extremely subtle, and honestly, my first impressions were proven wildly off time and time again. But an LLC or corporation has a certain heft. It hints that you're legally set up to grow, take risks, and protect yourself. Besides, coming up with an LLC name feels kind of epic and meaningful. While an LLC isn't for everyone or every type of business, turning your business into a separate, protected entity is definitely something to consider as you grow and work with bigger, more established partners.

You don't need to form an LLC straight out of the gate—you should ask around and do some research to see if incorporating ASAP is right for you. But if you sell a product, your customers might feel more secure and trusting if they spot an "LLC" somewhere on your site. If you're a freelancer and you render a service, having an LLC might hint that you have a larger team at play. If you want the freedom and protection to bring on a business partner, take any sort of investment or hire an intern, an LLC glow-up is definitely in order.

10. Own your customer experience

It can be scary to transition off platforms like Etsy or eBay or turn your Instagram community into an actual brand and website. But the closer you are to fully owning your customer, the better. If you have a platform-based business, like an Etsy shop or a Depop page, it might feel like there's no point leaving the nest. You've grown on those platforms and because of those platforms, and they've provided a safe environment for you to experiment and evolve.

That being said, if you want to expand your business, an owned-and-operated Shopify or Squarespace site might be part of your toolkit. Get your own domain. It doesn't need to replace whatever platform-based account you've built, it can simply supplement. You don't need to go all in and abandon the platforms that helped you launch and build a customer base. But take a crack at developing a site with your own look and feel. The site should feel like a cohesive brand identity is anchoring the whole thing, and it should highlight you as the business owner.

The more you can control your brand identity, communications, and customer service, the more you can control how you're perceived and how you scale.

EVERY GLOW-UP YOU INVEST IN SHOULD BE AN INVESTMENT IN GIVING YOUR COMPANY A REAL, UNDENIABLE CHANCE TO SUCCEED.

CHAPTER EIGHT

PRESS
≠
SUCCESS

Throughout my entire life, when I realized I was "good" at something, I became addicted to it. Partially because it can be fun to train and flex your skillset (I mean, if you got it, flaunt it!), but partially because I measured so much of my worth against external validation and heavy pats on the back. I think we all do, to some extent. There is something so reassuring about finding a craft or trade you can do well—consistently well—and getting some recognition and applause for it can feel like a delicious little cherry on top. Writing, for me, has always been a vehicle for satiating my need to learn and grow, but also satiating my need to be seen and appreciated. Throughout middle school and high school, I took the hardest English courses, joined the school paper, wrote short stories and poems in my spare time, and workshopped by writing with teachers after school let out. I found a skill I could sink my teeth into, and whether I was doing it privately or publicly, writing cured a loud, incessant craving for a sense of purpose and acceptance from my peers and my authority figures.

Running a company or launching any sort of entrepreneurial brand or project only intensifies this appetite for external, and in return internal, validation. I have met countless founders who seek big-name investors, impressive advisors, an infusion of venture capital, or hot press mentions just to give their business and their vision a golden stamp of approval. When you're launching something from scratch and risking so many hours and resources to make your dream a reality, any stamp of approval (particularly one with name recognition) can feel like major relief and help assuage any doubts you might be having about the future. Entrepreneurs can see press, specifically, as a way to signal to others and to themselves that their company is legitimate, thriving, and poised for greatness. Many also use it to build brand awareness with the right audience, or as part of their customer acquisition strategy.

And I totally get it. Because I've been one of those founders. Once I started running a business, "getting press" became a new muscle I liked to build and flex. It was a craft I was consistently good at, and my constant wins reassured me like warm milk at bedtime. As a wordsmith and persistent salesperson, I've always been extremely skilled at securing press for Bulletin: *Forbes, Fast Company*, Refinery29, Nylon, TechCrunch, the *Wall Street Journal*, and the freakin' *New York Times* have all covered Bulletin in some capacity.

All the while, I would faintly recall Y Combinator partners and other mentors urging us to avoid using press as a catchall solution to growth, brand awareness, and market validation. Seeking and subsequently getting press, they cautioned, could trick you into feeling like you'd accomplished way more than you actually had. It could poison you with a sense of complacency and slowly strip you of the hunger and drive needed to push your business forward in ways that were more effective. To quote Rudyard Kipling, "Words are, of course, the most powerful drug used by mankind." Press *is* a drug that can offer a brief jolt of gratification, but ultimately, obsessing over it or building your business around it can severely hurt or even kill your company. I've taken the drug, so I know firsthand.

You may be wondering: But how can you grow a company that no one knows about? As a twenty-four-year-old first-time founder, this question constantly plagued me as YC partners and other mentors advised we dedicate no more than 5 percent of our time getting press. This was back in 2016, when for the first third of the year, we were trying to drive site visits and sales for Bulletin 1.0, our "editorialized Etsy," and from springtime onward, we needed to bring foot traffic to our outdoor markets. I'd have a nudge in one ear, telling me not to focus on publicity, and in the other, a nagging whisper from deep inside asking, If a tree falls in the woods and no one's around to hear it, does it even make a sound?

To help bring site traffic and (hopefully) sales to our initial site, we chased down friends of friends who worked at Refinery29 and BuzzFeed. Alana and I both tried to build genuine relationships with these new press contacts. We wanted them to believe in Bulletin and in us—it was the only way these journalists would take a chance and feature a brand-new, completely unknown e-commerce site. After months of coffee dates and careful follow-ups, we got Bulletin 1.0 featured in a few Refinery29 gift guides and one of our most expensive products got a spotlight on BuzzFeed's social channels. I remember seeing the word "Bulletin" bolded in the Refinery gift guide and explicitly tagged on BuzzFeed's crazy viral Instagram account and feeling a surge of excitement and an overwhelming sense of triumph. Here we were, this tiny two-woman show with no PR department, not even a lone publicist, getting all this exposure with two highly regarded publications that aligned perfectly with our audience.

I felt exuberant and light and on top of the world! The main reason I was so excited is because, truthfully, press is helpful in building consumer trust in your brand. Refinery29 and BuzzFeed were giving us the stamp of approval, and making it safe and cool for their audience to shop our site. And it showed. As a result of both placements, we generated a handful of high-value orders attached to e-mail addresses we'd never seen before, so it started to feel like press was a free, direct line to brand-new customers who might not have learned about or trusted Bulletin otherwise.

In my mind, each placement took some serious time and mindshare, sure, but they led to trackable sales, helped legitimize the company with consumers, and served as excellent references for new brands we pitched the site to. I may have been dealing with mild cognitive dissonance: others' advice to minimize press efforts directly contradicted our own experience. So even though I knew on an intellectual level that press would never be a cure-all, I continued to hunt it down when the markets started. I used the same approach to secure press for our pop-ups in *Time Out New York*. I built personal relationships with journalists who were willing to take a chance and promote a pop-up market series that hadn't even started yet. And once we got started, each outlet *was* genuinely helpful in notifying New York that we existed, and convincing folks to come check us out.

The first weekend hosting in the Williamsburg parking lot, I asked certain market customers how they had heard about Bulletin, and many mentioned the *Time Out* feature. My earlier theory—that press could expand our reach in a meaningful way—proved true yet again. These were complete strangers, showing up and spending money with Bulletin because we were able to get noticed by larger platforms and build trust with their audience. To me, as long as I wasn't pining for press *so* badly that I was sacrificing my other responsibilities, I was in the clear.

I think press pushes like this are extremely valuable if you're building a brand and you have some sort of debut, major partnership, new line, or expansion to announce. If you have a huge event or update that can help legitimize your brand within your industry or build awareness with your target audience, go for it. But always have a goal or an outcome in mind so your push stays specific and your outreach stays strategic. The goal can be outlandishly vast or extremely precise. We needed people who cared about lifestyle and design to know Bulletin existed (let's label that "quite vast indeed"), hence our initial push to get products placed with Refinery29 and BuzzFeed. It helped generate sales. We needed people who lived in New York to show up for Bulletin Market the first weekend in July (as specific as it gets), hence our push for *Time Out New York.*

Across the board, it's smart to spread good news, and it's even smarter to own your story when it matters, like in the case of a pivot or a new product launch. If you need to place a story, then, at most, I would spend two hours a day for a full week researching publications, finding the right journalists, stalking their Twitter feed, combing through every word of their LinkedIn profiles, chasing down their e-mail addresses and pitching. I don't believe in a strict "only 5 percent of your time" rule. I think different businesses have to use different levers for growth, and in my own experience, consumer brands seem to need a bit more press than business-to-business (b2b), or non-consumer-facing, companies do.

Your press should perform for you, and should be done in thoughtful, strategic sprints. You shouldn't chase it for external validation, internal validation, or as a surefire, sustainable way to get customers or grow revenue. Press can be temporarily helpful in accomplishing short- and long-term goals, and within a tightly defined window of time, you should give it the time and attention it deserves.

There is only one major circumstance under which press—even if pursued deliberately and strategically, as advised—can irreversibly damage your company. This precious thing that you've worked so hard for means absolutely nothing if your product is shit. If you're serving up straight garbage, masked by the pomp and gravitas of a *Vogue* feature, you are still serving garbage, and now, way more people will know. Hi. Hello! Welcome to Total Nightmare Scenario! Your product or service need not be terrifyingly bad for a coveted press opportunity to go haywire, either. Press serves as a public debut—whether for your entire brand, a new product, or an important announcement—and butchering that debut can take many forms. I've seen founders go for broke on a huge press feature, or multiple features, and watched as their websites, software, or fulfillment centers failed to handle the volume of exposure. They simply hadn't prepared for the impact of the publicity, and it resulted in a range of lukewarm-to-negative outcomes.

In one instance, I watched a pair of founders fight tooth and nail for their product to go viral—they tapped press, TV, and influencers to build insane momentum around their launch and get as many pre-sales as possible. They generated millions of dollars in pre-sales and exceeded their goal by more than 200 percent, but when the time came to actually fulfill customer orders, the team was unable to ship product on time. Angry customers began ripping the brand apart on every social platform, and negative press about the fulfillment hiccups, product claims, *and* product quality (for those who did get the item shipped) started pouring in. I've watched services-oriented start-ups get written up, only to get overbooked the next day and spark utter outrage from potential customers as well as a slew of (new, but) irate press features.

THE STORY WOULD BE A FULL-STOP, POOP-YOUR-PANTS, POP-CHAMPAGNE DREAM COME TRUE.

While these instances are rare—truly, they are few and far between—they still stress how important it is to do press in a focused, methodical way. It is important to game out different outcomes, because your desired outcome may not happen. At Bulletin, I'd like to think (aka I tell myself every night before bed) that we've never backed a crappy product or served up straight garbage, so to speak. However, we *did* walk into a major press opportunity that we weren't prepared for, where our desired outcome just didn't happen. But what did happen fundamentally changed my thoughts on how, when, and why to focus on PR.

In the summer of 2017, Alana and I had developed a relationship with a writer from the *New York Times*. The journalist knew Alana from childhood and was a woman we respected and admired. She had a history of covering female-founded companies doing interesting things in tech and fashion. We had drinks with her a handful of times and I became obsessed with the idea of seeing Bulletin featured. I sent her e-mails detailing the company's history, our focus on female-founded businesses, how our business model worked, and how we had transitioned from markets to stores. The story would be a full-stop, poop-your-pants, pop-champagne dream come true.

For about six months, we did everything we could to further the relationship in the hopes of securing coverage. I invited the writer to every Bulletin event, sent her a long, insane e-mail detailing the entire history of the company, checked in periodically with invites to catch up over lunch or drinks. The *New York Times* story quickly evolved into this nagging, desperate dream that wouldn't die. I believed that article would change everything for Bulletin: it would quadruple our newsletter count, explode our number of Instagram followers, and spike online and in-store sales. Those were my desired outcomes. I soon became fixated, and I wouldn't—*couldn't*—let up until I saw Bulletin in the paper of record.

Come November 2017, it happened. My full-stop, poop-your-pants, pop-champagne dream *came true*. The *New York Times* piece was finally online and in print. I woke up early and spent the first two hours of that Thursday morning, crust in my eyes, running from bodega to bodega, trying to find copies of the paper, and buying up as many as I could. I needed one for the office, one for my mom, one for me, one for Alana, and dozens as backups. Throughout the rest of the week and weekend, we saw a ton of fresh traffic to the website, our online sales tripled, and a ton of people wandered into our stores because they'd seen us in the paper. We got resounding messages of encouragement and excitement from our customers via Instagram and e-mail. One older couple who lived in Nolita even cut out the article from the *Times* and brought it to our Prince Street store, mentioning how emotional and meaningful it was to see us profiled. For a few days there, it felt like we were taking off like a rocket ship! I felt like a hero. I got us published in the *Times*, which meant the business was, at long last, about to explode.

[*RECORD SCRATCH*]

The story had gone live on November 15, but by November 30, our website traffic, e-commerce sales, and in-store customer visits had all settled back to pre–*New York Times* numbers.

What the fuck?

I racked my brain over this for weeks and weeks. We had our fifteen minutes of fame and weren't capable of sustaining it. I felt deflated. *What went wrong?* Clearly many people had read our story—our site visits soared, our sales went up—but we weren't good enough to keep people's attention or get them to come back? My foregone, honest conclusion: we must be doing something very, very wrong. I was right, and Google Analytics confirmed it.

The *New York Times* piece forced us to take a magnifying glass to our old e-commerce website and glare at its flaws. We had gotten so good at opening physical stores that we forgot to give any love or TLC to our digital one. A ton of people had gone to bulletin.co that week—but they never came back. We lost most of them after the homepage, which meant the site wasn't very shoppable. Users didn't understand how to navigate the tabs to our different product categories. No wonder the *Times* traffic was a flash in the pan. We had spent so long desperately pining for the article, that we didn't think to perfect the platform we'd be driving customers to.

When I pause to remember the entire experience, I automatically think of the word "slipping." Because my fixation didn't happen overnight. I played by all my own rules. I wasn't forsaking other departments or lagging on other tasks for the *Times* story. I was just juggling a major PR opportunity along with my sales, strategy, and copy work. And I wasn't gunning for it blind—Alana and I had desired goals and outcomes in mind. I was trying to make the story a reality because we had our new Nolita store to promote, foot traffic to generate, and brand awareness to build! Sure, some of my desired outcomes seem outlandish now: even with an incredible website, would we have taken off like a rocket ship simply because of the piece? Were our in-store sales ever poised to triple indefinitely? Are anyone's? Or, does press always give a healthy boost that eventually (and sadly) wanes?

My excitement led me to a deep sense of optimism—maybe even delusion. The piece became something I wanted to win, rather than something I wanted to use. Had I stayed in a healthy headspace wherein the press was truly meant to support a larger company goal, like more online sales or newsletter signups, my focus would have immediately turned to the usability of the site. But I didn't stay in that healthy place. In my downtime, I thought about the story a lot. I wondered if the editor had read it yet. I wondered what they'd cut. If it would ever really make it to print.

When you're running a company, your headspace is everything. For me, that headspace should have been used to noodle on much more sustainable and impactful ways to grow. But the piece brought validation, and it brought recognition, and I slipped into a relationship with press that was ultimately unproductive. Actually, counterproductive. Both for me and for Bulletin.

WHEN YOU'RE RUNNING A COMPANY, YOUR HEADSPACE IS EVERYTHING.

Wanting press isn't inherently bad. Spending money and time on getting press can be a smart, strategic decision you make for your brand or your company. As I've experienced firsthand, press can help introduce you to new customers, validate you within your industry, and help you own your story during trying or exciting times. Press only veers into dangerous, unhealthy territory once you start to consciously—or subconsciously—use it as a barometer of your success. Just because your friends, industry experts, or journalists start to validate your business and think it's hot shit does *not* mean your brand or business actually *is* hot shit.

You know your brand from the inside out. You know its flaws and you know its magic. You should build your own personal barometer around your internal performance metrics, customer feedback, and traction. That way, if *Vogue* calls you the "it" brand of the moment, your excitement can feel like gratitude *and* motivation. Those feelings will keep you moving forward and push you to innovate and hustle harder. Because while you deserve to feel validated and you deserve to feel seen, having your own measuring stick will prevent you from conflating that validation with success.

JUST BECAUSE YOUR FRIENDS, INDUSTRY EXPERTS, OR JOURNALISTS START TO VALIDATE YOUR BUSINESS AND THINK IT'S HOT SHIT DOES *NOT* MEAN YOUR BRAND OR BUSINESS ACTUALLY *IS* HOT SHIT.

WHAT ABOUT PRESS?

LAURA SCHUBERT

FUR

When we launched in 2016, our two biggest expenses were a PR agent and inventory.

People trust press. That's why it has always been really important to us as founders and as a company, because we are an entirely new category and we needed people to trust *us*. In building this new category, we were asking people to use our oils in their pubic area. That's asking for a lot of trust from our customers. We wanted to communicate that the formulas were safe, they've been tested, and they work. That, and we didn't want to be some punny joke. We make products that care for pubic hair and skin—when we launched in 2016, it would have been easy for people to avoid taking us seriously. We didn't want to come off as some stunt.

I still work with my 2016 press agent today. I interviewed over twenty press agents and finally found the right person who believed in us and what we were doing with the brand. Your partners are your partners, whether they are agencies or internal. Those partners need to back you, your mission, and your vision. We pay a PR agent, but we don't do any paid placements. Back in March of 2017, Emma Watson told the beauty blog *Into the Gloss* that she used Fur, and it was this insane organic moment that boosted traffic to the site, sales, and the number of stores that wanted to carry us. She just loved the product and believed in the brand's message and what we were doing to legitimize body hair. It was definitely a huge moment in helping us build that consumer trust.

CYO NYSTROM

QUIM

As a cannabis business, you are incredibly limited in what advertising and marketing platforms you can use. You are limited in what payment processors and social media outlets you can use. We struggle to promote content or run campaigns on Facebook and Instagram. Mailchimp and SendGrid have shut down cannabis accounts. We can't buy ads in a lot of mainstream magazines. For all of these reasons, press was such an important way to get the brand message out there, but it wasn't something we invested in early on. Our watershed press moment was all about timing, really.

We launched in California six months before the state became the largest adult-use weed economy in the world. We began Quim in 2016, right when Trump was elected, and since then we've seen a 200 percent increase in millennial-targeted, feminine-focused wellness brands. Pretty quickly, *Vice*, a popular online publication, found us. At the time, we were trying to get into dispensaries and no one would take our call. We were assembling all the products ourselves. We were slowly fundraising and starting to apply to pitch competitions. Viceland changed everything.

In 2018, the TV host and producer Karley Sciortino, founder of Slutever, discovered Quim and did a whole piece in San Francisco about weed and sex. She included us and things really ramped up from there. We placed very high in various pitch competitions and ended up getting even more press. We were in the *Atlantic,* which then led to pieces in *Forbes* and the *Guardian*.

It wasn't until very recently that we decided to invest in a real PR team or service, because that initial press had led to more inquiries and dispensaries were finally lining up to sell the product. It was definitely really validating for the brand and the business and, given our limitations on other platforms, that type of press has been essential to our growth.

**JAMIKA MARTIN
ROSEN**

We've worked with two free-lancers and one agency, and we're working with a new PR freelancer now. It's been hard for us. Early on, we weren't seeing a ton of results. Maybe you get a quick write-up, but every founder's ideal goal is the type of piece: Look at this amazing entrepreneur and the brand they're building, look how they're disrupting XYZ industry. You invest and you invest in press support, and sometimes you don't get that write-up. You'll get included in roundups or gift guides, but it's very hit-or-miss as far as your returns. Press is just hard to crack. Last month, with everything going on and a push on social media to support Black-owned businesses, we saw a ton of people posting about us and we got a ton of press. I was talking to the team about our new higher average for daily sales. The press came with other things: we focused on our newsletter, ran our Facebook ads, and worked with influencers. But even while keeping those things the same, we've reached this new daily aver-age and have entered this new normal. What else changed? I mean, we have to look at the press stuff. But it's never a 1:1 ratio, like you'll get press and it will always make a significant difference.

MEENA HARRIS
PHENOMENAL WOMAN
ACTION CAMPAIGN

I didn't necessarily think press would be a major, important thing for my business, and instead I approached ways to scale by consulting with smart people, getting advice on what to do, and building brick by brick. In talking to some advisors and mentors early on, they suggested that I bring in a business development person, someone to stake out partnerships and vet incoming opportunities, so that's what I did. As a one-woman show still juggling a full-time job, I couldn't afford to pay and manage both a business development consultant and a PR person.

Not having an unlimited budget means you have to worry about your priorities. I decided to really start building out the communications and publicity side of the business, after the business development route didn't net the results I was looking for, and it ended up helping more than I imagined. But the role and significance of press varies from company to company. Because I was an individual who was already plugged into the media space, loved moderating and doing public speaking, and had done a ton of freelance contributing as a journalist and writer, it made sense for me to amplify my PR strategy with professional help.

Those things are unique to me as the founder, and further building out my profile helped build the business a profile. These days, consumers are paying a lot more attention to who's behind the business. They want to understand the values of the CEO. But what to invest and not invest in really depends on the business, and I still had to be really thoughtful, smart, and protective about when to push on PR.

JASMINE MANS
DESIGNER, POET, AND FOUNDER

One time, this amazing plus-size model got the "Don't have sex with a guy who won't eat you out first" shirt and posted it on Instagram. That day changed our lives as far as sales go. She helped us generate thousands of dollars in sales that we hadn't expected or anticipated. We were like, Oh shit—how do we get these shirts out? The PR was incredible, but it was this random viral moment and we had to act fast to make it work. We wanted to honor the model's promotion to her audience and fulfill every order; we didn't want her to get bashed because she was promoting a brand that couldn't fulfill orders on time.

We made it happen. It was one of these incredible moments that simultaneously made the company but also shut down the company for a period of time as well.

KRIS FRETZ
EMOJIBATOR

After launching our vibrators, *Cosmo* picked up the buzz and within a few days it was a huge story on their site. The press exploded our demand and we weren't prepared for it at all.

Once you get a feature like that, you have to immediately start thinking about how to live up to your customers' expectations *and* what happens once that press goes away. I have to build a world-class program for customer service. I have to create engaging content and connect with our community. Fulfilling the promises you make to your customers is *way more* important than the press itself.

CHAPTER NINE

THOSE WHO CAN'T DO, HIRE

Contrary to popular belief (or maybe just to my own psychosis), you don't need to be good at everything—not only as a founder or someone with a side hustle, but frankly, as a person. As a type-A overachiever with a self-titled stage mom from the Bronx, I always felt extremely pressured to perform at peak greatness at all times, in all things. I was pushed to excel at anything and everything thrown my way—and shit was thrown my way. My mom, the child of two German Jewish immigrants, wanted me to find my American Dream. My *thing*. As a kid, I took a wide array of dance classes; played piano, tennis, and soccer; took singing lessons; did student government, chorus, and the school newspaper; and was put in extracurricular computer classes and writing courses. Like throwing fresh spaghetti at the wall, she lobbed classes and courses and activities at me to see what would stick.

These were incredible opportunities and privileges that any child—or person for that matter—should feel utterly thankful for. And don't get me wrong—I *knew* this, which made me all the more eager to excel, and make her proud. This eagerness, however, can easily morph into pressure. And that nagging sense that I needed to be good at everything followed me through college, my early jobs, and, most severely, with Bulletin. From the outset, the business demanded I do a lot of shit I was good at—selling, strategy, copywriting, and public speaking. But it also demanded I do a lot of stuff I was bad at or had no clue how to do well: Excel whizzing, people management, product selection . . . I mean, the list goes on and on.

Obviously, this isn't just a "me" thing. In launching any business, starting a new role, or making a bold career shift, there will be moments where you totally shine, relevant skills in hand, and others where you're completely clueless. And while there is something to be said about rolling up your sleeves and doing tasks or filling roles that challenge you, the reality is, you can't be everyone. You can't do everything. And sometimes, learning what to delegate comes from realizing your shortcomings. Or, put more bluntly:

from realizing that you flat-out suck at something. Or many somethings. And then, asking for help. As a success-obsessed, hardworking hustler who tied her value to how much I could do right, I felt crippled by self-loathing any time something went wrong. I had to learn that it was okay to be bad at things—abysmally bad at things. And that denying my shortcomings could, actually, severely hurt my business.

BUILDING MUSCLE WHERE YOU HAVE FLAB

When we started opening physical retail stores back in 2016, I had to pitch and close all of the brands (sales! I got this) and do all of Bulletin's product selection and visual merchandising for the stores (umm . . . this looks cute I guess?). I don't come from retail. I had—and I can't stress this enough—no idea what I was doing. I mean, on a personal level, I was more of an excavate-the-bargain-bin-at-the-thrift-shop kinda gal. I didn't *ooh* and *ahh* at exquisite store merchandising or fancy fixtures or Pinterest boards packed with retail porn. I didn't understand the relationship between proper merchandising and the store's sales-per-square-foot. I didn't see product display as the delicate science that it is. I was building a business that let brands access turn-key, affordable retail space. Which, at the time, meant I was laser-focused on proving the model that brands would pay a monthly fee to place their product in a store—*and that's it.* I had the brands, I had the space, they had the products. And in my mind, it was up to them to showcase their wares as they liked—after all, they were paying a fee to have their goods sold with us.

I remember booking all the brands for the first iteration of our Williamsburg space and asking what products everyone would be selling and how much shelf space they needed for their stuff. We built a drop-off schedule so the brands could trickle in with their collections and display them as they liked. Every brand had their own dedicated little area in the store, whether it was a series of IKEA shelves or a small IKEA table (our stores got swankier,

I promise). Over the course of a few long nights getting the space in order, I did some *zhooshing* to make the space feel more cohesive. After all, we had about thirty different brands guiding their own visual display. With a bit of fine-tuning—voilà! We were good to go! I recall Instagramming the store with pride and sending loads of videos and pics to my friends, mom, and brother. It never even crossed my mind that I was an absolutely clueless, completely misguided and radically unskilled visual merchandiser.

Alana was busy doing all of our legal paperwork and negotiating leases for the store, hiring and managing part-time help for the build-out, designing the overall look and feel of the space, and managing our finances. I don't think either of us realized how grave our merchandising situation really was. I was proud of myself for booking thirty brands in under two weeks with a brand-new, innovative retail model, getting all their product in time for our launch, and tackling an unfamiliar role at my company. I felt like a boss-ass bitch. I thought the brands would be thrilled, and I anticipated hordes of customers throwin' cold, hard cash in our direction.

We opened in November 2016, so we actually had a pretty solid holiday season through December. Granted, we had absolutely no benchmark, but we were generating sales, seeing a steady flow of repeat customers, and had found a more sustainable, scalable, indoor way to help brands sell their stuff IRL. We didn't consult any experts with this first store (mistake). We didn't read up on store displays or merchandising hacks (mistake). We were gearing up for Y Combinator's core batch program, and thus, for fundraising, so our thinking caps and resources were occupied elsewhere. It wasn't until May of 2017 that I'd learn just how incompetent I was when it came to visual merchandising and product curation, and how desperately I needed to get the F out of the way and let someone else take the wheel.

It's funny: publicly failing at something had always been my biggest fear. Forgetting a line in a show, my voice cracking in chorus, botching a piano recital, losing a student government race. But, come 2017, when we hired an actual expert and I realized how hilariously bad I was at creating a compelling, shoppable store experience, I felt relief. I didn't feel an ounce of shame or self-loathing, despite seeing my flaws on full display in the stores. If anything, I was oddly thrilled to know I sucked, so I could give the store the retail guru She deserved: enter Maggie Braine.

Maggie brought visual display, assortment optimization, and store design muscle where Alana and I had mere flab. As a former merchandiser with J.Crew and C. Wonder and a true operations whiz, Maggie brought mastery to our product selection and inventory management. Maggie started her Bulletin career as a senior retail associate and grew intimately familiar with our weak spots in the stores. One day, she pulled me aside to simply say, "Hey, I can spot serious areas for improvement here and have the training and experience to make really positive changes. What do you think?" I relayed this to Alana, they met, and the rest was history.

We didn't even really have a merchandising role open, but Maggie's potential impact seemed so obvious, we made one. At first, I expected Maggie's expertise to worsen my insecurity and make me feel like an even greater failure. After all, I was the one who had set many of our broken processes in motion. Our slow sales, poor visual display, and reckless inventory management—the things Maggie was dead-set on fixing—felt like major blunders that had my fingerprints all over 'em. But in fact, her input had the exact opposite effect. I started to feel immense pleasure watching her excel where I had failed. Her expertise was apparent from the jump.

Rather than internalizing my shortcomings and judging myself for them, I felt a sense of fulfillment and achievement in giving my business the support it needed to improve and grow. Amid my ongoing impostor syndrome and self-doubt, Maggie's commitment to Bulletin and her ability to take my company's weak spots and turn them into strengths gave me confidence as a leader. I was thrilled that she spoke up, thrilled that Alana got on board, and thrilled that Maggie agreed to work with us. I started to understand that there's an expert for every department, with her own set of strengths and skills. It's important to find the experts who can tackle your areas of weakness, not just to plug holes in the business, but also to help *you* focus more exclusively on your secret sauce and set of skills that add magic to your brand and build traction for your company.

FINDING YOUR "SECRET SAUCE"

My secret sauce was always a blend of sales, community building, and copy-writing, and I have rotated through doing none, to just one, to all three at once (again and again!). But it's important to know when to really own a role or department, and why. Early on, I had trouble delegating the copywriting, because it was both the work I wholeheartedly enjoyed, *and* the work that made me feel the most secure and competent. In my eyes, my writing skills were my secret power, and I felt like no matter who we hired, *my* copy and *my* messaging would help the business succeed. I wrote every marketing e-mail, every Instagram caption, every store sign, every press release, every product description. My copy tentacles were anywhere and everywhere, and I was insistent on editing or approving any public-facing copy Bulletin produced. I knew how important it was to present a unified, cohesive voice early on. I knew that if we wanted to build a long-lasting company, whatever tone or personality we introduced up front would dictate the future of our brand identity. And, I knew that of anyone on the team, and of anyone I could hire, I was the most qualified person to do it.

In the early stages, every founder and entrepreneur should identify their secret sauce and unabashedly lean into it. Whatever magic you bring to the table, you need to know it, accept it, and find ways to do more of it. If you're a graphic designer launching a line of tees, you might want to design your

WHATEVER MAGIC YOU BRING TO THE TABLE, YOU NEED TO KNOW IT, ACCEPT IT, AND FIND WAYS TO DO MORE OF IT.

e-commerce website and create a unique, compelling site experience that stands out—because you can. If you're the ops whiz of a stationery brand but you're also really funny, you may want to start a funny illustrated newsletter for your customers. If you're launching a cupcake company and are addicted to Instagram, you may want to make behind-the-scenes content of you baking and throw it up on Instagram Live every other day to gain followers.

> WHEN YOU'RE FACING A NEW SKILLSET THAT YOU HAVE TO LEARN AND ADOPT, IT'S EASY TO GO INTO A TAILSPIN. THE VERSION OF YOU THAT KNOWS WHAT SHE'S DOING AND THE VERSION OF YOU THAT HAS NO CLUE ARE SO FAR APART.

It's important to know what your superpower is—the thing that no one else on your team, no freelancer, and no contractor could replicate. The thing that makes you different than all the other jewelry brands, graphic tee lines, coffee shops, consultants, tutors, babysitters, skincare companies. As best you can, use that superpower to differentiate your business and make it stronger, and find ways to delegate or share the other stuff so you can cultivate and disseminate that secret sauce.

NEW SKILLS BECOME HER

Let's say you know what you're great at and you know what you suck at, but what about new stuff? How do you know when you're bad at something new and should just accept it, versus when your weakness is just strength patiently waiting in the wings? We are all predisposed to be better at certain tasks than others, but it's important to spot the difference between work you should abandon and delegate, and the opportunity to dominate a new skill.

I recently had to make this exact calculation when it came to the product marketing for our new wholesale marketplace. Product marketing sits somewhere in between product development, marketing, and sales. In a product marketing role, you typically end up talking to a shit ton of potential and existing customers; funneling that feedback back to the product, tech, and design teams; working with salespeople to help them understand and pitch the product; and crafting product positioning and messaging with your marketing team. It's a doozy of a role, and one that requires a fair amount of technical copywriting and a lot of critical thinking. Over the past four years at Bulletin, I have produced tons of consumer-facing copy and done a fair amount of market positioning, but I have never in my life written web copy that positioned and sold a technical platform.

Needless to say, I was intimidated. In order to do the job correctly, I'd have to create and preserve an ongoing feedback loop with Alana, our art director, our growth team, and our customers—both brands and retailers— all of whom have entirely different needs and goals. Then, I'd have to use that feedback to finesse how we described the platform, how we pitched it to our two different audiences, and what we put in our sales collateral. I'm a confident marketer, a confident salesperson, and an experienced copywriter, but this whole product marketing thing felt like a bigger, more complex role I wasn't ready for. Shouldn't I hire someone who's brought a technical product to market before? Multitasking under pressure makes me anxious. If I take this on, am I literally inviting a mental breakdown?

Part of me thinks I was just afraid of the unknown or scared to fail again after my visual merchandising blunder. Clearly, it wasn't the first time Bulletin demanded I hone a new skill or build processes from scratch. I'd definitely fucked up last time. And to me, this felt like an even bigger call to make. What do we call the platform? How do we describe it? How do we get brands to use it? Get retailers to shop it? What do we build first? When you're facing a new skillset that you have to learn and adopt, it's easy to go into a tailspin. The Version of You That Knows What She's Doing and the Version of You That Has No Clue are so far apart.

But when I really thought about it, product marketing was really just the sum of a bunch of skills I already have and, for the most part, enjoy. It was different from the visual merchandising situation with our Williamsburg store. I had no prior store design experience, and I was preoccupied with selling memberships and booking brands. With product marketing, though, I wasn't tackling some out-of-left-field technical skillset or technique I would need years to study and master. I wasn't becoming a developer or graphic designer or SEO specialist. Yes, I needed to study product marketing, chat with veteran product marketers, and make sure I knew what the hell I was doing. But I saw the role as a chance to stretch my skillset, not chase down a new one.

> IDENTIFYING WHETHER YOU'LL BE GOOD OR BAD AT NEW STUFF MEANS GETTING A GRIP ON HOW NEW THE WORK ACTUALLY IS, AND CANDIDLY ASKING YOURSELF WHETHER THE NEW ROLE OR SKILL TAPS INTO YOUR STRENGTHS OR PREYS ON YOUR WEAKNESSES.

I could leverage and mold existing strengths to fit this new, immediate demand. Collecting feedback from retailers and brands—i.e., getting people to talk? I was a veteran sales genie and a Gemini. I could do that. Build an internal community of employees that prioritized constant user feedback? I had already built an external community of brands and community of shoppers that shared the same values. Building an internal community suddenly didn't feel so hard. Write copy for, pitch, and go to market with a new technical product? Well, I loved learning new things, a good copy challenge, and making a splash. Suddenly, the prospect of filling this role felt less overwhelming and kind of exciting. And once I dove in, I felt old muscles working hard to do something new.

Sometimes, assessing your ability to tackle a new role for the sake of your business means demystifying what that role actually is. In my experience, you can do this by breaking down the role into smaller components and simply talking to folks who have done it before. In reading about product marketing and the day-to-day elements of the job, I quickly realized it overlapped with a lot of the sales, marketing, and copy stuff I had been doing for years. In talking to other product marketers, I learned how to fine-tune my existing skills to do the best possible job, and got the reassurance I needed that yes, this was a new application of my strengths, but no, getting it right would not be impossible. Identifying whether you'll be good or bad at new stuff means getting a grip on how new the work actually is, and candidly asking yourself whether the new role or skill taps into your strengths or preys on your weaknesses.

I'm not telling you to give a new skillset the middle finger or to abandon the idea of adopting a radically new strength (like me pointedly deciding against becoming a visual merchandiser). I am all about stocking your professional toolkit with skills that are marketable, valuable, and relevant. I am by no means arguing to simply stretch your existing skillset. You can and should develop brand-new ones, whether to qualify for higher-paying roles, become a more well-rounded entrepreneur or employee, or simply shake things up and diversify your work experience. But you can use the same methodologies described above to determine what new skills and superpowers you should master.

I have a brilliant high school girlfriend, Emma, who went from being a data analyst to a software engineer at Foursquare. She had to determine whether coding would be fulfilling and something she'd want to sink her professional teeth into. Emma graduated college with a cognitive science degree after dropping out of a computer science program her first year at Berkeley, where she felt intimidated and behind. While working as a data analyst at Foursquare, she had to run repetitive data queries for the sales team. She felt like there had to be a way to automate the reports, so she got approval from her manager and built her own tool. She pushed the tool live, told her higher-ups she loved the project, and shortly after, they offered her a role on the engineering team. Emma, who once felt like a computer science impostor, had to do some coding on the job to realize she was, in fact, a computer science mastermind. Because of her data science experience, the work felt familiar enough and like it built on her existing strengths and way of thinking. She was lucky to have a few unofficial mentors along the way, too, which helped her do her first major coding project in a safe and encouraging environment. It was a skill she wanted to master, and one she had always felt held excitement and intrigue. With a small, low-stakes project, she learned that she could do it.

It can be hard to know what skills you should learn and develop, and what parts of your business you should outsource to employees, partners, contractors, vendors, freelancers, interns, or anyone else who's game to take this journey with you. I believe in delegating around your superpower, truly knowing and accepting your weak spots, and challenging yourself with skill stretching or new skill development. But most important, I believe in doing the work you actually love. I think you do the work you love better than the work you hate. You may not always love your superpower or the work that comes with it. I'm a great salesperson, but some days, I despise taking calls all day, pitching, and schmoozing to open closed doors. It's exhausting and soul-sucking and often painfully repetitive. So, despite my talents in that department, I'd rather not pile on these types of tasks. I don't do sales 24/7 or oversaturate my day with it because I know, after years of grinding, that I simply won't enjoy it. I've been lucky enough to delegate around it over time and outsource the sales-related processes and tasks I enjoy the least. You won't always be able to delegate or outsource, though. I couldn't for a long time. There will be periods of growing your business where you'll have to do so much shit that's completely foreign to you, superirritating to manage, and/or just flat-out unpleasant. But you should make it a goal to build up your business enough that you can delegate those tasks so you can focus on the work you love. You chose to start a business for a reason: to be your own boss, make your own money, have more agency and freedom, disrupt an industry, monetize your creativity. Whatever it is, by electing to fulfill roles and tasks you can't stand if and when you have the means to delegate, you're also choosing to be unhappy. Delegating is a privilege and a reward—it's something that often comes after years of juggling completely different tasks to make your side hustle or business a reality.

So, once you've hit that inflection point and can collect on your years of multitasking, make it a priority to focus on doing more of the type of work that brings you joy. And while you're multitasking, pay attention to the tasks that weigh you down, lift you up, benefit from your strengths, prey on your weaknesses, that challenge you in a good way and help push the business forward. The stuff you're both bad at and hate? If possible, find a financially feasible way to plug that hole and give your business the expertise and support that it needs. If you can't delegate just yet, make it a target milestone for you and your business. Nothing inspires hustle like making your venture successful enough to outsource the work you don't love or enlisting people with more expertise and experience to strengthen you where you are weak.

TAKEAWAYS!

IF YOU DON'T HAVE THE ANSWER, JUST FIND SOMEONE WHO DOES.

IT'S CALLED A SHORTCOMING, NOT A FATAL FLAW.

ENJOY WATCHING PEOPLE BECOME STRONG WHERE YOU ARE WEAK.

DELEGATING IS A PRIVILEGE AND A REWARD—IT'S SOMETHING THAT OFTEN COMES AFTER YEARS OF JUGGLING COMPLETELY DIFFERENT TASKS TO MAKE YOUR SIDE HUSTLE OR BUSINESS A REALITY.

CHAPTER TEN

"BRAND"

I didn't know, intellectually at least, how to build a brand. I didn't study it in school, I didn't pay for pricey panels with branding gurus, I didn't buy books on it or listen to podcasts. I had taken on a few branding-adjacent internships writing copy for IKEA or playing brand rep for Ann Taylor (*so many* free sheath dresses), but I had never really thought long and hard about how brands were shaped or manufactured. But halfway through my time at Condé Nast, my boss, Pat, told me to watch the 2009 documentary *Art & Copy*. I was in the marketing department, and I wanted to learn more about the strategy and processes behind all of the branded editorial we were doing. Well, *I* wasn't doing any of it—I was making copies and picking up Pat's chicken avocado sandwich from Pret most afternoons.

But to me, at twenty-two, there was something very *Mad Men* about the goings on at Condé, and I wanted some context. I wiggled into bed that night, glowing laptop on a pillow, and watched advertising giants give a retrospective on some of the most influential and iconic commercials, print ads, and slogans in history. After watching, I wanted to be one of those giants. Their jobs seemed so creative, challenging, and fun. Early advertising was this form of condensed-yet-powerful storytelling where captivating visuals, pithy copy, and ruthless consistency could build an "it" brand virtually overnight. I loved seeing all the puzzle pieces come together for a new print campaign or a product's first commercial: every frame, every color, every word was given so much thought and detail. In a world where you have limited time to communicate a powerful message or leave a meaningful impression, *everything* matters.

This type of short-form storytelling is something you'll need to do convincingly when running a business, but especially early on, when you can't hire a design agency, a PR firm, or a veteran copywriter to do it for you. You'll need to tell brief, compelling stories all the time: to your customers, to your audience, to potential investors, to your potential crowdfunders, to collaborators, new hires, partners . . . the list goes on. TLDR: whenever you need buy-in from someone, you need to tell them a story. And, like the advertising creatives in *Art & Copy* (minus their resources or experience), you'll need to do your best telling stories that are both deliberate and designed.

Bulletin was the first brand story I ever told. Back in 2015, I didn't know the step-by-step process of building a visual identity or brand persona or brand guidelines, and Alana and I definitely learned as we worked. The Bulletin brand has evolved dramatically and at times rapidly over the past few years, and the visual and verbal identity of the brand has gone through a careful process of refinement based on what we've learned about our audience and radical changes to our business model. But, when we started, we had no data, no audience, and no clue. We learned by studying and parroting brands we knew and loved. Alana did an internet deep dive on other relevant brands and made millions of Pinterest boards with inspo pics for our logo and design, while I devoured the copy—on packaging, websites, social media, you name it—from the same portfolio of brands.

At first, we saw ourselves, aka Bulletin, as a passive curator. We wanted the brands on our site to do most of the legwork and really shine. As such, Bulletin 1.0 was a sleek, black-and-white Squarespace site with a geometric, sans-serif logo and minimal personality. We didn't have any flashy colors or spunky text. As a birthday gift, Alana's then-boyfriend commissioned a local art celeb to make us a chunky alien logo (since we were all about brand discovery . . . aliens live in outer space . . . we search for new shit out there . . . you get it). But that was the only real custom or branded thing in the mix. Our e-mail newsletter was equally minimalist in vibe and lingo. We kept it cool and subtle, not wanting a flashy, loud point of view to overshadow our featured designers. With that in mind, I didn't make a real effort to craft a cohesive brand voice. I was too scared and inexperienced to write a pithy tagline or mission statement, and our About Us blurb was superclinical and uninspiring. That, and if you dug around, it was hard to tell if Bulletin had a real "why," or a reason for existing. Seems like a critical thing to be missing, right?

Alana and I knew we loved supporting these small businesses, and we were obsessed with their handmade products and stories and childhoods and kooky studio spaces. But we struggled to communicate that in our branding, which didn't compel our audience to share in our enthusiasm. We struggled to define exactly why our friends, family, and prospective customers should care as much as we did. There was no real messaging or branding that defined or differentiated us—there was nothing to fall in love with. And that became more and more obvious as we tried to get people—readers, brands, investors—to fall in love with what we were doing. We were unable to find funding, we struggled to generate traffic for the site, and our newsletter audience count stayed stagnant. We failed to tell the first Bulletin story on two fronts: we were unable to either articulate our mission or motivate buy-in for that mission.

WHAT, WHY, HOW

What Alana and I would both learn in due time is that the visual and verbal identify of your brand must be rooted in your "what," your "why," and your "how." The "what" is your purpose. As a statement, it succinctly and clearly addresses what your company does and for whom you do it. The "why" is pretty straightforward, too: it answers the question of what your brand or business is hoping to accomplish or what values you're trying to promote with your audience. It's your mission: it tells your customers why you're offering this product or service in the first place. The "how" answers, simply, how you want your prospective and existing customers to feel when they engage with your brand and your mission. The "how" will determine your brand's communication style as well as your visual identity. Every choice you make, every story you tell, will rely on your what, why, and how.

Have I what-why-and-how'd your mind into a salty little pretzel? No worries, let's break it down into a few short and easy examples:

> A new kitchenware company makes stylish appliances, pots, and pans for female millennials (what). They believe cooking is not only fun, but also offers an important, rare opportunity to feel fully present in the moment (why). They want customers to feel inspired when they shop for and use their products (how).

> A new kitchenware company makes sleek and durable pots and pans for millennials (what). They believe cooking is fun and a crucial part of crafting a healthier lifestyle (why). They want customers to feel confident and knowledgeable when they shop for and use their products (how).

These two companies both sell cookware to a millennial audience. But their branding, slogan, communication style, vocabulary, fonts, and personas will be radically different from each other. They will use different messages, they will leave different impressions, they will tell different stories.

Outdoor Voices, an activewear start-up based in Austin, offers a real-world example of a brand that's done a remarkable job of nailing down their what, why, and how.

Outdoor Voices is an activewear brand that sells fashionable, technical apparel to men and women (the what). They are "on a mission to Get the World Moving, because they believe Doing Things—moving your body and having fun with friends—is the surest way to a happy and healthy life" (the why, ripped straight from their website). Ty Haney, the founder, started Outdoor Voices to "free fitness from performance" and help customers see movement and exercise as recreational and fun (the why part two; it's okay to have more than one!). The brand wants customers to feel inspired and supported when they engage with the brand online and on social media, come into their stores, and make a purchase (the how, at last).

Some of this is from Outdoor Voices' website, and some is from published interviews with Haney, in all of which Haney articulates these values with precise consistency. Having these three pillars on lock helped Outdoor Voices stand out and initially explode in a highly saturated market. In addition to bringing completely new athletic wear styles and designs to market, the company introduced fresh branding and a novel brand voice that customers hadn't seen from household names (and direct competitors) like Nike and Lululemon. Every choice they made, every story they told, leaned on a "what," "why," and "how" the market hadn't really seen before.

As a brand, Nike is associated with extreme athletes, intense exercise, and reaching peak performance. We make these associations based on what we see and hear: the brand's colors, ad copy, its celebrity spokespeople, and even product names and descriptions. Customers are more likely to feel that Nike is for goal-oriented, self-identifying "fitness people" or athletes because of their copy and color choices. Lululemon feels like a brand for highbrow women who do yoga and seek self-improvement both physically and mentally. This perception is triggered by their higher price points, yes, but also by the motivational quotes and phrases scattered across their stores and shopping bags, the types of models they cast in their product and editorial photography, and the more serious, focused tone the brand takes on all digital channels. Customers are more likely to feel that Lululemon is for a slightly older customer who lives an all-around healthy lifestyle and has money to spend.

ENTER: Outdoor Voices launches with a friendly, almost tongue-in-cheek persona that defies the firm, supercharged tone of a Nike ad or the disciplined intensity of a Lululemon centerfold. The brand's casual air aligns beautifully with their "why" of making fitness less intimidating and more enjoyable. It shows up in their promotional copy, their social media presence, and their product descriptions. Their color palette gives off a similarly laid-back vibe. The brand leverages colors that are more neutral, soft, and understated compared to Nike and Lululemon's use of confident red, white, and black. Instead, Outdoor Voices leans on airy eggshell, beachy beiges, and Gap-y blues and grays. Where Nike and Lululemon use branding that leaves customers feeling motivated, challenged, and intense about their fitness goals and lifestyles, Outdoor Voices meets customers where they are, wherever they are—and doesn't assume customers have goals to crush or fitness lifestyles to uphold. The brand makes its customers feel motivated to get active and have fun, rather than feel pressured to exercise to lose weight or crush a marathon.

As Outdoor Voices proves, every color choice, marketing asset, product description, and brand decision should spoon-feed your customers a sense of who you are, why you exist, and how they should feel about you. And if you get it right, you may be able to compete with decades-old brands who are telling a completely different story.

"GOOD BRANDING" IS NOT ENOUGH

But you can't just rely on an amazing designer, revolutionary color palette, or agency to "get it right" for you. Whether a friend is helping you for free, you're hiring a freelance designer, paying an agency, or bringing a designer in-house, you need to learn how to communicate your "why," "what," and "how" to that graphic designer. The designer is not responsible for giving your company a soul, they are responsible for making sure others can see it.

Alana and I learned this firsthand. When we outgrew our funky, alien, minimalist branding and bland copy, we decided to hire a graphic designer to give us a proper glow-up, complete with a new color palette, logo, website design, icon set, and more. We met this partner through a mutual friend, and it was the first time we had ever solicited an outsider to help guide our brand direction. It was 2016 and we had just finished Y Combinator Fellowship, we were superfocused on building a business-to-business platform that helped brands access turn-key, affordable retail space in NYC. We had just launched Bulletin Market, and we needed a new identity. We had already started booking out booths at Bulletin Markets in Bushwick and Williamsburg, and we had a vague sense of the vibe we were going for. We wanted to build a brand that felt both technical and relatable, kind of like WeWork or Airbnb. We were in co-retailing after all, and thought it made sense to follow in the footsteps of the space-share giants that came before us.

THE DESIGNER IS NOT RESPONSIBLE FOR GIVING YOUR COMPANY A SOUL, THEY ARE RESPONSIBLE FOR MAKING SURE OTHERS CAN SEE IT.

Alana mirrored exactly what we'd done the year before: she drafted a comprehensive list of relevant brands we adored, made a Pinterest board of logos, colors, icons, and textures that felt right, and mapped out the various assets we'd need short- and long-term. We explained the business model to our graphic designer, we asked for wireframes for our booking platform, and met in person a few times to give feedback or review new ideas. After many months of back-and-forth and a handful of in-person meetings, we received our final brand book. The designer gave us a color palette, font hierarchy, some icons, site design ideas, and a few mockups. Neither of us were ecstatic about the end result. At the time, we felt like we'd provided our graphic designer a wealth of guidance and direction, in addition to various rounds of e-mail and in-person feedback. Why were the deliverables so disappointing? We paid up, used the guidelines for about a year, and eventually started from scratch.

In digging through my e-mails from 2016 and reliving this entire saga, I realize that I was to blame for the lackluster results we got from our outsourced designer. Because, despite feeling so passionate about this community of makers and wanting to celebrate them and their products, we didn't relay that passion to our graphic designer directly. While Alana provided an endless sea of colors, logos, brands, and images she loved, at no point did I provide any insight into why we built Bulletin and how in awe we were of our brands. We so deeply admired every designer and entrepreneur we met for early Bulletin interviews and photo shoots. We hung out in their studios, transcribed what they had sacrificed, and learned why they made what they made. We both thought more people should know about them and their work. But our designer had no clue.

FOR A DESIGNER TO TELL A DELIBERATE VISUAL STORY FOR YOUR BRAND, YOU NEED TO BE DELIBERATE WITH THE STORY YOU TELL THEM.

The push to "make it feel like WeWork" or "mimic Airbnb" worked as a stand-in for making it feel original or true to our mission and what we built Bulletin for. I'm not a designer, and I don't consider myself a visual person. Alana, on the other hand, is a branding expert and is more inclined to appreciate and understand design. But neither of us knows everything, so she hired our graphic designer to fill in the blanks. The lesson here is to leave no blanks. We left too many blanks. No matter how badly you need a designer to elevate and shape your brand, no matter how shitty you are at whipping up basic graphics, no matter how much help you need—only you can guarantee that your brand has a soul. If you hire a designer and they don't have a what, why, and how to anchor to, your branding will feel hollow. Because it kind of is! You need to spoon-feed your graphic designer a thoughtful, detailed breakdown of your vision, your purpose, and your target audience if you want anything approaching magic. Simply offering up adjacent brand names or logos or colors you like isn't enough. Telling your graphic designer to "make it feel like this" or "copy the vibe of that" is no substitute. For a designer to tell a deliberate visual story for your brand, you need to be deliberate with the story you tell them.

YOUR BRAND STORY

Barring a pivot or major rebrand, the what, why, and how of your business will stay the same, but the way you tell your story will always vary depending on your audience, which we've kind of hinted at already. That means you must package and deliver your story differently to your customers, investors, potential partners, and the press. The way you talk about your company to a potential manufacturing partner is not the way you should talk about it to your crowdfunding campaign audience. You'll need to design elevator pitches, grabby one-liners, fundraising presentations, Instagram captions, and more. Early on, you may feel a gut impulse to "just wing it." If you know your vision, purpose, and mission like the back of your hand, how hard can it be to explain your company at a cocktail party? At a networking event? To a mentor who might invest? To the bank that might approve a loan? But the question isn't really how hard can it be? The question you should be asking is, "How *effective* can it be?"

Knowing your business like the back of your hand is, for starters, your number one job. But, more important, it is not the same as knowing how to build brand awareness with or get buy-in from different stakeholders. To do that, you'll need to understand each audience in maniacal detail, and tell a deliberate, thoughtful story about yourself and your business that they can each latch onto and believe in.

Telling your brand story to your beloved customers is partially handled by your visuals and design, as we've already discussed, but your actual brand voice and the copy you commit to rounds out the whole experience. I have structured and overseen Bulletin's brand voice from the very beginning and have had to ruthlessly tweak and retool it as we've grown—and flat-out changed—the business. Throughout every iteration of Bulletin, our brand voice has played a huge role in how our customers feel about our company and about themselves. But we're no exception. I believe that brand voice has the power to either cement a company's identity and reputation with its customers or completely alienate and lose them. If your design choices give customers their very first impression of your product or service, brand voice rushes in pretty quickly to either confirm or confuse that impression. Brand voice doesn't just live in your tagline or About Us, it's the way you announce a product launch, communicate via customer support, present information on a label, respond to an Instagram DM, handle a delicate e-mail complaint, and explain a cool new feature. *Brand voice is your company's personality.*

BRAND VOICE DOESN'T JUST LIVE IN YOUR TAGLINE OR ABOUT US, IT'S THE WAY YOU ANNOUNCE A PRODUCT LAUNCH, COMMUNICATE VIA CUSTOMER SUPPORT, PRESENT INFORMATION ON A LABEL, RESPOND TO AN INSTAGRAM DM, HANDLE A DELICATE E-MAIL COMPLAINT, AND EXPLAIN A COOL NEW FEATURE. BRAND VOICE IS YOUR COMPANY'S PERSONALITY.

Building and evolving Bulletin's brand personality has been the most enjoyable and fulfilling project, and it's one that never seems to end. Once I got my sea legs and felt more comfortable guiding our consumer-facing persona, I fell in love with this idea that Bulletin could really mean something to our customers and our audience. I wanted Bulletin to deserve a customer's affection and respect. I wanted to build a brand voice that helped women feel good about themselves. I wanted Bulletin to encapsulate the power of female financial agency. I wanted Bulletin to be slightly self-deprecating, slightly superficial, curious, and big-hearted. I grew up with so many retailers—their mannequins, ads, catalogs, attitude—telling me what to wear and how to wear it. They felt stuffy, bossy, and conservative. I wanted Bulletin to take itself a bit less seriously and encourage the customer to explore all parts of herself. The brands we hosted in our stores all had their own values and personas: some products were explicitly political, like the graphic tees; some were explicitly sexual, like the lube; some were fun, like the makeup; and some were mystical, like the candles and rose quartz. Our typical customers were not just metropolitan millennial women, our customers were *themselves* political, sexual, fun, mystical creatures. I wanted our audience and our customers to know that we didn't live in a box, and we'd never put them in one, either. So, in that sense, I wanted our brand persona to line up with our store experience and help women feel fully seen, heard, and appreciated for all of their beautiful traits. Like a best friend who knows and adores everything about you—no questions asked—and doesn't expect you to look or be a certain way.

> I WANTED OUR AUDIENCE AND OUR CUSTOMERS TO KNOW THAT WE DIDN'T LIVE IN A BOX, AND WE'D NEVER PUT THEM IN ONE, EITHER.

After locking down how I wanted our customers to feel about Bulletin and how I wanted customers to feel about themselves, I then had to ask myself, Okay, so how do I communicate this? And how do I manifest these feelings? As I noted earlier, *brand voice is your company's personality* and it shows up everywhere: launch announcements, Instagram captions, homepage copy, yada yada. I knew each individual copy moment had to feel strong and on-brand, and all of the copy together had to feel familial. I found it helpful to first outline words or phrases Bulletin would never say: "babe," "ladyboss," "she-e-o." When words didn't fit, I could feel it in my gut. I also workshopped adjectives I'd use to describe Bulletin as a person: warm, friendly, approachable, excitable, in-the-know, picky, and inquisitive. And I studied other brands who, I thought, had crafted a distinct, identifiable brand voice that resonated on all platforms: Glossier, the Infatuation, Reformation, Seamless, and Slack. I'd look at their newsletters and websites and Instagram Stories to learn how they adjusted to each format. I'm a writer, so this customer copy puzzle was a fun challenge and something I wanted to tackle myself. I enjoyed writing about my business and trying to help her shine. But, if you don't identify as a wordsmith of sorts or feel cozy using copy to convey your "what," "why," and "how" to your audience, then now is the time to hire a copywriter! Like we discussed with design, make sure this partner has all the necessary tools and insights from you to do a fabulous job. Because *good* copywriters are like highly skilled Jedis (shoutout to all my Jedis!), and, like designers, they wage serious influence over your customer.

I hired a new copywriter for Bulletin, and it was like handing over plane tickets to a waterfront vacation with Chris Meloni (yum). I did it quite begridgingly and knew there was only one woman for the job. Rachel, who had long run sales and social media for Bulletin, spent two years trying to encapsulate the Bulletin brand voice in short Instagram captions, and ultimately, she became the defining voice of the now-folded consumer brand. Rachel was our microphone, so I knew it was time to let her take some control of the message. While relinquishing my involvement with e-mail copy, site copy, press interviews, and more, I wanted to make sure we were in good hands. We did a formal handoff with some training and editing, despite trusting her implicitly, because I knew how important the work was. I knew it would take a Jedi. If you find the right person, they'll feel out your brand's impulses and instincts and create a persona that feels authentic, natural, and familiar across all channels.

Before we move on to telling your investor, partner, and press stories, I want to stress one very important thing about your customer-facing copy: it is critical that you keep your customer story concise and consistent. As the tenured copywriter and communications lead at Bulletin, I often struggled with giving our customers concise and consistent messaging about who we were, what we did, and what we stood for. At times, I found it hard to write simple, straightforward things like an About Us blurb, a company bio, and an Instagram bio, or do strategic and fun things, like craft a bigger brand persona or communication style. For long stretches of time, there were so many layers—and often competing layers—to Bulletin, as both a business and a brand.

In 2017, we billed ourselves as the "WeWork for retail," a platform that gave brands affordable, turn-key access to shelf space in any of our New York stores. But we only featured women-owned businesses in our stores. And we hosted events all the time. And we donated 10 percent of all store proceeds to Planned Parenthood of New York City. And we sold products with in-your-face, unapologetic slogans, many dripping with sexual inuendo. Were we a tech company? A retail company? A brand? A real estate company? What was Bulletin? In the same way Bulletin believed our shoppers—and our brands—were not one-dimensional, Bulletin itself held multitudes. That would often lead to these stressful situations on the copy front. For something as simple as a Twitter bio, I'd have no idea what to write. In both Williamsburg and Nolita, I had to write copy for our mission wall and try to encompass all things Bulletin for our new and returning shoppers. It was a nightmare. I didn't know what parts of our story to disclose, or what parts to emphasize. When an old classmate would ask, "So what's Bulletin?" I couldn't give a straight, consistent answer. Sometimes I'd say "I run three feminist stores in New York," not even knowing what a "feminist store" is or means. I still don't. Other times I'd say, "I run a retail technology company, it's like WeWork for retail," and immediately wonder, Wait, is WeWork even a technology company? I feel like . . . no? Turns out I was right.

As a retailer, we sold dildos and weed pipes and cards covered in titties. We hosted events about safeguarding women's reproductive rights, we did a panel on the meaning of sex and pleasure. We also had venture funding, traditional tech investors, a Crunchbase profile, and the early days of a new

inventory management platform. We were political, progressive, provoca-
tive, and, for those aware of our many layers, confusing. From 2017 to 2018,
Bulletin didn't have some neatly packaged, one-sentence catch-all. No crisp,
clean way to cinch it all together. Merging the co-retailing technology bit
with the female-led brands focus with the Planned Parenthood of New York
City commitment was always a tussle. It was impossible to make it concise,
and a lot of messaging to keep consistent.

BULLETIN DIDN'T HAVE SOME NEATLY PACKAGED, ONE-SENTENCE CATCH-ALL.

I mentor other brands that struggle with similar messaging riddles: beauty
brands whose products have both digestive and skin-clearing benefits, not
knowing which benefit should take center stage; two-sided marketplaces
that don't know who their website copy should speak to, because they help
chefs do local delivery and give customers access to high-quality, home-
cooked meals; a sustainable clothing brand with an impressive, revolutionary supply chain and inclusive sizing up to size 25, clueless as to what they
should market front and center.

Across the board, you need to optimize for messaging that is going
to help you accomplish your larger goals. If you're the aforementioned beauty
brand, do some market research and see which market—the digestion or
acne-care market—has more white space. Or the larger market size and
growth potential. Or simply spend some time thinking about which of the two
solutions you care about and relate to the most. Make that your centerpiece.

If you're the marketplace founder, decide what you're trying to accomplish, and what you need to build up first: supply or demand. Do you need to
recruit more chefs? Will a consumer waitlist help you do that and generate
excitement? If so, maybe the site should be consumer-facing to start. Focus
on demand. Are you approaching a seed round and investors want to know

you have the right roster of chefs to meet proven consumer demand? Maybe you need to focus on supply, then.

As for the clothing brand, you need to accept, first and foremost, that you can't be everything for everyone. Sometimes it feels like that's not the case. Mass outcries on social media often beg brands to be size-inclusive, sustainable, ethically produced, affordable, and, of course, hyper-transparent, all at once. I'm not saying brands shouldn't aim for those features, but the reality is, if you're starting something from scratch, you can't hit all those notes straight out the gate. And even if you are optimizing for incredible features like sustainability and inclusivity, like our friends at the unnamed clothing brand, you'll likely still need to pick a primary and secondary marketing focus.

Customers want to know who you are and what you are about the most, what you're the best at, what you can uniquely offer. For that reason, every business needs an angle, a bull's eye to focus their communications, copy, marketing, and strategy on. If you have any cobwebs getting in the way of that clarity—competing value propositions, too many layers to the business model [*cough, cough*]—you have some ruthless decision-making to do.

INVESTOR PITCH BASICS

If your customer story is what you do, why you do it, and how you make your customers feel, your investor story is what you do, why you're worth the risk, and how you're going to scale and make them boatloads of money. While investors appreciate sharp design and thoughtful copy, they prefer compelling founders, industry-disrupting ideas, high-margin businesses, and untapped markets. You should keep all of this in mind when crafting your investor pitch. Whether it's a small check or a big check and no matter who it's from, you'll need to tell a story that makes their money seem meaningful. For friends or family, it's important they know where their money is going and what it will help your business achieve. For institutional investors, it's important they know how you're going to turn their money into even more money. Most investors want to know important things like: Why are you the person to bring this product or service to market? What are your margins? How big is the market opportunity? Of course, they'll want to learn more about the brand story: why the brand voice is so innovative, the inspiration for your logo, stuff like that. They'll definitely sink their teeth into your mission and your vision, too. But the guts of your investor story—the one you'll have to pitch at networking events, in formal meetings, over e-mail, or for accelerator applications—is all about innovation, growth, and cash.

IF YOUR CUSTOMER STORY IS WHAT YOU DO, WHY YOU DO IT, AND HOW YOU MAKE YOUR CUSTOMERS FEEL, YOUR INVESTOR STORY IS WHAT YOU DO, WHY YOU'RE WORTH THE RISK, AND HOW YOU'RE GOING TO SCALE AND MAKE THEM BOATLOADS OF MONEY.

In explaining to investors what you do, make, or sell, it is important to weave in why your company is bringing something new to the table. If your company name is your title, so to speak, consider your "what you do" one-liner as the subtitle. These subtitles are usually captivating, direct, and aspirational. In 2017 and/through 2018, while we were running multiple stores on our rent-share model, our pitch decks started with: Bulletin, the WeWork of retail space. Before that, when we ran Bulletin Market, we tried: Bulletin, the Airbnb of retail space. We all know Glossier as a cult direct-to-consumer skincare and makeup brand. Their Crunchbase profile, however, says they are a "beauty company that leverages content and community to power a superior shopping experience." I know and use Stripe as a payments and billing platform, but their About Us says Stripe is a "global technology company that builds economic infrastructure for the internet." There is something hefty to these one-liners, because they don't just explain what the company literally does, they are hinting at why it matters or why it's big.

If you're thinking of raising from angel investors, joining start-up pitch competitions, applying for grants, or seeking any funding whatsoever, you'll need to come up with a subtitle that quickly communicates what sets you apart. Are you the first to create the product? Serving a brand-new market? Leveraging a new ingredient? Building new technology? Allbirds, for example, raised on the fact that they made stylish sneakers, yes, but also on the fact that they invented a "revolutionary wool fabric made specifically for footwear." Whatever makes your company innovative, disruptive, or special, make that as blatantly obvious as possible and make the point as soon as possible in any pitch collateral you're putting together.

There are plenty of other important stories to highlight for your investors, and they all carry equal importance. Each industry and, frankly, each individual investor, will want something more or something different, but your investor story must always address the basics. Investors will want an overture on why you decided to launch the business, details around the problem you're solving and data on your market size (aka the total number of potential customers you can charge), spreadsheets showing how much money you're spending and earning, and transparency around your traction thus far (which is code for how many users you have and how much money you're making). You can google around and find tons of pitch decks from various companies at various stages of growth: seed pitches, Series A pitches, Series E pitches. You can go back in time to dissect successful Kickstarter campaigns and watch companies pitch to the public. You can watch *Shark Tank*! Studying these publicly available documents (and *Shark Tank*) is the fastest, easiest way to understand what a pitch deck or fundraising campaign looks like, and what questions you'll need to answer.

I've pored over pitch decks from technology companies like Airbnb, Gusto, and DocSend. In my time at Bulletin, I've also reviewed and edited fundraising decks for lifestyle brands and direct-to-consumer companies. These pitches span different industries, target different investors, and tell different stories, but they all cover the same ground. Any type of investor— or anyone who scans the deck for that matter—should be able to recite your company name, remember what you do, and think you might get rich. That's where pitch decks usually fall short: not because they're missing data or they're formatted wrong, but because they aren't clear or compelling enough. If you learn anything from the Airbnb deck or any of the others I know you'll find, I hope it's that simplicity has Big Deck Energy. It has conviction. None of the billion-dollar-start-up decks are wordy or hard to understand. They are straightforward and direct. They're simple. We must learn from our wiser, wealthier, more successful entrepreneur elders.

SIMPLICITY HAS BIG DECK ENERGY.

If you've built a business that you're proud of and you have defined, thoughtful reasons for raising capital, you should be able to present your company and your market opportunity with direct statements, clean data, and genuine optimism. That's how a pitch deck stands out in the crowd. That's how you leave an investor pitch (mostly) unscathed. That's part of how you run a successful crowdfunding campaign. As the failed WeWork IPO and their wordy pre-public filing with the SEC made loud and clear: if you veer off into convoluted or bloated explanations, projections, or fluff, you may seem full of shit.

CAN OUR BRANDS BE FRIENDS?

Brokering successful partnerships is absolutely critical to growing your brand, so the story you tell your potential partners—and what they will gain by working with you—needs to be airtight. Bulletin has partnered with nonprofits, influencers, celebrities, other brands, media outlets, charities, and more. Thoughtful, well-executed partnerships can have useful outcomes: you can grow your Instagram follower count, bump up revenue, acquire new customers, build your newsletter list, and, frankly, learn a lot about your audience. We brokered tons of partnership activations that didn't pan out or lead to any of these positive outcomes, but, in the process, we learned who our customer *was*, who our customer *wasn't*, and how to better spend our time and money in the future.

Newsflash: if you explore partnerships as a way to grow, which you should, you are destined to broker shitty deals and partner with brands, people, or events that ultimately don't move the needle for you. That's okay. Know that now. But you need to lock in your partner-facing story so you can pitch and secure the partnerships you want to test.

Over the past few years, I've learned that constructing an effective partnership story is all about audience. Your potential partner is essentially sitting there and assessing what they can gain from getting exposure to your audience and customer. In the same way you're hoping to increase your number of newsletter subscribers or increase sales, your potential partners have the same hopes and dreams and are sniffin' out whether you've got the goods. For your partnership story, you'll need to use your design and copy muscles to make a general partnership deck, and, on occasion, you may need to make a proposal specific to the partner or client. Regardless of whether your partnership story lives in a general deck or a hyperpersonalized pitch, the most important part of this story is your audience overview and your audience data. This is stuff you'll need for your investor story, too—clear, easy info around who your customer is—but in your investor story, it's part of the pie, and in your partnership story, it's the main ingredient.

I was able to broker dozens of effective, smart partnerships with other companies, people, and organizations because we had straightforward customer data and, ultimately, an audience that our partners were hungry to get in front of. We partnered with Broadway shows like *Mean Girls*, rappers like Saweetie, shows like *Broad City*, and brands like Dirty Lemon. Across the board, these partners were interested in building brand awareness with our store shoppers and Instagram followers. I was always able to tell a really clean, concise story about our community by looking at Google Analytics, our Shopify e-commerce data (back when we had consumer-facing e-commerce), and Instagram data.

TO THIS DAY, I WANT TO UNDERSTAND—I LITERALLY NEED TO COMPREHEND—WHY ANYONE WOULD LIKE AND GIVE MONEY TO MY COMPANY.

When we ran our stores, our consumer audience was 90 percent female and we had two distinct audience buckets. One bucket was Gen Z/Young Millennial—they bought more items but spent less money at the time, used Instagram as their primary social media platform, and primarily engaged with our pop culture, sex-positive, and funny, irreverent digital content and products. We also had a slightly older bucket, between the ages of twenty-six and thirty-four, and they bought less but spent more, also used Instagram as their primary social media platform, but engaged more heavily with our political and brand-building content and products than our younger audience did.

These were key details our partners needed in order to vet us and decide if they were going to give us money, let us use their logo, utter their name, or coordinate a co-produced event. Sponsors, especially, need this type of data in spades! Every liquor and wine brand or food vendor that donated product to a Bulletin event wanted to make sure their free, in-kind product was in the right hands. The more customer and audience data you provide, the more legit you'll seem, while also signaling to the potential partner that you take the collaboration seriously. In many cases, folks on the other end who are brokering partnerships need to justify to their higher-ups—a VP of marketing or head of partnerships, or even a founder—that the partnership is worth the work. Typically, once the partnership is signed and sealed, both parties will need to do some form of cold, hard labor: graphic design work, event prep, a press release, you name it. Your partner needs to be bought in, and thoughtful, organized data around your audience and customer can have a huge hand in making that happen.

Beyond poring over your Google Analytics, sales, and Instagram data to mine deets on your audience for your partnership story, it can be super-helpful to survey your followers and customers to add more depth and color to your audience profile. This seems superobvious, but for a while, we never did this. Our iconic two-year intern, Nadira, was the one who suggested we give it a shot back in 2017, and it has become a normal practice ever since (even though we are running a very different business!). In our surveys, I always find it helpful to ask what other brands our customers follow and love, what their shopping pain points are, and how they themselves would describe a Bulletin customer. These questions will breed helpful data points you can share with the team, sound bites you can toss into partnership decks and pitches, and yummy insights you can use to guide important partnership decisions. If users describe your new smoothie company customer as a geriatric senior with missing teeth, you may not want to partner with a tween gymnastics champion on social media straight out of the gate. Do you see what I mean? I think the most important thing these surveys offer, though, is perspective. To this day, I want to understand—I literally need to comprehend—why anyone would like and give money to my company.

I ask similar questions of our job candidates in applications and interviews. I need to comprehend why someone would bet their paycheck on us. I'm not a user research expert, so I could definitely frame my questions more scientifically, no doubt. But even getting a rough sketch of how you are perceived can be wildly helpful. I've found that in the face of impostor syndrome and a growing number of problems to solve, it is harder for me to find pride in what we sell. In what *I* sell. This phenomenon sounds absolutely ridiculous, I know, but it isn't new.

CUSTOMER FEEDBACK WILL HELP YOU SEE YOUR COMPANY THROUGH THE LENS THAT MATTERS MOST AND GIVE YOU PERSPECTIVE WHEN YOU'VE LOST SOME.

Back in 2018, the year we partnered with Comedy Central and Showtime and my influencer crush Ally Love, I didn't really understand or accept that we were worth partnering with. Our stores were frequently packed, and we were Instagram darlings, and we wrote funny e-mails to tens of thousands of people in New York, but still, I struggled to latch on to what our partners would get out of working with us. In my darkest moments, those surveys and our Instagram DMs and our customer e-mails and our intern applications were my guide. They still are. That user research tells me who my customer is, what they care about, what they get excited about, and helps me navigate where we fit in. User research will give you the data that helps you pitch and broker effective, productive partnerships, but it will also help anchor you. Customer feedback will help you see your company through the lens that matters most and give you perspective when you've lost some. They will tell you what real estate you take up in your customer's mind, and who your neighbors are.

YOUR PRESS PERSONA

Your press pitch is the final story you'll have to tell, and for anyone to give a shit, you'll have to make it good. I've been Bulletin's PR agent from day one, and it's no real shock or coincidence that I happen to be a salesperson, a writer, and a storyteller. Being good at PR requires all three. I always joke that I could've been the Jewish Samantha Jones. Quick reminder, though: PR can be helpful, but it isn't some holy grail or magic potion you can use to grow a business. So the following advice (and suggested workload) only applies when you're launching a new brand, unveiling a new product, promoting a game-changing partnership, or any of the other exceptions we made way back in Chapter Whatever. For when you absolutely need to scream through the noise and get someone to listen. I'm still figuring stuff out, but there are a few things I know for sure.

We've discussed the importance of summarizing the pure, unadulterated "what" of your story to level-set with consumers and bag investors, but the "why" is most critical for your press pitches. With PR, you are telling your story as a way to convince other people—journalists—that they should tell it, too. For that reason alone, it is so much easier to build a compelling story around your business if the service or product is somehow true to who you are and what you care about. That's what you need to focus on. Successful, effective press pitches get journalists to believe in you and want to share your story.

Polly Rodriguez, the co-founder and CEO of powerhouse sex tech company Unbound, founded her business after battling colon cancer for multiple years. Once in remission, she struggled to find a high-quality, affordable sex toy brand that nurtured her libido and sense of sexuality. So, she began Unbound as a sexual wellness and pleasure subscription box, selling other brands' products, but turned the biz into a brilliant, viral phenomenon that makes its own sex toys—and with personality to boot. In press pieces about Unbound, Polly is forthright, candid, and comical. She speaks consistently and incisively about her vision and why her diagnosis ultimately led to starting a sex toy and accessories company in particular. In conducting serious user research and doing her own vibrator shopping, she realized that, on the whole, she felt embarrassed and ashamed hunting for these products. There was no real consumer brand or company that made shopping for sex toys a cheeky, exciting, and fun experience. Her "why" is meaningful: she was compelled by personal experience but empowered by a compelling market. Meanwhile, her forthright attitude and excitement about Unbound make it nearly impossible for a journalist to feel anything but goodwill toward the company.

At the end of the day, journalists are just people. They may carry this scary, aloof aura (sometimes I'd look at a journalist's e-mail address and work myself up into a sweat figuring out what to say to such a distant, yet influential person). But they live lives like you and me; they eat, sleep, drink, fart, and cry. They also receive dozens upon dozens of pitches and ruthlessly decide who gets the limelight and who doesn't (so much power!). But ultimately, your press pitch must be designed to convince a thinking, feeling, busy human being to pause, take interest in your company, and consider that maybe—just maybe!—more people should take interest in it, too.

AT THE END OF THE DAY, JOURNALISTS ARE JUST PEOPLE.

At Bulletin, I always did my best to humanize our impact, which often made our business more interesting and easier for journalists to understand. I always dialed in to *why* we started the business, *why* our work mattered, and *why* the journalist should give a shit. I reviewed old press stories I had written to try to extract the most effective tactics and copy that got journalists to actually reply or agree to cover us:

- I used testimonials a ton to show our real-life impact on brands and their founders. I would include quotes from brands discussing how we helped them build their business or how we helped them learn more about their products or their customer.

- I focused on our origin story a lot and what inspired us to toss our six-fig salaries out the door in favor of launching a company that supported small businesses.
- I would indicate why and how their potential coverage might differ or stand out from previous coverage. Ripped straight from a pitch: "I'm contacting you because while Bulletin's tech and business model is democratizing brick-and-mortar retail and giving online-only brands access to shelf space for the first time ever, no major pub has written a very huge story about this. We've gotten a fair amount of lifestyle coverage, but no publication has addressed our Big Picture mission + how we plan to grow this concept."
- I would hyperpersonalize the pitches and reference another company the journalist had just covered, a piece they just published, a tweet they recently posted, or a general theme or industry they seemed genuinely interested in and excited about. Ripped straight: "We think given our new product direction and your focus on direct-to-consumer brands and the future of retail, you might be interested in what we're building next. Alana and I thought you would be the ideal reporter to speak with about the latest at Bulletin including: our Series A financing, recent executive hires, and new wholesale platform."

As you can see, there are many ways to skin a press pitch, and it will take some trial and error (and a whole lot of cold e-mails) to find the one that really lands. Back in 2016, when we were running the Bulletin magazine, for example, I tried pitching Bulletin as a small, local business; Bulletin as an Etsy competitor; Bulletin as a bold content/commerce play; Bulletin as a new type of media company; Bulletin as a master curator; Bulletin as the defender of indie designers. I chose the template depending on the reader and depending on what was and wasn't getting replies.

Once you have a press pitch you think might work, you need to become (1) shameless, (2) persistent, and (3) tactful in getting that story out there. As I know all too well, it can be hard to muster up the chutzpah to become your own cheerleader. In a world that judges us in mere milliseconds, it feels risky to promote yourself, and it's scary to stand out. It's also easy to feel a nagging sense of impostor syndrome and think you haven't accomplished enough to e-mail *Forbes* or tweet at a Refinery29 beauty editor. And maybe you haven't. But you won't know until you try. And, I should mention, every big-name brand with press cred started out as a no-name brand in some journalist's inbox. Which means the time is nigh to get shameless and start pitching like there's no tomorrow.

IN A WORLD THAT JUDGES US IN MERE MILLISECONDS, IT FEELS RISKY TO PROMOTE YOURSELF, AND IT'S SCARY TO STAND OUT.

Not shameless by nature? That's okay. You will learn shamelessness. Because you need it to succeed as an entrepreneur. As a salesperson, I was accustomed to selling and schmoozing to get what I wanted. In my mind, getting press coverage for Bulletin was synonymous with closing a deal. And why shouldn't it be? A successful PR push requires the same two key ingredients as a successful sales strategy: relationship building and follow-through.

If you have a test pitch on lock and you're down to get a little shameless, then it's time to get your story out the door and into the ether. Here's how I did it: first, I searched the internet for journalists who might be predisposed to lending an ear. I wanted to e-mail people who were plugged in to our industry and covering similar companies or ideas. How do you find journalists who might actually give you a shot? You have to google and Twitter stalk your brains out. For example, when we were a shoppable magazine, I used to find journalists who repeatedly covered Etsy news, featured local Brooklyn businesses, wrote indie brand gift guides or tweeted about the relationship between content and commerce. I then used plugins like Hunter.io and other hacks to get their e-mail addresses and pitched them. Any accurate e-mail address became a viable lead. I'd send a carefully worded, personalized e-mail and follow up consistently until I heard back. If I had not heard back by a third follow up, I'd DM them on Instagram. If I didn't hear back via Insta, I'd respect their privacy and move on (gotta gtfo before you cross the creep threshold, ya know?).

NOT SHAMELESS BY NATURE? THAT'S OKAY. YOU WILL LEARN SHAMELESSNESS. BECAUSE YOU NEED IT TO SUCCEED AS AN ENTREPRENEUR.

My e-mails were both shameless—gotta be!—and tactful. The copy and cadence of your press e-mails can make or break your chance of being featured. A lot of start-ups use PR firms because they have time-tested, solid relationships with the press: editors, producers, writers, etc. But in our DIY PR scenario, those relationships are not bought, they are made. And you can't force them, which means that sometimes you have to be patient and strategic about your outreach. As you read up top, I'd often compliment the journalist's other work to show I was familiar with their byline and position Bulletin in a way that resonated with them specifically. But the final trick? Always insert an easy, low-key call to action. Ask for a quick fifteen-minute call or invite the journalist to sign up for your newsletter.

When I started, I never asked for coverage straight-up or expected to close the deal right away. During Bulletin's digital magazine days, we'd send an initial cold e-mail and ask the journalist to pick one free product from the website, on us. Sometimes, if we didn't get a reply, I'd stalk the journalist's Instagram to personalize their gift and send something I thought they'd actually like. I'd add a cute card with one easy call to action: "Let's get in touch," and throw in my e-mail. If that got their attention and they wrote me back, we'd have an entryway for conversation and a subject—my obnoxious gift!—to build off of. We'd get on a quick call or have a snappy e-mail dialogue, and I'd explain more about the businesses and pitch ways to feature our website or our products.

When Bulletin was doing pop-ups, I'd invite journalists to Bulletin Market and comp their visit, with food and drinks on me. We'd get to spend a little time together and get to know each other beyond the obvious, transactional "my-brand-wants-press" conversation. I always made sure to tell the Bulletin story in as much detail as seemed appropriate. I found that candor and real conversation often went a long way. In fact, a lot of journalists enjoyed talking to me over a typical publicist, and they said as much. If you're yourself, calm, and collected, it won't feel like you're in some stressful business meeting, begging a journalist to bring you some exposure.

WHEN YOU DO LAND A STORY, IT'S USUALLY A SAFE MIX OF GOOD LUCK AND GOOD TIMING.

I did this over, and over, and over again. Not every lead converted, but a few did. When you do land a story, it's usually a safe mix of good luck and good timing. I remember pitching *Time Out New York* because I had googled "what to do in New York" during our Bulletin Market days. *Time Out New York*'s suggestions were always ranked numbers one and two by Google, and I wanted Bulletin Market to make the cut. I pitched Jennifer, their Things to Do editor at the time, over e-mail. For months. And finally, as a local Brooklynite, she decided to pop by Bulletin Market one day when she had a friend in town. I, of course, offered some free rosé and a "private tour" of the "grounds" (LOL @ our radioactive parking lot). It happened to be one of our packed weekends, the sun was out, and Jennifer independently liked supporting Brooklyn makers. She loved the market. Knowing Jennifer well now, I realize she was likely amused with my lame but heartfelt tour (which was basically just me walking her from vendor to vendor). She has become a longtime friend and Bulletin advocate since then. But had I not been persistent, Jennifer and I may have never met. Shamelessness is key, and shamefulness is easily avoidable. As long as your outreach is persistent but not pushy (those casual, low-lift calls to action can be a huge help) and tactful instead of tacky (study your list of journalists, be thoughtful with your words and respectful of their time), you're in the clear.

Crafting and telling your brand story are some of the most creative and energizing parts of starting a business, but as this nearly ten-thousand-word chapter proves, that process requires a lot of thought and audience segmentation. While the "what," "why," and "how" of your company should stay static and anchor your brand voice, vibe, and aesthetic, you'll need to highlight different parts of your story for different groups of people. The story you tell your customers is not the story you tell your investors is not the story you tell your partners is not the story you tell the press (out of breath here!).

And no matter what story you're peddling, it may not hit right away. You will go through a painful process of optimization and refinement on all fronts, so it's important that you analyze the effectiveness of your copy with no ego or sunk-cost bias in the mix. Be ruthless and honest when things aren't working: if your customer acquisition is slowing, if investors aren't biting, if potential partners aren't replying, if press searches go cold. And when you're stuck and feeling like no one gives a shit about your business? Talk to and survey the people who do. Even if there's only five of them. You may know your story best, but your customers, Instagram followers, and even intern candidates can shed light on the story *they* fell in love with.

TAKEAWAYS!

YOUR STORY DEPENDS ON YOUR AUDIENCE.

LEAN ON WHAT'S WORKING.

BE SHAMELESS WHEN IT COUNTS.

BUILDING A BRAND STORY ISN'T ABOUT TELLING YOUR CUSTOMERS WHO YOU ARE, IT'S ABOUT CRAFTING WHO YOU WANT THEM TO SEE.

WHAT'S YOUR BRAND STORY?

ALEXIS ROSENBAUM
ROSEBUD

In 2017 I started using cannabis for the first time in my life. I had spent all my life against cannabis, like totally hardcore against it. I had just sold my other business, so I was in this interim, anxious period of like, Okay, what's next? I'm a really type-A person and I get bored really easily, and it causes my anxiety to get much worse. My husband and I were infertile, and I had been going through an IVF round, which cost us a lot out of pocket, and we walked away empty-handed. The month of the egg transfer was the most stressful month of my life. I knew I had to do something. I was going to lose my mind. While I didn't birth human life, I did end up birthing this business in 2018.

I was finally using cannabis—my sisters had told me it would really help with my anxiety—and I started to watch the landscape as it was growing and growing. I was watching all these brands get started, and I was thinking about their quality standards, their cluttered, "bro"-looking packaging, and if I could maybe pocket some extra pocket cash by selling CBD. I was curious what that would look like. I wasn't necessarily thinking of building my own brand. I found the farm I now work with and thought at first that maybe I'd be a sales rep. But by March of 2018 I had built up a clientele of more than two hundred people selling CBD on Instagram and Venmo, and I was calculating how many I sold to, how much money I had coming in. I asked myself, Alexis, what are you doing? Are we going down this path, are you building another business? I figured if I could sell to two hundred people in someone else's packaging with someone else's story, I should make my own brand, with my own packaging, and tell my story. If I do that, I can sell to four hundred people. I used all the profit from those first customers to build the brand, and I launched in April 2018.

When I was developing the first iteration of the brand, I thought a lot about the product and why someone would bring CBD into their life. I questioned what I had seen in the cannabis space that just wasn't clicking with me: a lot of cluttered design and cluttered packaging. The packaging was overwhelming and overstimulating, especially for a product that is supposed to reduce stress. I wanted to do the opposite and launch a brand with packaging that was simple, with clean lines, and I wanted it to feel welcoming and warm and inviting. I put myself in the shoes of a first-time user—what would I be nervous to ask about the product? Would I be like, What's CBD? Is this weed? Are we rolling a joint? Is 420 a thing that relates to this? Do I sound dumb? I wanted Rosebud to make you feel like it's totally cool if you know nothing, we are in this together and I want you to know this plant is here for you when the time is right. No pressure, and we can answer any questions you might have. I was thinking about the stigma around cannabis, and how it can lead to negative feelings or emotions, and I wanted to simplify everything.

These CBD products with aggressive packaging aren't speaking to the Midwestern woman who isn't comfortable in a smoke shop or a vape shop. She looks at those products like, These are scary. Are these going to fuck me up? I wanted the brand to carry a more feminine look and tone, to almost feel motherly. Like you're going to be taken care of.

TRINITY MOUZON WOFFORD
GOLDE

From the beginning, Issey and I always had a superclear vision of what we wanted for the brand and how we wanted customers to feel. The brand has been refined over time—we are always changing the packaging, even if slightly—but that feeling we're trying to share with our customers has always stayed the same. Early on, it was about figuring out how to communicate a real sense of warmth and maximalism. We really wanted to go against the minimalist, luxury, black-and-white vibe everyone was seeing on Instagram and with other brands in our category. I wanted customers to engage with Golde and feel like they were suddenly smiling, like a ray of sunshine had come out. That feeling is what informed all our early decisions around packaging, the voice, the formula. I wasn't scared to go against the grain; I honestly just had the most anxiety about making sure we didn't rip off anyone. Now, Golde is in a place where we end up on some mood boards. You can see that we're influencing other brands, and that's great. But what I keep saying is, You need to figure out the problem you're trying to solve with your products or your brand. You have to be the one to solve that problem for the customer, and that becomes your brand. Copying another brand isn't helping you add value, and really, consumer goods force a conversation between brands and customers. That's why it's important to be and feel original.

**VICTORIA ASHLEY
LAUNDRY DAY**

I built the brand I was looking for but couldn't find. I've always known what I was looking for with the label and logo and palette. Those things are very important. I only work with people who understand the direction and the vision. I did the first round of branding myself, but now, it's important that I take the time to do other things. The photography style really provides the atmosphere I've always been going for. I wanted to capture a vibe that didn't reflect mine, or where I was necessarily. It is all about the beauty of where we are right now—to this day, no one ever knows where we are based. The photography—I love it. It's like, Are we in LA? Is it . . . New York? No one really knows, and I have a lot of fun playing with that. It lets anyone connect with the brand.

I focus on modern fonts and modern colors. I want the brand to feel welcoming and approachable, but also beautiful. I think of someone shopping in a brick-and-mortar boutique, and I see her getting a candle and a blanket and Laundry Day, and creating this full mood. As we've grown, I've also wanted it to feel luxurious and sustainable, like something you want to hold on to. My experience working with the right designer, Mark, has been priceless. We never spoke on the phone, we exchanged one or two e-mails, but he knew exactly what I was looking for. Finding someone who shares your vision is important. It saves you time and lets you free up to work on new things. Next, I want to focus on reaching a new group of people and building a brand that's even more elegant and elevated, more of an experience.

JACLYN FU
PEPPER

We wanted to start a company that represented a cheekier, bolder, and more fun approach to undergarments. The brand names already out there were very feminine: ThirdLove, Victoria's Secret, Adore Me. We had a really hard time finding a name for our concept. We were at lunch picking up random objects: a sandwich, salt. Lia Winograd, my co-founder, said, "Pepper!" and we knew we had it. It has alliteration with "petite," and then there's "peppercorns," which pack a nice, spicy punch. The brand itself I would say is characteristic of the word. It's for this community of women who are simply done being ashamed of having small boobs. For women who ask, Why can't I celebrate this? I am sick of being called a pancake or getting boy-body insults. It is a brand that rallies with these women and says enough is enough. We wanted the brand to capture the essence of that early community. The site and colors are bold and loud. We try to feature as many community stories as possible. Every interaction, all customer service, it feels like you're talking to a really great girlfriend and you leave the conversation feeling confident and complimented. We sign off every support e-mail with a meme and a compliment. When you order a bra, we send a handwritten thank-you card. Every touch point should make you feel great about yourself and your body. That's where the brand story really lives.

JAMIKA MARTIN

ROSEN

I've always had acne-prone skin—it's just something I've always dealt with, and I accept that this is the skin I have. Before starting ROSEN, my skin was in really rough shape, and I just couldn't do Accutane a third time. I was really into clean skincare at the time, and a lot of indie brands were launching in the space. They all had black-and-white, super-minimalist, apothecary-type packaging. I loved these brands, but they weren't meant for my skin. I wanted to develop my own brand. I didn't initially think ROSEN would be such an acne-focused brand.

I launched ROSEN with a similar minimalist vibe, with that indie apothecary-type packaging, but we're moving away from it. Because now, acne is really at the forefront of the brand messaging and brand story. My personal journey is what helped the brand finally come together. In 2018, we started writing about skin positivity on our blog, and we had guest writers being really candid, and I was so inspired by what they were sharing. Every time I would read what they'd post to the site, I realized I could relate to their stories. Even if we didn't have an identical experience, that feeling of looking in the mirror and crying because of your skin, or not wanting to leave the house because of a breakout, sucks for everyone!

I didn't want to be a brand that's like, your skin is terrible and this is why you need us. We want to be skin-positive, bold, unapologetic, casual, and educational, like the older friend who you're down to kick it with, but they're also a great source of knowledge for you. We try to be approachable but not super "cool girl." That was always the case on voice, but because we know more about the customer now, we want to step out of the current visual branding and go for a younger feel: more of a retro, colorful aesthetic, something that feels nostalgic and futuristic at the same time, and really fun. I tell a lot of people, the brand identity is a continuous, working document. You will launch with something, but the faster you educate yourself about your customer, get their feedback, and really know how they receive your messaging, the stronger the brand will be. People will start to grasp and understand it better.

CHAPTER ELEVEN

HARD DECISIONS

'm writing this chapter on the front lines of 2020. I've watched seem-
ingly invincible companies go belly-up in the span of two months; on call
after call, I've heard our small business customers complain that they can
barely make payroll or may have to shut down entirely. I've watched savvy
CEOs—meticulous planners who forecast for dear life—fail to predict what
will happen. They've stopped hiring. They've stopped paying themselves.
They've stopped forecasting. All around me, the small businesses I used to
frequent—the late-night beer and sliders joint, the neighborhood gift shop,
the place I went to have my eyebrows dyed—they're just gone. Some have
signs up, passionately stating that they're closed for now, they miss us, and
thanking us for all our years together. Some have simply disappeared, and
ominous gates obscure any indication of the business that once was. All
the while, I am acutely aware that behind every start-up, restaurant, hair
threading salon, and storefront that died with the pandemic stood a business owner that, under harsh light, said, "I have to kill you now."

Shutting down is a shitty and painful decision, but if you're lucky, it
appears at the end of a long journey riddled with shitty decisions and unfore-
seeable forks in the road. At any point in time, you might have to lay off a
lot of people, hire a lot of people, stop paying yourself, start paying yourself,
turn down an investment, take an investment, spend more money than you
thought, lose more money than you thought, pivot, postpone a launch, fire
someone who does good work, abandon your business partner, or find a new
one. These are all what we call "hard decisions," regardless of whether they
suggest your company is rising or falling. No one goes into entrepreneurship
to *make* these hard decisions (maybe second- and third-time founders do,
and for that, I commend you! *And you're a little sick*). But they come with the
territory if you're pursuing a dream, or building something from nothing,
and fighting with every piece of yourself to keep it alive. That's what this
chapter is about.

Ultimately, you make hard decisions because you have no choice—the company won't survive either in the short- or long-term unless you pull the trigger. These are typically do-or-die situations, even if they don't feel like it in the moment. Often, you may only realize you made a hard decision after the fact. That's because some hard decisions are clear-cut, like the ones many business owners had to make as COVID-19 bulldozed through the entire world: If I don't lay off half my team, we'll run out of money in six months. If I don't close my store, I'll go into tens of thousands of dollars of debt. If I don't postpone this launch, we'll lose our credibility. Alana and I had to make a few of those painful judgment calls ourselves.

Other hard decisions, however, are a bit more nuanced, but difficult all the same. These decisions are sometimes even *shittier*, because they require an element of self-sacrifice. They require that you say "no" to something that might make your life easier or put more money in your pocket: turning down an investment, firing a high-performing employee, or walking away from a lucrative partnership. In the first category, you're just trying to survive. In the second, more elusive category, you have to lose in the short-term to gain in the long run. Both types of hard decisions require a lot of you: a level head, a heart full of conviction, and sustained empathy, dignity, and vulnerability with your team and with yourself.

A LEVEL HEAD

I am not cool, calm, and collected by nature; I tend toward anxious, and my mind races when things go wrong. I start playing out every worst-case scenario and planning for five different doomsday outcomes all at once. In our hardest times—closing stores, laying off half our team, pivoting for survival—that quiet panic lives in my body every day, at all times. In fact, at the end of 2018, as the realization that we had to pivot *yet again* fully crystalized for both me and Alana, I started to notice physical manifestations of it.

I started losing hair in the shower and developed a sudden and tender herpes outbreak on my left fingertips. I remember going to my dermatologist and feeling so confused; this had never happened to me before. I had no idea herpetic whitlows were even a thing. He sat down across from me in the bright white room and asked, "Are you stressed?"

When you're in the midst of making a hard decision, you're both praying you did the right thing and living to make it so, and a level head doesn't come easy. You have to work for it. I learned this from Alana, by serving as her partner and watching her lead. For the first couple of years, before I really knew her and understood her as deeply as I do now, I always thought she was just stoic by nature. I thought she had a much higher tolerance for the lows and had this well of calm and logic she could draw from at any time. When I spun out, she'd reassure me. When I didn't know what was going to happen next, she told me everything would work out. When I introduced her to my herpetic whitlows, she told me, through laughter, to "go get a fucking Band-Aid" and "keep my hands away from her."

When I was alone, my mind could go so dark so fast, but Alana would bring a sense of levity and warmth back to the frame, and my rambling thoughts would even out. We had to lay off a portion of our staff in order to extend our runway and get through COVID-19, and while in the shower, lying in bed, or pouring coffee, I could *not* stop stressing over how to do it, when to do it, and how it would impact the wider team. I felt like I wouldn't even know what to say, or how to act. And I couldn't shake the emotional weight of cutting off someone's income. In the midst of a global pandemic. I felt like a perpetrator—like I was knowingly inflicting pain. Here I was, completely frantic, and Alana was as cool as a cucumber. Throughout that period, she guided the way, with every text, phone call, nod, and hug, working to anchor us both. She brought stability not only to our partnership, but to our leadership—and still does to this day. When we struggle, she never lets the team sense even a whiff of distress. She leads every meeting like nothing is wrong, pursues our fundraising or next milestone with the grit of a prehistoric hunter, and keeps us all on track. I know Alana better now. I know she isn't magical because she just "doesn't feel the stress" or "has so much conviction"—she's magical because she feels it all, just like I do, but she *decides to project* the level-headedness we need to make it out alive.

Every time we've had a hard decision to make, a failure to overcome, or our backs up against the wall, she's refused to indulge in a full-blown break-down. Or at least, she doesn't let me see it. She bolts into action; she'll make each problem definable and do everything she can to get a handle on the situation. She makes pro and con lists, she calls up advisors and mentors we trust, she makes diagrams (she loves diagrams), and she makes space to think and talk it out. She processes, and then she plans. By being her part-ner, I've learned how to organize my thoughts and feelings when things get scary. I've learned how to feel it all—the anxiety, the suspense, the regret—and think and plan and breathe at the same time. She's given me the gift of clarity in crisis.

I think a lot of this clarity comes with time. It comes with facing a crisis and surviving, again, and again, and again. Alana doesn't let the crisis define her—or us—so when things go wrong, she sees it as a problem we're equipped to solve, not evidence of some quiet incompetence. When you effectively navigate a crisis once, and then twice—and you make it out alive—the third is much less anxiety-inducing. The fourth and fifth don't rattle you in the same way. You can start to take the ego out of it, and you start to unglue your self-worth from the problem at hand.

Alana ran a successful business years before I met her. She was CEO in the years I was still just Bulletin's editor in chief. She had scars I didn't have, and she'd won battles I never fought. I think you gain this level of clar-ity by making many hard decisions, for many years, while training to keep your confidence and conviction in place, even in the face of hardship. By just staying in the ring.

Alana *does* have a well of calm and logic she can draw from after all, but she had to claw for it. Fight for it. She muzzles her inner chaos so she can keep our leadership levelheaded, and our team in check. It's an art form you'll have to learn, too, to make productive, sound decisions under fire. As with anything, it takes time and experience.

CONVICTION

Once you've leveled out, made a few lists, and taken some time to acknowledge and address your anxiety, it's time to build some real conviction around whatever comes next. You're going to need it, and your team will, too. You can't corral your team around a new direction or motivate them after a round of layoffs if you're processing or pouting. Pitching a half-baked plan that you're still "coming to" can be painful and unnerving for both you and your team.

In late 2018, we were building our wholesale marketplace with brute force while still running three stores in New York City. Our newest investors kept asking what the plan was: Were we going to keep the stores open, or would we walk away from our leases? At the time, we thought it might make sense to keep the stores open and run the marketplace simultaneously. The stores could act as lead generation, like a showcase, and show our retailers the quality of brands and products in our community. This wasn't *totally* delusional: in trying to get beta testers—retailers who would join the platform early, before it was really "ready"—the store played a huge role in helping us get buy-in. Many of our beta testers were New York City–based store-owners, and as entrepreneurs themselves, they wanted to help and support us. They knew about Bulletin because of our stores—they'd either come in and shopped or seen us on Instagram—and because of that, they trusted *us* and our brand selection, even if the platform itself was, as we say, "janky." They were eager to use our marketplace, even in its infancy, to find new products and brands for their shelves. And so, Alana and I decided that yes, for the time being, we *will* keep the stores open, because they give us the authority and brand awareness that we need to launch this platform; they are living proof that we *know* retail and retailers; they don't bleed us dry; and many months they *make* us money. We tied up our myriad justifications with a neat little bow and forced a smile. We were off to share the plan with our team.

> YOU CAN'T CORRAL YOUR TEAM AROUND A NEW DIRECTION OR MOTIVATE THEM AFTER A ROUND OF LAYOFFS IF YOU'RE PROCESSING OR POUTING. PITCHING A HALF-BAKED PLAN THAT YOU'RE STILL "COMING TO" CAN BE PAINFUL AND UNNERVING FOR BOTH YOU AND YOUR TEAM.

I remember that day. It's still this crisp little memory that jumps out and screams if I think about the green knit sweater I wore and just close my eyes. We had just completed our Series A right before the new year, and change was afoot at Bulletin. You could sense it, but the holidays and travel and consecutive days off, with the stores closed, kept us all from coming together as a company and getting aligned on what came next. I knew that as soon as we possibly could, we had to *personally* share details about our new wholesale marketplace and overall pivot to our retail team. If any of our brands or retailers were to come to the stores, this team would be on the front lines explaining what Bulletin is and what we do. They knew we had just successfully raised a new round of funding and heard murmurs here and there about the new platform, but our part-time team associates didn't have the full picture. Not even close. If anything, they were confused. They were on the ground and in the stores selling "F*ck Trump" T-shirts and vibrators while Alana and I flew to Sand Hill Road in Silicon Valley to pitch a technology company they knew nothing about. It was time to share our conviction around what we were building next and why it mattered. They needed to be convinced, to be motivated. That's what the day was all about.

I don't know that it worked. Alana and I gave a presentation on "where we've been, where we are now, and where we're going." We revisited our Bulletin Market days, regaled them with stories from our first HQ in Alana's old apartment, did all the mythologizing and, frankly, selling we could muster. But it didn't land. Something in the room felt flat and hollow. The company I was describing was not necessarily the company they agreed to work for, and I think it was obvious that the stores were swiftly becoming secondary to something else—something the retail team was far away from. *Even if* we said they played a key role in our success, *even if* I told them nothing would change, I believe that our mythologizing and explaining and selling was received in direct response to how it was given: tepidly, and coated with a quiet panic. Because I did the thing: I pitched a half-baked plan that I was still "coming to."

In the deepest layer of my being, on that very first sheet of soul lasagna, I knew we had to close the stores. I knew it the whole time. But for some reason, I grabbed on to my justification about the beta testers. If the platform was going to scale nationally—and fast—why would we need three stores in New York? In what universe would even a single New York store help retailers in Arkansas decide what keychains to buy for *their* customers? It didn't make any sense.

Maybe I motioned that we keep the stores open because I felt like closing the stores would be embarrassing—we had just been in an *Inc.* magazine reality series about the flagship store launch and practically wailed that it was a dream come true. I wondered what my friends would think, too; what other founders would say. But beyond the humiliation, there was obviously a sentimental element to all this. We ran those stores for almost three years. We held events there, built community there, and designed, staged, and opened them ourselves. They were a creative tissue connecting Bulletin employees at every level, and for me and Alana, they felt like part of us. But the fear of embarrassment and nostalgia is not what kept me trapped in months and months of processing. We were struggling to find and create conviction around the decisions that were best for the business—to focus on the marketplace, close the stores, lay off our store team—because we knew how many people those decisions would hurt. We would hurt our part-time retail employees—they would lose a portion of their income, many of them students or brand-new to New York City. I knew what that felt like. We would hurt our landlords—they'd lose a tenant and that reliable rent check. We would hurt our corporate team—they worked tirelessly to make each location a success. It would hurt us, as the perpetrators. The harm-doers. It would send shockwaves. And it would put a sudden, sharp end to an era we all shared together.

WE WANTED TO MOVE FAST WITHOUT BREAKING THINGS.

I was grieving, and Alana was grieving, when we pitched our entire team on Bulletin 3.0 that fated day. I did not have, and therefore could not manufacture, conviction with the team. We wanted to move fast without breaking things. But on my most cellular level, I knew there was grief waiting around the corner for so many of us—the layoffs, the tears, the cardboard boxes, the empty hangers getting plunged into trash bags. Things had to break for us to move forward. It was a patchy year as we decided to close Williamsburg, then the flagship, and finally, Nolita. First, we thinned out the retail team, then we did a round of layoffs, and then we gave everyone notice. Our merchant team packed up three stores in the course of ten months; stores they spent hours perfecting. Years improving. Nights dismantling in the dark.

Once you've made a hard decision, you may have to sell the company all over again—to your investors, your team, but most important, to yourself. You can't get buy-in from those around you if you're endlessly revising the pro and con list in your head. Or tripping over yourself with guilt. Or grasping for an ounce of confidence due to impostor syndrome, the shame of a big pivot, or fear of the unknown. You need a heart full of conviction to be an effective leader through your company's darkest times. You need it to manage from strength, not insecurity, to make uncomfortable decisions that may hurt people, and to get everyone excited about building your new rocket ship. Don't pitch the vision until you've fully bought in yourself—and take whatever time you need to get there. I wish I had. Consumed by the anxiety and the guilt of our retail staff not having full transparency into the future of the company, I rushed a presentation that Alana and I weren't ready for and that ultimately raised more questions than it answered.

Right when the pandemic hit in early March, Alana and I did a round of layoffs, and then regrouped with the remaining team at Bulletin HQ. Unbeknownst to us, it would be the last time we'd see our team in person that year. A month later, we'd abandon our office lease. *That* conversation—that pitch to our remaining employees—*had* conviction. It wasn't self-conscious, or tepid, or half-baked. By then, the governor told us to work from home and avoid the subway. Rumors were swirling that they might quarantine everyone in New York. And our sales were slowly fading. The pandemic wasn't coming—it was here—and our industry would take one of the biggest hits. Laying off our team members saved the business we'd worked so hard to build over the past five years. We needed to survive, but more important, we needed our remaining team members to *want* to help keep us alive. With enough deep breaths and long runs in the park, that knowledge gave me all the motivation and conviction I needed to reimagine the company all over again, and to have a compelling, honest conversation with our smaller team about the future of Bulletin and their role in building it. To manage from strength.

EMPATHY

Okay . . . but how do you make hard decisions knowing you'll hurt people? How do you process that? Just like finding levelheadedness, you're going to have to drag your ass to the well. Hurting people should not come easy. When we've had to lay off people, terminate a partnership, or fire a consultant, I try to think about their experience of what's going on. I reflect on times when *I've* lost control of my income, or of my life. I think about the shock of thinking things were one way, and one minute later, realizing I was wrong. That my reality was not guaranteed.

I spent so many years out of control, out of the driver's seat, with both my family and with work. When my dad needed his second kidney transplant, our family was pushed through a door that led to nights filled with false hope, financial insecurity, and lingering uncertainty. We all waited through years of dialysis, machines cleaning his blood when his kidneys could not. There was nothing any of us could do. The ripple effects were more like tidal waves, dragging us even farther away from everything that felt familiar and secure. Marital strain, car accidents, divorce, constant fighting, financial collapse, and almost a decade-long estrangement between me and my father soon ensued. I worked as a hostess at a popular West Hollywood sushi restaurant and got fired for standing up for myself with a drunk customer. I juggled four part-time jobs at once to put myself through school the next semester, tallying every paycheck with a calculator. Throughout my teenage years and early adulthood, it felt like I was getting tossed around like a coin in the dryer. I know what it's like to feel like the life you planned is slipping away from you. Or what it feels like to get fired and immediately start freaking out about how you're going to pay for this bill or that repair. I know what it feels like to live beyond your means, not because you're indulging, but because life costs money, and a lot of jobs just don't pay well. I know what it's like to count on a paycheck, and I know what it's like to lose it.

But at some point, I went from counting to cutting. To laying off people. At no point in my life did I think I'd be running a company that serves as the main source of someone else's income. I never thought I'd be on the other end of that dynamic. There are a lot of things I don't know. There are plenty of experiences I have never and will never have. There are things you've experienced and wrongs you've suffered that I'll never understand. But if you've lived a life, you definitely know what it feels like to get bad news, or feel stuck or anxious about your future. We've all felt those things, no matter what side of the dynamic we're on.

You have to accept that when you make certain decisions to preserve your business or your dream, you are going to create those emotions in others. You will disappoint people, make them fearful, or leave them behind. If you're successful, and you're growing, these things are inevitable. If you're struggling, you may have to do these things for survival. If you are in the thick of a decision like this and feel overwhelmed and you don't know what to say or how to do it, just breathe deep and make it simple. When you give the bad news, remember what it feels like to lose control and get scared. When you plan a round of layoffs or do salary cuts, move slowly and methodically through every single step. When you fire someone, give shelter to their dignity; put yourself in their shoes. Remember that they spent time and effort on *your* idea. If you can do this you will know what to say, and how to say it. Then try to help them land, if they ask, and if you can. Some companies share public databases of laid-off workers looking for new roles, some may connect you with recruiters, while others take a more 1:1 approach. I wish I could give more tactical advice on how to properly lay off someone or remove a co-founder or any other choice that negatively impacts members of your team, but beyond getting excellent legal advice on how to best handle those procedures, all you can do is bring some humanity to the interaction.

THE LIKEABILITY DILEMMA

Sometimes when I'm faced with a daunting choice, *even if* I bring all the empathy, all the conviction, and every ounce of bravery to the table, I feel exposed and anxious about the fallout. Because as a woman, you feel this constant, prickly sense that you're being judged, both internally and externally, *not only* on your merits as a forceful businesswoman, leader, and decision-maker, but that you're being judged on something a bit more . . . elusive. The closest word to approximate that elusive "something" is probably your *likeability*; but I think it goes so much deeper than that. As tech journalist and Recode co-founder Kara Swisher puts it in her recorded Zoom call with Jessica Lessin, editor in chief of the Information, there's an expectation that "women should create different companies from men, [companies] that are nicer." This sit-down, titled "How Female Founders Are Treated by the Tech Press," goes on to explore why the press might disproportionately "take down" female founders and CEOs, compared to male founders and CEOs exemplifying the same bad, or even *worse*, behavior. We don't have to look too far for our answer, though: to quote Swisher again, "It is sexism."

In talking to dozens of female founders throughout the pandemic and hundreds of female founders in my time running Bulletin, it has become quite obvious that women suffer from a particular breed of anxiety and indecision that is informed by a fear of being disliked or discredited. This is not surprising to me, because I think Swisher is right: I think there's a quiet, subtle, misogynistic expectation—from employees, former employees, investors, the media, Twitter—that women should cultivate and carry "feminine energy" as leaders. Maternal energy. And often, that means big, impactful decisions that will shock, disappoint, and harm people—like laying off half your team or shutting down a project—can feel even *more* stressful. You want to stay clearheaded and calm and confident and empathetic, but the pressure of how you'll be received and perceived sneaks its way in and takes up some room. You are simultaneously managing the stress *and* worrying about how you'll be judged under said stress. Those voices inside your head can get loud and messy.

Twitter was set aflame reading through the Verge's account of Steph Korey's forceful, insistent instructions to her customer service team at Away, the company she co-founded at age twenty-seven after leading supply chain operations at Warby Parker and Casper. Many were demanding that she step down as CEO or get booted from the company altogether. I have worked at male-founded companies with a similarly obsessive and abrasive emphasis on customer support—it is a demanding and often thankless role. As investor Charlie O'Donnell points out in his blog, Amazon founder Jeff Bezos notoriously asked employees on his customer success teams, "Why are you wasting my life?" "Are you lazy or just incompetent?" "Did I take my stupid pills today?" His "explosive" reactions, "hyperbole," and "harshness" make him a "brilliant founder" and "visionary," according to *The Everything Store: Jeff Bezos and the Age of Amazon*, a book about his life—and the press coverage that followed. And at Tesla, Elon Musk's enterprise, workers have complained of dangerously long hours, a toxic work environment, and unsafe factory conditions that push people to exhaustion, where sometimes, they end up in the hospital. This is still happening—these workers are still complaining. But I have yet to see a social media or press campaign that has effectively removed Elon Musk as Tesla CEO. He's still there. So is Jeff. Steph Korey is not. A few months after the Verge piece on Away, BuzzFeed ran a story with anonymous quotes from former Outdoor Voices employees about founder and former CEO Ty Haney's tone—*literally*—publishing, "Ty would say she didn't like something, but said it in a way that gave you a lot of anxiety." Unlike Jeff, the reporting didn't reveal that she called anyone lazy, or stupid, or incompetent. But her tone was mentioned over and over again. Even if a former employee offered up this opinion, I am not sure that publishing commentary on her tone was the best way to open up an investigative piece on Ty Haney's effectiveness as a leader, or the company's HR policies.

We can discuss those items without commenting on her tone. Or take the *New York Times* article and anonymous quote that shamed Audrey Gelman, co-founder and former CEO of the Wing, for saying a CEO should not be doing dishes during a high-profile event. Again, do we need to know this? The piece was about the tension between capitalism and feminism, the struggle to scale as a mission-driven company, and where the Wing fell short on its promises through certain policies and its organizational structure. I am not sure what the anecdote is trying to do. Like Steph Korey, Audrey Gelman and Ty Haney no longer run their companies, due in large part to the fallout from these articles.

In all these articles, the journalists are sure to indicate that employees, often female employees, were "left in tears." And in many instances, journalists share that former employees at these female-founded companies, and others, lament being "silenced" by severance agreements that might include an NDA, non-disparagement clause, or other terms around confidentiality. Meanwhile, these types of severance agreements are standard and used by companies of all sizes all over the world—they are not special muzzles used by female CEOs or their HR departments. I can't help but think that the journalists know that. And if they don't, that might be even scarier.

I truly do believe in leading with empathy and a baseline gratitude and appreciation for your team. And I am not going to absolve these founders of the cracks in their leadership or other incidences surfaced in these articles and others. Employees and former employees were right to speak up and share accusations of workplace racism, unreasonable and inhumane workloads, and negligence from leadership at these companies. Just like the Tesla employees were right to speak up, and to keep speaking up. These founders should not be put in some glass cage because they're women. I have always appreciated when my employees and former employees have shared constructive feedback or major grievances, whether they still worked with us or shared their thoughts after they left. As a young first-time founder who has worked hard to establish a positive and thoughtful culture, I know not everyone will get it right all the time—because I've fucked up, too. Running an organization, especially a growing organization, is difficult. Put any company under a microscope and observe it under bright light for a year, two years, three, or more, you will find things that are broken. And good on those employees for speaking up about what was broken and striving for change.

I simply read these articles and wondered, If these women were male founders, would they receive the same *coverage*? The same press. The same framing. Would we get special mention of the "tears"? Would their anonymous employees share some of these specific anecdotes? Would we get anonymous quotes about tone and "how something was said"? Would we read about a male CEO who didn't want to be washing dishes in his co-working space while coordinating a recorded tour with Amex and Venus Williams? Would reporters make such a hoopla about standard, completely conventional severance agreements at male-founded companies? Would we get the same megawatt spotlight on the founders themselves, versus the organization as a whole? Or the venture capital system at large, and the incentives to grow at all costs—*even* at the cost of your employees and their well-being? My research says "no." Because for years, members of the press—journalists in New York, in Silicon Valley—and investors either knew about or heard reports of Adam Neumann and Travis Kalanick's behavior at WeWork and Uber, respectively. There were allegations of sexual harassment, drug use, pregnancy discrimination, and legal retaliation against employees who spoke out. Yet, these men were lauded for being "crazy" and "hypercompetitive" and "ruthless." They got even more funding. This reward for bad behavior just serves to illustrate the point: the definition of "leadership" and the consequences for poor leadership are starkly different for female entrepreneurs and their male counterparts.

Female founders at every stage—small business owners, venture-backed growth junkies, e-commerce experts, and especially aspiring entrepreneurs—read these pieces, internalize the lessons, and are changed in ways we can see, and ways we can't. Many active founders I've spoken to recently over-worry about how their team will react or perceive them after a bombshell decision, like a major round of layoffs or team-wide pay cuts. Will I seem rash? Will my former employees put me on blast on Glassdoor? Like Alana and I, they tinker with every major team-wide communication, announcement, or assignment to make sure they sound authoritative but not intimidating, understanding but not docile, critical but not cruel, disappointed but not angry. It's this "likeability" thing, the measuring stick of "feminine energy." It feels, in times that require sharp thinking, bravery, and ruthlessness, like an anxious stagehand tiptoeing up to the curtain and whispering, "Hey, um . . . don't forget to perform your womanhood." It's this voice that fogs you up and warps your vision, and sometimes it gets really loud when you most need it to shut the fuck up.

THE ELEPHANT IN THE ROOM

My intention is not to make the press's more emotional treatment of female founders the central issue, or even a central issue, in tech—far from it. In fact, I sense that sometimes, the press's specific focus on female founders—the one that yields dozens of headlines about this female founder's social media statements, or that one's tone—might be distracting from more serious conversations and coverage about those companies, their actual policies and business models, and other aspects of Silicon Valley that need serious dissecting, like how board members and investors, who are often white, and male, play a role in governing these high-growth companies, or conveniently overlook the harm they caused. Or the fact that all these venture-backed women—myself included—are ourselves white, able-bodied, and conventionally beautiful. Women of color don't even get a full 1 percent of venture financing. Only 2.8 percent of venture capital goes to women, 1 percent goes to Black founders, and less than 2 percent goes to Latinx founders. I was hard-pressed to find any data on venture investments in Indigenous founders, or founders with disabilities, which speaks volumes in and of itself. Maybe the press should look into that with as much gusto and consistency and hold the male founders of various firms and funds accountable for the insular, exclusive club that is Silicon Valley.

Another thing: all the women I've mentioned were first-time founders but had veteran investors and board members. As we discussed earlier, if you take venture capital, then you are, by definition, giving up equity—or ownership—in your company. And that means that how you grow, and what you prioritize, isn't always up to you. These founders had competing stakeholders to answer to—and competing promises to keep. They had to grow like a rocket ship but preserve the mission. Hire incessantly but screen without error. Manage impeccably with decreasing oversight. But the pieces I read in the *New York Times*, BuzzFeed, the Verge, and more never took these realities into account. Instead of using these founders and their failings as a way to inspect and dissect the balancing act of running a "nicer" but rapidly growing company while appeasing both investors and employees, these stories were, as most things are these days, painted in black and white, with a lone assailant at the center. As a venture-backed female founder myself, I know what it can be like to juggle those competing priorities and to try and hit your growth benchmarks without compromising company culture. I've been in those exact trenches for five years now, and those complexities define my experience. It was odd to see this angle entirely absent. We of course must hold these leaders accountable. But if they failed, then *so did* their boards. *So did* their investors. *So did the system.*

We need to decide and declare that the system itself is problematic, not just the founders within it. I don't work at a news organization and I am not part of the media landscape—not one iota. But from afar, I've noticed that as soon as one outlet releases a piece about a well-known female founder and her mistakes, or her company's shortcomings, dozens of outlets follow suit. Journalists paraphrase the first piece and package it with a salacious, eye-catching headline of their own. Because these stories do get clicks. They get pored over. They get tweeted, and re-tweeted, and obsessively Instagrammed. I simply wish other important coverage—diversity at venture firms, diversity among limited partners, the tension of scaling to meet investor demands while preserving company culture, the fact that 90 percent of all funding goes to white guys—came in just as hot and had the same viral impact among journalists and us, their captivated readers.

The "likeability" struggle is compounded by race—for both men and women—and Silicon Valley, despite pledges and platitudes, is still powering white entrepreneurship. I can't speak to everyone's experience, but many of us are both living through and seeing the inequities in venture capital and notice that white dudes who fail emerge a bit more unscathed, or that they don't get the same heated coverage as their female counterparts, or that women have to back up their pitches with more data than their male counterparts, and women of color, even more so. Being a female founder, you may feel like you represent all female founders. If you're a nonwhite founder in venture capital, and especially a nonwhite woman, you may feel a floodlight on you and your journey. We all have inner voices that challenge us, and external forces that push us down, some more than others. All the while, you have so many hard decisions to make—maybe not yet, but if you keep going, you will soon.

If you're able to see clearly and plan thoughtfully, feel genuine conviction about your decisions, and feel empathy for yourself and your team, you will . . . maybe . . . probably . . . hopefully . . . be okay. The voices don't disappear, but you persist in spite of them.

SOURCES

Azevedo, Mary Ann. "Untapped Opportunity: Minority Founders Still Being Overlooked." Crunchbase. February 27, 2019. news.crunchbase.com/news/untapped-opportunity-minority-founders-still-being-overlooked/.

Campbell, Alexia Fernández. "Elon Musk broke US labor laws on Twitter." September 30, 2019. vox.com/identities/2019/9/30/20891314/elon-musk-tesla-labor-violation-nlrb.

Chernikoff, Leah. "Are All These Female-Founder Takedowns Fair?" The Helm. May 14, 2020. thehelm.co/female-founder-takedowns-outdoor-voices-away-the-wing/.

Clark, Kate. "US VC investments in female founders hits all-time high." TechCrunch. December 9, 2019. techcrunch.com/2019/12/09/us-vc-investment-in-female-founders-hits-all-time-high/#:~:text=Female%20founders%20raised%202.8%25%20of%20venture%20capital%20this%20year&text=Venture%20capital%20investment%20in%20all,latest%20data%20collected%20by%20PitchBook.

Edwards, Jim. "These Are the Sarcastic Things Amazon's Jeff Bezos Tells Employees When He Gets Angry." October 10, 2103. businessinsider.com/things-amazons-jeff-bezos-tells-employees-when-he-gets-angry-2013-10.

Helft, Miguel. "How Travis Kalanick Is Building the Ultimate Transportation Machine." *Forbes*. December 30, 2016. forbes.com/sites/miguelhelft/2016/12/14/how-travis-kalanick-is-building-the-ultimate-transportation-machine/#17974d1c56ab.

Hess, Amanda. "The Wing Is a Women's Utopia. Unless You Work There." *New York Times Magazine*. March 17, 2020. nytimes.com/2020/03/17/magazine/the-wing.html.

Lessin, Jessica and Kara Swisher. "How Female Founders Are Treated by the Tech Press." The Information. March 24, 2020. Video Q&A. theinformation.com/events/female-founders-media.

Lessin, Jessica E. "The (Pink) Elephant in the Tech Press." The Information. March 14, 2020. theinformation.com/articles/the-pink-elephant-in-the-tech-press.

Matousek, Mark. "Ex-Tesla employees reveal the worst parts of working at the company." *Business Insider*. February 20, 2020. businessinsider.com/ex-tesla-employees-reveal-the-worst-parts-of-working-there-2019-9#the-toxic-environment-elon-musk-creates-1.

O'Donnell, Charlie. "The Double Standard of Female CEOs Moving Fast and Breaking Things." *This Is Going to Be Big*. November 15, 2020. thisisgoingtobebig.com/blog/2020/11/15/the-double-standard-of-female-ceos-moving-fast-and-breaking-things.

Sacks, Brianna. "Outdoor Voices Became a Staple for Millennial Cool Girls Thanks to Its Chill Aesthetic. Employees Say They Were Drowning." BuzzFeed. March 11, 2020. buzzfeednews.com/article/briannasacks/outdoor-voices-ty-haney-employee-allegations?origin=web-hf.

Schiffer, Zoe. "Emotional Baggage." The Verge. December 5, 2019. theverge.com/2019/12/5/20995453/away-luggage-ceo-steph-korey-toxic-work-environment-travel-inclusion.

Simon, Morgan. "Racial Bias in Investing? Just Look at the Data." *Forbes*. September 24, 2019. forbes.com/sites/morgansimon/2019/09/24/racial-bias-in-investing-just-look-at-the-data/#6e5cc4afa8e6.

"The Venture Capital World Has a Problem with Women of Color." Girlboss. girlboss.com/read/venture-capital-woc-women-of-color.

Wong, Julia Carrie. "Tesla factory workers reveal pain, injury and stress: 'Everything feels like the future but us.'" *Guardian*. May 18, 2017. theguardian.com/technology/2017/may/18/tesla-workers-factory-conditions-elon-musk.

Zipkin, Nina. "Out of $85 Billion in VC Funding Last Year, Only 2.2 Percent Went to Female Founders. And Every Year, Women of Color Get Less Than 1 Percent of Total Funding." *Entrepreneur*. December 12, 2018. entrepreneur.com/article/324743.

I'M
STILL
BUILDING

I've been writing this book for more than two years, and it's been a wild, unpredictable, exhausting ride. I've run different businesses while writing this book. When I started and wrote chapter 1, I was running a co-retailing company with two, then three stores. I was working out of the back of our Nolita office, squished in with eight other women. We had twenty-five part-time retail employees. We didn't have a wholesale platform or software or a VP of engineering. And our stores? There are none left. We've gone all-in on our wholesale marketplace and closed our final space right before COVID-19 ravaged retail and the US economy. We're all working remotely now, and there are only ten of us. But our pivot worked.

While writing the chapter on pivoting, I was plagued by a major company pivot of my own, and an uncertain future that made me doubt myself, and doubt whether I even deserved to write to you. I've written to you about impostor syndrome, and how to silence it, while feeling it in my veins every single time I struck my keyboard. I've laid off, fired, and hired lots of people, and many different faces have worked hard to launch my rocket ship. To build my empire. This book has been like a time capsule for me, and earlier pages remind me of a younger Ali who still had so much learning to do, and so, *so* many mistakes to make. And now, here, as I write my conclusion, I feel like a haggard-ass bitch who's lived through sudden tragedy and put out brutal fires. And the scariest part is I know there are plenty more to come.

Though Bulletin's journey may be jagged and imperfect, I think there has been one consistent through-line in our story. I truly believe that Bulletin has been able to exist, in all its forms, because we asked people to believe in our vision, whatever it was, and people said *yes*. While writing this book, I have been consumed with so much gratitude. Our magazine existed because a bunch of strangers, the coolest designers in New York and beyond, agreed to give us their time and do an interview. They trusted me to write editorial about them and put their stories into words on the internet. Our markets, up and live in just a few weeks' time, were booked and busy (most of the time,

LOL) because dozens of local vendors and creators agreed to post-up and sell with us. Our stores worked and we sold great inventory because brands agreed to join. We've been able to open stores, build software, sell product, and grow a business because of a loyal, hardworking team that shows up every day and fights for us to keep going. I am here because, even though I didn't ask, Alana believed in me, and still does. She has taught me to love myself and value my skills, and her trust, friendship, and partnership have made me a better founder and person.

Customers buying our stuff, users using our product, and employees doing good work were not givens, not foregone conclusions, which I know firsthand, because I know what it feels like to have nothing: no business model, no traction, no hope. I am deeply appreciative and thankful for every brand on our platform, every retailer using our site, and every employee who gives or has given us their all. Getting buy-in is the hardest thing to do, and it should be treated like a delicate, precious treasure once you have it.

Our employees, brands, contractors, retail customers, and store shoppers made Bulletin happen. If you're launching your own thing, it too will take a village. It will take co-founders challenging your assumptions, friends cheering you on, customers giving you feedback, freelancers doing good work, designers making your logo, a bank approving a loan, and investors cutting a check. I've read other books that position the founder as some mega-genius, a far-reaching overlord who turns all parts of the company to gold. And I've seen other founders talk about themselves this way too, and act like they alone are the secret sauce to their successful business. *That's not how empires get built.* You will delegate, to Upwork helpers and interns. You will hire a copywriter, or a manufacturing partner. You will find a part-time assistant to help you ship product. Or a friend to help you screen-print tees or run your outdoor markets when you just need that one day off.

The point is: your business is the sum of its parts. You can't build alone, and you must find a community, no matter how big or small, that will work hard to move your business forward. Whether you're running an Etsy empire, a coffee shop, or a software company, it's important to find good, talented people who trust and believe in you. And who bring critical skills and new perspectives to what you're building. You cannot, and will not, be giving this your best shot if you settle on mediocre help or don't get the help you need. Vet your leads, ask for sample work, and whether it's your friends, external partners, potential investors, lovers, employees, or interns, know that you're entrusting them with a piece of your baby, because they are all on this journey with you. While you're not the mega-genius overlord (I know all the stinky shit and bad mistakes you're about to walk into, *sorry*), you are the one who stands to either lose or gain the most from this journey. Make sure your village gives a shit.

I am not sure why you came here. I don't know what you thought I'd say, or what you hoped to learn. But I'm excited for you. I hope, in some small way, I've helped you expand your sense of self, and your potential, like what Alana did for me. I hope you have an idea you're excited about, whether it's a career change or a new brand or a YouTube channel. A lot of what we've covered—PR, sales, pitching, branding, risk-taking—applies to any and all new adventures. Not all of us are running a retail technology company (a show of hands?), but we are all trying to build something fulfilling, get other people to like it, and have some wiggle room to grow it, *if we want.*

And that last part is really important. Because as the dozens and dozens of brand interviews show, you should build your empire on *your* terms. Want to run a brand part-time? Totally fine. Go fuckin' get 'em. Want to gun for a venture-backed business and build the next Glossier with a crazy huge team and worldwide offices? You obviously have to try. And you should.

Want to start making resin plates with your best friend and sell them at a local craft fair? You should obviously call yourselves the Resinettes and get a cute logo on lock ASAP. Empires come in all shapes and sizes, and how big you build it is a personal choice. One that requires serious consideration about your lifestyle preferences, feelings about money, risk appetite, and current obligations. But if you're inspired to think bigger after reading this little ditty, so be it.

The hardest lesson I've learned is one that I hope you learn with haste and excitement. I struggled to call myself a founder, own my shit, promote my business, internalize my successes, and write this book. I delayed opportunities because of it, and if you're a sheepish, insecure damsel like me, you'll lose opportunities, too. So, listen up. If you want to sell a few prints on Instagram, just for kicks, while secretly longing to see what happens and how many you'll sell . . . then screw the secret. *Act* like you take your prints seriously. Because by pining, you're taking them seriously already. Listen to that. If you have a side gig, make it known. If you're dabbling in music, make it known. If you're an aspiring author, make it known. I did.

Don't worry about what they'll think or how it seems or stress you aren't far enough along. You get far by sharing, networking, and holding pride in your work, whether it's a two-hour-a-month passion project or a full-blown side business. I still have to remind myself of this. Because every day, I don't feel successful enough, or ready. But fuck it.

I'm in the ring. And you are, too.

ACKNOWLEDGMENTS

First and foremost, I want to thank Alana Branston, my co-founder and Bulletin's CEO, for supporting me throughout this process and sharing a wholehearted "yes" when the opportunity arose. Alana, we have spent more than five years building together, and throughout two of them, I frantically juggled my responsibilities to our company and to these chapters. You have been my biggest champion, my best friend, my role model, and my hype girl through it all. Your ongoing, undying belief in me and support of me as a person and partner has completely changed my self-perception, which is the gift of a lifetime. Thank you for letting me use these chapters to get candid, be vulnerable, and tell parts of our story.

To Elias Altman, my literary agent, who found a piece on Bulletin in the *New York Times* and changed the course of my life with one e-mail: thank you for giving me the opportunity to write for an audience; weeks before you e-mailed me and Alana, I had, internally, bid adieu to my dreams of doing so. As an entrepreneur, I accepted that writing professionally in any capacity was out of reach indefinitely. I am so grateful that you saw something in me, and in our story. And—quick aside here—thanks to Leslie Bennetts for realizing you sent your initial e-mail to us at @bulletin.com, not @bulletin.co. Without Leslie, it may have been too late!

To Becky Sweren, my literary agent at Aevitas, and everyone at ACM: thank you for making this dream possible. You kept me sane and optimistic from proposal through publication and encouraged me to write the book brewing inside me, not the book I thought people would "want to read." Becky, I will never forget you telling me that I was a Writer, capital "W" and all, despite negative self-talk trying to convince me otherwise. Like Alana, you too have changed my self-perception, and it means more to me than you know.

Thank you to Samantha Weiner, my editor, who has watched me cry over half-eaten salad, fielded a zillion panicked e-mails, and answered the phone every single time I called or texted. You were right by my side through Bulletin's pivot and through my own bouts of extreme insecurity and doubt, but no matter how frantic I got, you believed in me, and in my writing. Thanks to every single person at Abrams who worked on this book and gave it so much love and attention despite delays, a pandemic, and the world turning upside down. To every copy editor and graphic designer, and everyone on the marketing team and beyond: I appreciate it. I am so grateful to all of you.

Thank you to everyone who helped make Bulletin a reality and gave us their time and headspace to build our rocket ship. Without the support of Y Combinator—specifically, Kevin Hale and Adora Cheung in our early Fellowship days—Alana and I would not have made it this far. To Jonathan Ehrlich and Foundation Capital: thank you for believing in us and challenging us to think bigger. And to Nick Chirls at Notation Capital, our first investor: thank you for being the one we call when shit hits the fan, and then sprays blood and mucus everywhere. Every founder needs an investor like you, and not many of them exist. You're a good dude.

To everyone on the Bulletin team, past and present, I am so grateful for your thoughtfulness, your talents, and every ounce of optimistic energy you brought to work every day, even when things were an absolute shitshow (aka always). I am honored that you've made Bulletin part of your career story, and we would not be in business right now without your contributions and your efforts. To Lisa Bougie, our advisor and mentor: thank you for your perspective and giving just a little bit to me and Alana every time we talk. You calm us down, ask the right questions, and keep us squarely focused on our own company and the outcomes under our control. Sam Safer: thank you for being my wholesale guru and training me Rocky-style before and during our pivot. Creating a functioning two-sided marketplace out of thin air was a daunting task and our day-long whiteboard sessions made it feel just a bit more manageable. I am still shocked that we pulled it off. Thank you for believing in us and seeing the light, even when I felt like everything was totally futile. You kept me going.

To all my friends who worked Bulletin Market, shopped our stores, indulged my stress tantrums, and provided pockets of fun amidst a few very grim years: thank you for buying into my delusions and cheering me on from afar. To Sara

Ramanuj and Maggie Braine: thank you for running Bulletin Market on weekends when Alana and I were about to break. Alison Monk, Eden, and Jacob: thank you for spending so much money at Bulletin stores over the years and opening your home to me in 2013. My entire New York story starts with you. I love you so much.

I am forever indebted to the University of Pennsylvania, the financial services department, and the Class of 1954 Scholarship for making my college education accessible. Thank you, Kelly Writers House, for feeding me, nurturing my love of literature, and giving me strong, brilliant women to look up to and learn from. Erin, Jessica, and Michelle, I wanted to be all of you when I grew up. I still do. I am also extremely grateful for the Milken Scholars Program, which partially financed my college education and has given me an enduring sense of community and professional support.

Every time I sat down to write, I thought of my most influential teachers: Jerry Martin, Amy Frangipane, Jonathan Krauss, and Gi Haller. I loved learning from you, I loved writing for your classes, and I lived to impress you. I am so thankful for every lesson you gave, every paper you edited, and every word of encouragement you sent my way. School was my safety when things were challenging at home, and entering your classrooms felt like such a blessing.

Before Alana, there was Jana Kozlowski, and before Jana, there was David Getman. Jana, you were my first adult "collaborator," if we can call it that; the first person I ever teamed up with for a creative project post-college. We were only twenty-two or twenty-three, running around the country to film our small documentary on a mere $5,000 budget. You took me seriously, and you helped build my work ethic. I love you so much and am so proud of us both. To the late David Getman: I carry your electric-yet-gentle energy with me everywhere I go. Our memories got me through late nights writing on fumes. I thought of your infectious smile every time I wanted to give up. I thought of the white flowers you brought to my door the last time I saw you. I live to make you proud, even though you aren't here. I write because you can't. And I keep going because you saw my potential before I ever could, and I want to get there, for the both of us.

To Nick: thank you for giving me steam when I had none. You were my late-night co-conspirator, pumping me up at 10 P.M. to write a few more pages, making me a full-blown gourmet dinner when I turned in my first manuscript, and telling me I was worthy when I felt so, so far from it. You have been with me on the front lines while I battled my impostor syndrome and worried I had no right telling this story. You were the affirming, motivating voice in my head when everything inside me screamed: What if Bulletin failed? What if every chapter's horseshit? What if I don't finish? Nobody else had a front row seat to the chaos, or the breakdowns. You hugged them tight and made me strong. And to Winnie, our stinky little beagle: thanks for the incessant licks, cuddles, and happy snorts. I know you'll probably chew at this book and make it your next victim, but I think you've earned it.

To Ben: thank you for making me laugh, for believing in me, and for calling late at night to make sure I was okay. Throughout this entire process, it felt like you were the older sibling, and I was the younger, lost sibling who couldn't get my shit together. In spite of our tumultuous childhood, you have become a stabilizing force. I love you so much, and your support has made me feel a lot less delusional and a little more capable. To Dad: I know we have a unique relationship and there's a lot for us to unpack at a later date. Regardless of our history, my ability to write comes directly from you, and I am so eternally thankful for that. Though it's been years, I feel connected to you when I write, and that makes me happy,

And finally, to my gritty, resilient, and slightly delusional Momma: thank you for every sacrifice, every writing workshop, every extracurricular, every word of encouragement, every word of constructive criticism; for the depths of your commitment to me and Ben; and for setting me on a path of fulfillment and, most important, opportunity. You are the most special person I know. From such an early age, you nurtured my talents, told me to shoot for the stars, and stressed that if I worked hard enough, I could do the impossible. I would not be the woman, business partner, person, or writer I am without your support and guidance. I love you! We did it!